The Opposing Self

THE WORKS OF LIONEL TRILLING

UNIFORM EDITION

LIONEL TRILLING

THE OPPOSING SELF

Nine Essays in Criticism

A HARVEST / HBJ BOOK

HARCOURT BRACE JOVANOVICH

NEW YORK AND LONDON

First published in 1955

Printed in the United States of America

LIBRARY OF CONGRESS CATALOGING IN PUBLICATION DATA

Trilling, Lionel, 1905–1975.

The opposing self.

(The works of Lionel Trilling)

(A Harvest/HBJ book)

Bibliography: p.

1. Literature, Modern—History and criticism—
Addresses, essays, lectures. I. Title.

II. Series: Trilling, Lionel, 1905–1975. Works.

PN710.T66   1979   809   79-10362

ISBN 0-15-670065-4

First Harvest/HBJ edition 1979

A B C D E F G H I J

To James and Elsa Grossman

Preface

MOST of these essays were written as introductions to books, and all of them were written for occasions which were not of my own devising. The occasions were quite discrete from one another, the subjects are in some ways diverse, and I wrote the essays with no thought of achieving an interconnection among them. In each case my intention was only to serve the given subject, to say what makes a particular book or author interesting and valuable to us. Yet inevitably an interconnection among the essays does exist—apart, I mean, from whatever coherence is to be found in their writer's notions of what constitutes the interesting and the valuable, of what constitutes "us." The essays deal with episodes of the literature of the last century and a half, and they all, in one way or another, take account of the idea that preoccupies this literature and is central to it, and makes its principle and its unity—the idea of the self.

There have always been selves, or at least ever since the oracle at Delphi began to advise every man to know his own. And whoever has read any European history at all knows that the self emerges (as the historians say) at pretty frequent intervals. Yet the self that makes itself manifest at the end of the eighteenth century is different in kind, and in effect, from any self that had ever before emerged. It is different in several notable respects, but there is one distinguishing characteristic which seems to me pre-eminently important: its intense and adverse imagination of the culture in which it has its being.

I speak of the relation of the self to *culture* rather than to *society* because there is a useful ambiguity which attends the meaning of the word culture. It is the word by which we refer not only to a people's achieved work of intellect and imagination but also to its mere assumptions and unformulated valuations, to its habits, its manners, and its superstitions. The modern self is characterized by certain powers of indignant perception which, turned upon this unconscious portion of culture, have made it accessible to conscious thought.

One of the essays of this book, that on Dickens' *Little Dorrit,* remarks on the frequency with which the image of the prison appears in the imaginative works of the nineteenth century; and this, as the essay goes on to say, seems natural enough when we remember that the new age was signalized by the fall of a very famous prison, the Bastille. The attack on the Bastille was an attack on the gross injustices and irrationalities of the social system. These gross injustices and irrationalities were not wiped out in 1789, nor were they forgotten in the years that followed. But as soon as the Bastille had fallen, the image of the prison came to represent something more than the gross injustices and irrationalities. Men began to recognize the existence of prisons that were not built of stone, nor even of social restrictions and economic disabilities. They learned to see that they might be immured not only by the overt force of society but by a coercion in some ways more frightful because it involved their own acquiescence. The newly conceived coercive force required of each prisoner that he sign his own *lettre de cachet,* for it had established its prisons in the family life, in the professions, in the image of respectability, in the ideas of faith and duty, in (so the poets said) the very language itself. The modern self, like Little Dorrit, was born in a prison. It assumed its nature and fate the moment it perceived, named, and denounced its oppressor.

And by this act it brought into being not only itself but also the idea of culture as a living thing with a fate of its own, with the possibility, and the necessity, of its own redemption.

The best account of the strange, bitter, dramatic relation between the modern self and the modern culture is that which Hegel gives in the fourth part of his *Philosophy of History*. Few people nowadays have a good word for Hegel, and I—who am not, I had better say, a Hegelian—have no doubt that he is in everybody's bad books for the right reasons. But if we think of Hegel not in his political aspect but simply as an observer and describer of the developing culture of our time, we cannot but recognize his power. It was he who first spoke of the "alienation" which the modern self contrives as a means for the fulfillment of its destiny, and of the pain which the self incurs because of this device of self-realization. And it was he who, speaking of the principle of culture, and of course speaking in its defense, referred to it as the *terrible* principle of culture.

Hegel understood in a remarkable way what he believed to be a new phenomenon of culture, a kind of cultural mutation. This is the bringing into play in the moral life of a new category of judgment, the category of quality. Not merely the deed itself, he said, is now submitted to judgment, but also the personal quality of the doer of the deed. It has become not merely a question of whether the action conforms to the appropriate principle or maxim of morality, but also of the manner in which it is performed, of what it implies about the entire nature, the *being,* of the agent. This is what Hegel had in mind when he instituted his elaborate distinction between "character" and "personality," the latter term having reference to what we might call the manner and style of the moral action.

His perception of this new mode of judgment Hegel in part derived from his reading of the new literature of his day, and it was one of the things that led to his giving to art an importance quite without precedent in moral philosophy. For Hegel, art is the activity of man in which spirit expresses itself not only as utility, not only according to law, but as grace, as transcendence, as manner and style. He brought together the moral and the aesthetic judgment. He did this not in the old way of making morality the criterion of the aesthetic: on the contrary, he made the aesthetic the criterion of the moral.

Much the same thing was done in a simpler way by a literary critic who never, I believe, read Hegel. Matthew Arnold said of literature that it was a criticism of life. No doubt there is extravagance in the statement. Literature has perhaps not always been, and is not in its essence, a criticism of life. But as the statement refers to the literature of the modern period, it is strikingly accurate. It lost a good deal of its authority with us after T. S. Eliot's adverse comment on it in the preface to the second edition of *The Sacred Wood*. Arnold framed his famous sentence in two versions, sometimes with "literature," sometimes with "poetry" as its subject, and of Arnold's having called poetry a criticism of life Mr. Eliot observed that "no phrase can sound more frigid to anyone who has felt the full surprise and elevation of a new experience of poetry." This may be true, and perhaps Arnold's phrase needed to be roughly handled because it seemed to license a dull way of reading poetry. But if now, after the passage of a good many years, we look again at the words which Mr. Eliot used to discredit Arnold's phrase, we see that they actually serve to explicate and to justify it. They tell us precisely in what way Arnold thought that poetry was a criticism of life. *Surprise and elevation:* set the words over against Arnold's sense of our life in culture, against his sense of modern culture as a kind of prison (so he called it) and we know very well what Arnold meant. The "frigidity" of his phrase could not have been wholly lost on Arnold himself. When he said that poetry was criticism—which in any ordinary meaning it so obviously isn't—he meant to shock us. He meant to say that in our modern situation the surprise and elevation of poetry can serve to bring to mind some notion of what is the right condition of the self—in general, and not merely when it is having the experience of poetry. He was proposing to us the idea that our culture is hostile to surprise and elevation, and to the freedom of the self which they imply.

He meant, in short, that poetry is a criticism of life in the same way that the Scholar Gipsy was a criticism of the life of an inspector of elementary schools. Our habits of feeling have changed since the time when Arnold's poem had a special place in the world's affection—we are no longer quite suited by the large sadness with which it speaks of the loss of peace and joy. And yet there isn't, I think, a more comprehensive and comprehensible delineation of the modern self in its relation to the culture than that which Arnold makes in this elegy for his own youth. We are all likely to be aware of the Arnold of duty, the Arnold who tried to enforce upon his readers the importance of morality, and the pain and suffering that the moral life entails. But in "The Scholar Gipsy" we have an Arnold who represents duty as a grim second-best, who speaks of the "patience" which the life in culture requires as "too-near neighbor to despair." It is the despair of those who, having committed themselves to culture, have surrendered the life of surprise and elevation, of impulse, pleasure, and imagination. The Scholar Gipsy *is* poetry—he *is* imagination, impulse, and pleasure: he is what virtually every writer of the modern period conceives, the experience of art projected into the actuality and totality of life as the ideal form of the moral life. His existence is intended to disturb us and make us dissatisfied with our habitual life in culture, whose nature his existence defines.

We recognize him as one with the free-ranging boys of Wordsworth's poems, upon whom the shades of the prison house are inevitably to fall, upon whom custom, or culture, is to lie "like a weight,/Heavy as frost, and deep almost as life." He has a clear affinity across the Atlantic with the boy who started from Paumanok, "the boy ecstatic" whose intensity of selfhood was to serve him as "hardest basic fact, and only entrance to all facts." For us of the immediate present he has his avatar in the legendary figure of Yeats. There is perhaps not much of Arnold's poetry that, at the present time, can be related to Yeats's, and we are likely to be startled when we come on the record of a little pilgrimage which

Preface

Yeats undertook in the year in which he published his first volume
of poems—on a visit to Oxford, as he says in a letter of 1889, he
spent a long day "going to the places in Matthew Arnold's poems
—the ford in the 'Scholar Gipsy' being the furthest away and the
most interesting." The poem, of course, is a prefiguration of Yeats's
whole career; it gives us the terms of his long quarrel with the culture, which, more than anything else, made his passion and his
selfhood. Such quarrels with the culture we recognize as the necessity not only of the self but of culture.

I have dealt in these essays with more novelists than poets, but
of course the novelists in their own way of particularity and cir-
cumstantiality are no less committed than the poets to the modern
imagination of autonomy and delight, of surprise and elevation, of
selves conceived in opposition to the general culture. This imagination makes, I believe, a new idea in the world. It is an idea in the
world, not in literature alone. If these essays have a unity, it is because they take notice of this idea, and of its vicissitudes, modula-
tions, and negations.

Most of the essays have been revised since their first publication,
but none has been radically revised. I am grateful to the publishers
and editors who have permitted me to reprint them here.

1955   L.T.

Contents

The Opposing Self

The Poet as Hero:
Keats in His Letters

I

IN THE history of literature the letters of John Keats are unique. All personal letters are interesting; the letters of great men naturally have an especial attraction; and among the letters of great men those of the great creative artists are likely to be the most intimate, the liveliest, and the fullest of wisdom. Yet even among the great artists Keats is perhaps the only one whose letters have an interest which is virtually equal to that of their writer's canon of created work. No other letters, for example, have ever been the occasion of such a warning as F. R. Leavis felt it necessary to give a few years ago. Dr. Leavis said that in thinking about Keats as a poet we must be sure to understand that the important documents are his poems, not his letters. No one will wish to dispute the point with Dr. Leavis. When we think about Keats as a poet, his letters are of course illuminating and suggestive, yet in relation to Keats as a poet they are not primary but secondary; they are no more than illuminating and suggestive. The fact is, however, that because of the letters it is impossible to think of Keats only as a poet —inevitably we think of him as something even more interesting than a poet, we think of him as a man, and as a certain kind of man, a hero.

To be sure, no hero, no man who fully engages our attention, is

ever a man in the abstract but is always marked and distinguished
by some particular role. We know him as he is a lover, a husband,
a father, a son, and it is so much the better if we also know him
through his profession, as, say, a king, or a soldier, or a poet.
"Othello's *occupation*'s gone!"—the famous pathos of the cry reminds
us that in tragic story men are first vulnerable not in their abstract
humanity but in the particular commitments of their lives. And so
we cannot think of Keats as a man without thinking of him in his
occupation of poet. At the same time, when once we have read his
letters, we cannot help knowing that his being a poet was his chosen
way of being a man.

    The charm of Keats's letters is inexhaustible, and we can scarcely
hope to define it wholly or to name all its elements. Yet we can
be sure that some part of its effect comes from Keats's conscious
desire to live life in the heroic mode. In a young man this is always
most winning. Keats was situated in a small way of life, that of the
respectable, liberal, intellectual middle part of the middle class; his
field of action was limited to the small continuous duties of the
family; his deportment was marked by quietness and modesty, at
times by a sort of diffident neutrality. He nevertheless at every
moment took life in the largest possible way and seems never to
have been without the sense that to be, or to become, a man was
an adventurous problem. The phrase in his letters that everyone
knows, life is a "vale of Soul-making," is his summing up of that
sense, which, once we have become aware of its existence in him,
we understand to have dominated his mind. He believed that life
was given for him to find the right use of it, that it was a kind of
continuous magical confrontation requiring to be met with the
right answer. He believed that this answer was to be derived from
intuition, courage, and the accumulation of experience. It was not,
of course, to be a formula of any kind, not a piece of rationality,
but rather a way of being and of acting. And yet it could in part
be derived from taking thought, and it could be put, if not into a
formula, then at least into many formulations. Keats was nothing if
not a man of ideas.

His way of conceiving of life is characteristic of the spirited young man of high gifts—except that it is also characteristic of the very great older men whom the young men of spirit and gifts are most likely to take seriously. Its charm in Keats is the greater because its span is so short and so dramatically concise. Keats is twenty when the letters begin, and he is twenty-six when they end. But he was strikingly precocious—I am inclined to think even more precocious in his knowledge of the world than in poetry. He was one of that class of geniuses who early learn to trust themselves in an essential way, whatever moments of doubt they may have. He was remarkably lucky, or wise, in finding a circle of friends who believed in his powers before he had given much evidence of their existence beyond the communicated sense of his heroic vision, and these friends expected him to speak out. He therefore at a very early age passed beyond all self-conscious hesitation about looking deep into life and himself, about propounding the great questions and attempting the great answers, and about freely telling his thoughts. And so we have the first of the vital contradictions which make the fascination of Keats's mind—we have the wisdom of maturity arising from the preoccupations of youth. This wisdom is the proud, bitter, and joyful acceptance of tragic life which we associate preeminently with Shakespeare. It explains the force, as the sense of adventure explains the charm, of Keats's letters.

II

Bernard Shaw does not seem the likeliest person to help us toward an understanding of Keats as a man, and indeed the little essay on Keats which he once contributed to a memorial volume is for the most part perfunctory. Yet in the course of this essay Shaw speaks at some length of a quality of Keats which, at least for our time, may well be the one which we ought to recognize before any other. This quality is what Shaw calls Keats's *geniality*.

The word is not in good repute nowadays. It is seldom used in common speech, and when it is used at all it is likely to be associated with men of middle age or of hale old age—to many readers it will imply precisely what is not young and fervent, and it will have overtones of a mediocre good will that verges upon a vulgar lack of personal discriminativeness. It will suggest anything but the dedication and impatient creative energy of a young poet. But the word was not always limited by these connotations. It was not thus limited in Keats's own time. It was then a word clearly applicable to a young man: Wordsworth speaks of "the genial sense of youth." And it was precisely applicable to the idea of creativeness: when Coleridge wants to express the idea that he has lost his creative powers, he says that his "genial spirits fail," and one sense of the word that he here intends is that which derives from *genius*.[1]

The word is rich in other high meanings that will be worth noting in relation to Keats. But it will not do for us to ignore the single rather commonplace meaning which we now assign to it, the meaning of simple good-humoredness and sociability. Our notions about "the" poetic temperament being what they are, the sensitive reader is likely to shrink from Shaw's description of Keats as "not only a poet, but a merry soul, a jolly fellow, who could not only carry his splendid burthen of genius, but swing it around, toss it up and catch it again, and whistle a tune as he strode along." This is certainly not the way to describe Keats, yet it is righter than the impulse to consider this description of a poet somehow blasphemous. Nowadays our theory of poetic creation holds that the poet derives his power from some mutilation he has suffered. We take it for granted that he writes out of a darkness of the spirit or not at all. But this was not the belief of the great poets of Keats's own time, and it was not Keats's belief. Wordsworth and Coleridge thought

---

[1] For the Romantic poets the English word was no doubt reinforced by the German word, although *genial* in German had meanings that would not have recommended it to Wordsworth and Coleridge—when G. H. Lewes, in his *Life of Goethe*, describes the wild life of the young men of Weimar and their free sexuality, he says that their actions were understood and forgiven as being typical of the *genial* period and adds in a footnote: "It is difficult to find an English word to express the German *genial*, which means pertaining to genius. The genial period was the period when every extravagance was excused on the plea of genius." Even Goethe's bad spelling, as George Eliot notes in one of her letters from Germany, was spoken of as *genial*.

that poetry depended upon a condition of positive health in the poet, a more than usual well-being. Keats himself seems to have had no analogous theory of the right circumstance for creation, but it is clear that for him the writing of poetry was first a regular work, his occupation, which he practiced with sober diligence, and then a great joy. For several obvious reasons, he was much concerned with health; the word occurs very frequently in his poems, and he hated ill health, whether physical or mental. Like any person, he had times of depression; and like any person of intellect, he might give expression to these moods in gloomy generalizations. Like any literary person, he had times when he seemed to feel nothing at all, in which he was without impulse and almost without personality. But he set no store by his dark hours. He was sure that negation was not of his essence, and that it must pass for him to be himself again. He writes to his brother George of a method he had devised for dealing with depression: "Whenever I find myself growing vapourish, I rouse myself, wash and put on a clean shirt brush my hair and clothes, tie my shoestrings neatly, and in fact adonize as I were going out—then all clean and comfortable I sit down to write. This I find the greatest relief—."

"In fact adonize as I were going out"—how much this tells us about Keats. He never, he said, wrote a line with public intention, and yet when he wishes to summon up his most private faculties and bring them to high pitch, he does so by preparing himself as if for company. He had a passion for friendship and society. It is a statement that needs modification, but as at first we see him he has not the least impulse to hold himself aloof from the common pleasures of men—the community of pleasure, the generality of geniality, are an important part of his daily life. And for quite a long time he believed that the development of his mind was scarcely less communal than were his pleasures. He felt that his friends, most of whom were older than he, had much to give him and were liberal in their giving. And very likely he was right. If we suppose that Keats's own large generosity perhaps estimated at too high a rate what they did give, we must also suppose that his generosity had the actual effect of calling forth a respondent generosity from them.

In his lively sense of social connection Keats was sharing a quality of his time: the life of art and intellect was then more genial than it is now. Men of the same artistic craft, or practitioners of different crafts who stood in the same relation to the public and to the established traditions, thought it becoming in them to admire and defend each other and to be often in each other's company for professional discussion, or merely for puns and jokes. Quarrels and jealousies of course developed, as we find them developing in Keats's circle, but the impulse was stronger than it is now toward the coterie, the *cénacle,* the little group that understood the purposes and legitimate ambitions of each of its members. The Romanticists revived the ideal of friendship, of comradeship in arms, which had been so commanding both in the Middle Ages and in the Renaissance. It was an ideal appropriate to a time that necessarily thought of new art as a political act, almost as a conspiracy.

To this strong tendency of sociability and friendship Keats happily contributed, and the quality of his letters is in part to be explained by it. Not all of Keats's friends were artists, but all lived in the ambiance of the ideals of art and intellect, which, for young men, is likely to have the coloring of bohemianism. And the delicacy of feeling and the cogency of observation of Keats's letters would scarcely have appeared had not Keats been able carelessly to entrust his thoughts to his friends—and not his second thoughts but his first. We owe the wonderful, misspelled immediacy of the letters not only to confidence between friend and friend but also to the free manners of the group, which are of a piece with the generality of the masculine manners of the time. Men then, it would seem, made more occasions for exclusively masculine social diversion, and their habits were livelier than now. The set that Keats consorted with was by no means unmannerly. In the nature of the case, to be sure, there could be no emphasis on "family," and the claims of some of its members to be considered gentlemen might be disallowed by the old, almost technical definition of that rank. Nevertheless gentility was of its essence; and Keats himself, the grandson of a livery-stable keeper, the son of a former ostler and of a mother whose behavior and status became more than questionable, put a high value upon manners, and his own were, I think, exquisite. Yet Keats insisted on manners that were comfortable, and he happily tolerated those that were rowdy. Out of his admiration of Wordsworth the poet, he had every wish to excuse the failings of the man, but toward Wordsworth's stiffness in society no one could have been more severe than he. And with what enjoyment he writes of the raffish dinner of January 1818, with its extreme and elaborate sexual joking and its larking about chamberpots. Keats would not have understood the ideal of delicacy of the later nineteenth century, which so far as it manifested itself in the society of men, would have seemed to him strange and foolish.[2] The Regency manners did not in the least offend him, they suited him very well, and they account in some part for the directness and vigor of his correspondence. He and his friends attended bear-baitings and were fond of the raffish world of the prize ring. Keats, among whose books was a volume called *Fencing Familiarized,* was an excellent boxer, and he did not, we know, hesitate to engage a heavier opponent in earnest and with bare fists; he did very well on this occasion. For all his passion for what he called "abstractions," for all the ideality of his poetry, Keats loved the actuality of life; its coarseness and commonness delighted him. "Wonders are no wonders to me," he wrote in November 1819. "I am more at Home amongst Men and women. I would rather read Chaucer than Ariosto." His sense of actuality was quick and racy and in the line of the English poetic humorists from Chaucer and

---

[2] It did not manifest itself quite so thoroughly as we have come to believe—the unpublished portions of Samuel Butler's notebooks give an enlightening account of the actual habits and conversation of the gentlemen of his period. But no doubt Butler's having been at such pains to record the facts suggests what the dominant behavior was.

Skelton to Burns. "Dawlish Fair" and "Modern Love" are no
doubt to be called exceptional among Keats's poems, but they are
of the very stuff of his temperament as the letters show it.

In speaking of Keats's social geniality we shall not be accurate if
we do not recognize that there was an element of his personality
which acted to check it. His illness, of course, embittered him,
separating him, as he grew more certain of his death, from those
who still had the prospect of life, making him suspicious and jealous. But even before his illness he had already begun to withdraw
from sociability. It was perhaps to be expected. Early in his career
he had expressed to Bailey his confidence in his understanding of
the springs of human action. It was an understanding which he
was willing to say was exceptional. "As soon as I had known Haydon three days I had got enough of his character not to have been
surprised at such a Letter as he has hurt you with." "Before I felt interested in either Reynolds or Haydon—I was well read in their
faults." But with the quick understanding of human failing goes
a most profound tolerance: "—Men should bear with each other—
there lives not the Man who may not be cut up, aye hashed to
pieces on his weakest side." And the sure way of friendship, he
says, "is first to know a Man's faults, and then be passive—if after
that he insensibly draws you toward him then you have no Power
to break the link."

The tolerance was as affectionate as the understanding was undeceived, yet an understanding so undeceived could not allow
Keats's social life to be a simple one. There came a time when he
found that he was embarrassing himself and annoying his friends
by replying not to their spoken remarks but to their unspoken
intentions.

Modest as he was in all his relations, inclined as he was to a quiet
generosity of admiration, Keats had nevertheless a lively and jealous pride. He early withdrew from Leigh Hunt because Hunt
spoke patronizingly of his poetry. He was always cool to Shelley,
suspecting condescension. He began to see that one reason for his

being liked was his retiring quietness, a certain courteous withdrawal from social competitiveness which he practiced. "Think of my Pleasure in Solitude," he writes, "in comparison of my commerce with the world—there I am a child—there they do not know me not even my most intimate acquaintance—I give into their feelings as though I were refraining from irritating a little child—Some think me middling, others silly, others foolish—every one thinks he sees my weak side against my will, when in truth it is with my will—I am content to be thought all this because I have in my own breast so great a resource. This is one great reason why they like me so; because they can all show to advantage in a room, and eclipse from a certain tact one who is reckoned a good Poet—." And again: ". . . I suffer greatly by going into parties where from the rules of society and a natural pride I am obliged to smother my Spirit and look like an Idiot—because I feel that my impulses given way to would too much amaze them—I live under an everlasting restraint—never relieved except when I am composing—so I will write away."

Keats's separateness must indeed be mentioned but it must not be exaggerated. In part it was but what we all feel. Keats might say that he admired human nature and disliked men, but everybody says that, or says its converse, or both. We are all naturally not satisfied by the society around us. It never really lends itself to our purposes and expectations. Of Keats this was especially true. For him there was perhaps only one man, Shakespeare, who ever satisfied his notion of what men might be. But his separateness must also be understood as a normal aspect of his genius. It came to him in the natural course of his growing awareness of his power and identity, of the work there was for him to do and the destiny he must fulfill. The remarkable thing is not that he was separate, that he held the social world at some small distance by means of his knowledge of it, but rather that he was not more apart. His knowledge of men checked and controlled and dignified, but never limited, his geniality. Up to the end it expresses itself in his letters like an animal potency, strangely manifesting itself even when, in the bitterness of approaching death, he experiences spasms of hatred of the friends he loved.

III

When we think about Keats's social geniality, it is easy and natural for us to suppose that it is the development of his relation to his family. If Keats is genial, he is so in one of the elementary meanings of the word: he is of the *gens,* the family, and, by extension, the tribe, ultimately the nation. "I like I love England," he said. Solitary as he might be in his mind, he was never a man for physical solitude. Company gave him pleasure. He lived but little alone. He could even compose in the same room with someone else. He liked, we may say, to reconstitute the family situation.

In the nineteenth century it came increasingly to be believed that alienation from the family was indispensable to the poet's growth, and nowadays our mythology of the poetic personality takes this for granted. But Keats would not have understood what we so easily assume. In him family feeling was enormously strong and perfectly direct. Or at least this is true of his feelings toward his brothers and sister. Of what he felt for his deceased parents we can speak only speculatively. But his affection for the brothers and sister is a definitive part of his character and legend. He devoted his life to the care of young Tom in the long last months of the boy's tuberculosis. His letters to George in America are those in which he most opened his heart and mind. To his sister Fanny he was unremitting in tenderness, and, so far as the Abbeys would permit, in solicitude; it was her image, together with that of the other Fanny, that haunted him on the Italian voyage. His familial feeling amounted to what he called a passion.

There is yet another aspect of Keats's geniality of which we must take account. This is his geniality toward himself. We cannot understand Keats's mind without a very full awareness of what powers of enjoyment he had and of how freely he licensed these powers. The pleasure of the senses was for him not merely desirable—it was the very ground of life. It was, moreover, the ground of thought. More than any other poet—more, really, than Shelley—Keats is Platonic, but his Platonism is not doctrinal or systematic: it was by the natural impulse of his temperament that his mind moved up the ladder of love which Plato expounds in *The Symposium,* beginning with the love of things and moving toward the love of ideas, with existences and moving toward essences, with appetites and moving toward immortal longings. But the movement is of a special kind, perhaps of a kind that the orthodox interpretation of Plato cannot approve. For it is not, so to speak, a biographical movement—Keats does not, as he develops, "advance" from a preoccupation with sense to a preoccupation with intellect. Rather it is his characteristic mode of thought all through his life to begin with sense and to move thence to what he calls "abstraction," but never to leave sense behind. Sense cannot be left behind, for of itself it generates the idea and remains continuous with it. And the moral and speculative intensity with which Keats's poems and letters are charged has its unique grace and illumination because it goes along with, and grows out of, and conditions, but does not deny, the full autonomy of sense.

But it is not enough to speak of Keats's loyalty to sense, nor is it even enough to speak of his loyalty to the pleasures of the senses. *Sense* and *pleasures of the senses* may apply as well to Wordsworth as to Keats. We must make no mistake about it: when it comes to sense and pleasure, Keats is Wordsworth's disciple, and the great difference between the ways in which they understood the two words must not blind us to the similarities. Here, however, we are concerned with the significant difference. Our language distinguishes between the sensory, the sensuous, and the sensual. The first word is neutral as regards pleasure, the second connotes pleasure of varying degrees and kinds but is yet distinguished from the last, which suggests pleasure that is intense, appetitive, material, and which usually carries a strong pejorative overtone and almost always an implication of sexuality. For Wordsworth the pleasures of the senses are the clear sign of rightness of life, but virtually the only two sense-faculties of which he takes account are seeing and hearing, and, at that, the seeing and hearing of only a few kinds of things; and the matter of the senses' experience passes very quickly into what Wordsworth calls the "purer mind" and has been but minimally sensuous, let alone sensual. For Keats, however, there was no distinction of prestige among the senses, and to him the sensory, the sensuous, and the sensual were all one. Wordsworth would have happily concurred in the sentiment which Keats expresses when, writing to his friend Brown, he speaks of the "pleasures which it was your duty to procure," for Wordsworth had identified the "native and naked dignity of man" with the "grand elementary principle of pleasure, by which he knows, and feels, and lives, and moves." But Wordsworth would have withdrawn hastily when Keats urges Reynolds to "Gorge the honey of life" in his prospective marriage. Particularly because of the sexual context, but not because of that alone, he would have been dismayed by the appetitive image and the frankness of appetite amounting to greed.

But it is, of course, exactly the appetitive image and the frankness of his appetite that we cannot dispense with in our understanding of Keats. Eating and the delicacies of taste are basic and definitive in his experience and in his poetry. The story of his putting cayenne pepper on his tongue in order to feel the more intensely the pleasure of a draft of cold claret is apocryphal. Yet it is significant that Haydon, who told the story, was sufficiently aware of Keats's disposition to have invented it. It does not, after all, go beyond Keats's own account of his pleasure in the nectarine. "Talking of pleasure," he writes to Dilke, "this moment I was writing with one hand, and with the other holding to my Mouth a Nectarine—good god how fine. It went down soft slushy, oozy—all its delicious embonpoint melted down my throat like a large beatified Strawberry."

We are ambivalent in our conception of the moral status of eating and drinking. On the one hand ingestion supplies the imagery of our largest and most intense experiences: we speak of the wine of life and the cup of life; we speak also of its dregs and lees, and sorrow is also something to be drunk from a cup; shame and defeat are wormwood and gall; divine providence is manna or milk and honey; we hunger and thirst for righteousness; we starve for love; lovers devour each other with their eyes; and scarcely a mother has not exclaimed that oh, she could eat her baby up; bread and salt are the symbols of peace and loyalty, bread and wine the stuff of the most solemn acts of religion. On the other hand, however, while we may represent all of significant life by the tropes of eating and drinking, we do so with great circumspection. Our use of the ingestive imagery is rapid and sparse, never developed; we feel it unbecoming to dwell upon what we permit ourselves to refer to.[3]

But with Keats the ingestive imagery is pervasive and extreme. He is possibly unique among poets in the extensiveness of his reference to eating and drinking and to its pleasurable or distasteful sensations. To some readers this is likely to be alienating, and indeed even a staunch admirer might well become restive under, for example, Keats's excessive reliance on the word "dainties" to suggest all pleasures, even the pleasures of literature. It is surely possible to understand what led Yeats to speak of Keats as a boy with his face pressed to the window of a sweet-shop. The mild and not unsympathetic derogation of Yeats's image suggests something of the reason for the negative part of our ambivalence toward eating and drinking. The ingestive appetite is the most primitive of our appetites, the sole appetite of our infant state, and a preoccupation with it, an excessive emphasis upon it, is felt—and not without some reason—to imply the passivity and self-reference of the infantile

[3] The phrase "manna from heaven" is a common one, but no one ever says "quail from heaven," even though the quail were just as important as the manna in the diet which was divinely provided for the Children of Israel in the wilderness; manna, we might say, was but the divine dessert. Yet because manna was evanescent and is not to be identified with any known edible thing, it has come to serve as a metaphor for miraculous sustenance and spiritual comfort; the quail, being all too grossly actual, have been quite forgotten!

condition. No doubt that is why Ciacco, the glutton of the *Inferno*, although not accounted the worst sinner in hell, is, as it were, the most dehumanized—not the most *inhuman* as we habitually use that word, but the most disgusting; he has not even grown into the adult activity which might lead to aggressive wickedness, but sits passive under the fall of stinking snow: his is the peculiar horrible-ness of a grown man who is still an infant. And religious satirists of modern life, such as Aldous Huxley, T. S. Eliot, or Graham Greene, when they wish to make a character represent the malign infantilism of our contemporary materialist culture, ascribe to him an undue and detailed interest in eating. In this connection it is worth noting that we consent to be delighted by the description of great feasts as in Homer, Rabelais, and Dickens; the communal aspect of the eat-ing implies "maturity" and allays our fears of infantile narcissism. This is especially true if the food is plain and hearty and does not suggest cosseting, and if the appetites match it in this respect, for largeness of appetite has a moral sanction which fineness of appe-tite can never have.

But Keats did not share our culture's fear of the temptation to the passive self-reference of infancy. He did not repress the infantile wish; he confronted it, recognized it, and delighted in it. Food—and what for the infant usually goes with food, a cozy warmth—made for him the form, the elementary idea, of felicity. He did not fear the seduction of the wish for felicity, because, it would seem, he was assured that the tendency of his being was not that of regression but that of growth. The knowledge of felicity was his first experience—he made it the ground of all experience, the foundation of his quest for truth. Thus, for Keats, the luxury of food is connected with, and in a sense gives place to the luxury of sexuality. The best known example of this is the table spread with "dainties" beside Madeline's bed in "The Eve of St. Agnes." And in that famous scene the whole paraphernalia of luxurious felicity, the invoked warmth of the south, the bland and delicate food, the privacy of the bed, and the voluptuousness of the sexual encounter, are made to glow into an island of bliss with the ultimate dramatic purpose of making fully apparent the cold surrounding darkness; it is the moment of life in the infinitude of not-being. As an image of man's life it has the force of the Venerable Bede's apologue of the sparrow that flew out of the night of winter storm through the warmth and light of the king's ale-hall and out again into darkness. Keats's capacity for pleasure implies his capacity for the apprehension of tragic reality.

It also serves his capacity for what he called *abstraction*. I have said that he was the most Platonic of poets. Ideas, abstractions, were his life. He lived to perceive ultimate things, essences. This is what appetite, or love, was always coming to mean for him. Plato said that Love is the child of Abundance and Want, and for Keats it was just that. In one of the most remarkable passages of his letters he says that the heart "is the teat from which the Mind or intelligence sucks its identity." The first appetite prefigures the last; the first ingestive image is constant for this man who, in his last sonnet, speaks of "the palate of my mind," and who images the totality of life by the single grape which is burst against the "palate fine."

IV

What I have called Keats's geniality toward himself, his bold acceptance of his primitive appetite and his having kept open a line of communication with it, had its decisive effect upon the nature of his creative intelligence. It had an effect no less decisive upon his moral character.

In speaking of Keats's appetitive inclination, we cannot ignore the element of heredity. There has been ascribed to his mother's father an extravagant concern with food—Mr. Jennings was said to have been so extreme in his love of eating that his wife and family spent four days in the week preparing for the Sunday dinner. His daughter, Keats's mother, was said to have resembled him in this gormandizing character, "but she was more remarkably the Slave of other Appetites attributable probably to this for their exciting Cause." The witness, to be sure, is Mr. Abbey, Keats's guardian, who was no doubt narrow in his views, and admirers of Keats naturally dislike him and allow him little credit or credence. Yet it was to the admirable John Taylor, Keats's publisher and loyal friend, that Abbey told his story; Taylor was an intelligent man and he must have known in some detail of the dealings of Abbey with the Keats children, yet Taylor speaks of Abbey as "kind hearted" and "good," and did not, as we are inclined to do, dismiss his testimony out of a pious partisanship but, on the contrary, thought him a man worthy of belief. And although Abbey may well have been exaggerating, he was not necessarily making it up out of whole cloth when he said that the young Frances Jennings was so ardent in her passions that it was dangerous to be alone with her, and that at an early age she had told him that she must have and would have a husband. We make what discount we will for Mr. Abbey's susceptibility and for his narrowness of view, even for his spite, and still we cannot but suppose that Frances was of a lively and straightforward sexual temperament. Abbey said that she was a pretty little woman (but Cowden Clark says she was tall) with regular features, although her mouth was too wide. He remembered that she troubled a certain shopkeeper on rainy days because she held her skirts too high in crossing the street, showing "uncommonly handsome legs."[4]

Whether or not Frances Keats was, in the conventional sense, a good woman and a good mother is a hard judgment to make. The piety of biographers inclines to say that she was, or at least that she was not bad, and explains her second marriage three months after the death of her husband as a necessary practical step to maintain the livery stable, and dismisses as a mere canard Abbey's story that

[4] Abbey's account of Mrs. Keats is reported in a letter of John Taylor as given in *The Keats Circle,* edited by Hyder Edward Rollins (Cambridge: Harvard University Press, 1948). The testimony of George Keats and of Reynolds, cited in the following pages, is from the same source.

after leaving Rawlings, the unendurable second husband, she formed a liaison with a Jew named Abraham and became addicted to brandy. Yet it is a remarkable fact that in all of Keats's letters, many of which are to his brothers and sisters, there is but a single reference to their mother, and this but a trifling one. (There is no mention at all of his father.) Keats was fifteen when his mother died (nine at the death of his father) so that he was certainly not without memory of her. We might suppose that in the normal course of things he would speak of her, that, in his tender letters to his sister Fanny, he would try to keep the mother's image alive in the little girl's mind. But we have not a word. There was much, it would seem, to be forgotten.

Yet it would also seem that there was much to be, in some fashion, remembered. Reynolds tells us that when John, at school, received the news of her death he was inconsolable. "When his mother died, which was suddenly—he gave way to such impassioned and prolonged grief—(hiding himself in a nook under the master's desk) as awakened the liveliest pity and sympathy in all who saw him." And George Keats, in a letter to Dilke, makes what is, I believe, the only significant reference by one of the Keats children to their mother: he says she "resembled John very much in the face, was extremely fond of him and humored him in every whim, of which he had not a few." He adds: "She was a most excellent and affectionate parent and as I thought a woman of uncommon talents."

We may take George's estimate of his mother as the expression of filial decency; or as the truth; or as some part of the truth. Yet there would seem to be no reason to question, there is indeed reason to suppose, her affectionate and indulgent nature—what we may call a biological generosity. It is then not difficult to understand the genesis of Keats's preoccupation with a felicity of "dainties," kisses, and coziness.

But how are we to understand the heroic quality of Keats, the quality of moral energy? In part, it is clear, by reference to Keats's temperamental endowment. We read of the violent child of five

who armed himself with a sword and brandished it on guard at the
door and refused to let his mother leave the house; the story in this
form is given by Haydon, who is not reliable, though usually apt,
in the stories he tells; another version of the story is that Keats used
the sword to keep anyone from entering his mother's room when
she was ill. We read of the schoolboy who would fight anyone—he
offered to fight one of the ushers who had boxed his brother Tom's
ears—and of whom it was said that anyone might easily fancy he
would become great, but rather in some military capacity than in
literature. The traits that make up what Plato calls the "spirited"
part of the soul were early and extreme in Keats. But Keats himself
made, as we may, a clear genetic connection between felicity and
manly energy. He who had stood guard at the door—whether to
keep his mother safe from invaders or to keep her captive—wrote in
Endymion of the happy pastoral people of Latmos as those fair
creatures "whose young children's children bred / Thermopylae its
heroes," and omitted all mention of any intervening period of Spar-
tan training. When he laid down the program of his development
as a poet, he stipulated that the first phase of his life in poetry be
devoted to sensual felicity as a prelude to his confrontation of the
noble pain of existence.

It is possible to say of Keats that the indulgence of his childhood
goes far toward explaining the remarkable firmness of his character, what I have spoken of as his heroic quality. This is not the
occasion to engage upon a discussion of the theory of child-rearing.
Such discussions, as conducted by laymen, and even as conducted
by experts, are all too likely to be unmodulated, contrasting an
unqualified indulgence or "permissiveness" with an equally unqualified disciplinary attitude. Indulgence is of many kinds and may
be given in many contexts. Strength of character is also of different
kinds, and it is necessary to ask what kind of strength our method
of rearing seeks to inculcate. Thus there can be no doubt that a
vigorous and strictly disciplinary training can indeed produce
strength of a kind, even of an admirable kind. But, granting the

complexity of the subject, I would yet venture to deal with it to the extent of proposing the idea that the person who was happily indulged as a child can in maturity—to use Keats's words—"bid these joys farewell" and "pass them for a nobler life," doing so of his own volition, with the moral advantages which attend upon free choice. His need of the childish joys has been satisfied, his will has not been fixed upon them.

"How strange it seems," says John Taylor after having retailed Mr. Abbey's account of Keats's parents, "that such a creature of the Elements as he should have sprung from such gross Realities—But how he refined upon the sensualities of his parents." How he refined indeed, but his relation to the "gross Realities" is not strange at all, or not strange in the way that Taylor meant. For the great and remarkable thing about Keats is that he did not refine by negation but by natural growth, by the tendency of life *to* refine. And when he had reached the top of the Platonic ladder of the appetites and had come as close as he could to what he called "fellowship with essence," he had no wish to kick over the ladder by which he had climbed. He felt free at any moment to climb down to the bottommost rung, to put himself in touch with his first appetites. He was, as Taylor says, "a creature of the Elements," but he never forgot, as Taylor apparently did, that the elements include not only air, fire, and water, but also earth.

This license to put himself in touch with his first appetites, this unquestioning faith in pleasure, has played an important part in the developing estimate of Keats. It accounts for the need felt by certain of his partisans to insist that he was really a very manly young person. As the biographical and critical studies accumulate, the insistence is ever more strongly made, but even at its strongest it carries the implication that Keats was very manly *after all,* that we can see the manliness if we look close: the boy with his face pressed to the sweet-shop window is the image that persists, if only to be corrected.

But the fact is that Keats's mature masculinity is not something that is to be discovered by special perceptiveness. It is the essence of his being. One hesitates to say what one means by mature masculinity when the cultural anthropologists have been at such pains to disturb our old notions of it, and when in modern culture so much confusion exists about its nature and its value. Yet we may venture to say that in the traditional culture of Europe it has existed as an ideal that implies a direct relationship to the world of external reality, which, by activity, it seeks to understand, or to master, or to come to honorable terms with; and it implies fortitude, and responsibility for both one's duties and one's fate, and intention, and an insistence upon one's personal value and honor.

It is impossible to read Keats's letters without seeing that this was indeed his personal ideal. And the way he held it, the grace of his holding it, suggests to me that it grew easily and gently out of his happy relation with his infant appetites. To insist upon the growth of this ideal as a natural thing, and upon its not having negated what it grew out of, is not to deny all conflict. After all, Keats did institute a kind of antagonism between the idea of luxury and the idea of energetic morality. But in a complex and difficult culture the development of personality, even at its easiest and most natural, proceeds always by conflict—Freud speaks of the erroneous belief of laymen that all neuroses (i.e., psychic conflicts) "are entirely superfluous things which have no right whatever to exist." We may not unreasonably suppose of Keats that both the seductiveness and the disorderliness that attended his mother's biological generosity made conflict the more necessary and the more lively. But what is characteristic of Keats is that the conflict is never to the death, is never cruel. He seems never to have wished to injure or destroy any part of himself. The conflicting ideals seem to understand each other and to wish to come to terms with each other.

As good an instance as any of the firmness, the developed strength of Keats's character is his simple probity in money matters. Even to himself this simple virtue seemed of great significance. It was often necessary for him to draw upon his publishers, Taylor and Hessey, who treated him with a generosity which was no doubt made the easier for them by Keats's financial punctiliousness. To Taylor he writes of "the sense of squareness . . . in me" and of his "desire to be correct in money matters." He generalizes upon this exactitude in a striking way: in August of 1819 he writes to Taylor explaining why, in taking an advance, he prefers to secure the money by a note endorsed by his friend Brown. "I must observe again," he says, "that it is not from want of reliance on your readiness to assist me that I offer a Bill; but as a relief to myself from a too lax sensation of Life—which ought to be responsible which requires chains for its own sake—duties to fulfill with the more earnestness the less strictly they are imposed."

I have referred to the remark made by an old schoolfellow that Keats was a boy whom anyone might easily have fancied would become great, but rather "in some military capacity than in literature." And there is indeed in Keats's character a sort of ideal military virtue whenever he confronts the difficulties of life. What he calls the "flint-worded" letter of August 16, 1819, to Fanny Brawne, is full of military references as he discusses their situation, his lack of money, his powers of work. "This Page as my eye skims over it I see is excessively unloverlike and ungallant—I cannot help it—I am no officer in yawning quarters." He is, that is to say, in action. He says he cannot, will not, be careless of his friends' money. "You see how I go on," he says, "like so many strokes of a Hammer. I cannot help it—I am impell'd, driven to it. I am not happy enough for silken Phrases, and silver sentences. I can no more use soothing words to you than if I were at this moment engaged in a charge of Cavalry." He is hard at work—as he says, "in the fever." "I would feign, as my sails are set, sail on without interruption for a Brace of Months longer." The sailing image is in his mind because he is about to tell Fanny of an incident of naval fortitude which had moved him to admiration: the ship in which he was sailing to Southampton had with its bowlines snapped the top of the mast of a Navy launch. "Had the mast been a little stouter they would have been upset. In so trifling an event I could not help admiring our Seamen—Neither officer nor man in the whole Boat moved a Muscle—they scarcely notic'd it even with words—Forgive me this flint-worded Letter, and believe and see that I cannot think of you without some sort of energy—though mal a propos."

This is Keats's characteristic tone when he confronts the necessity of action. We know with what dread he contemplates the Italian journey, but, as he writes to Shelley, he will undertake it "as a soldier marches up to a battery," and he uses the same image to Taylor. Poetry was his life, yet when he wishes to praise poetry he says, "I am convinced more and more day by day that fine writing is next to fine doing the top thing in the world. . . ." With him the deed comes before the word. The deed is, as it were, the guarantor of the word. Even the dull action of getting a living was charged for him with heroic meaning. Disappointed in the expectation of a financial competence and faced with the necessity of supporting himself, he came to understand that he could live only by his own exertions and self-denial. "I had got into a habit of mind of looking towards you as a help in all difficulties," he writes to Brown. "This very habit would be the parent of idleness and difficulties. You will see it as a duty I owe myself to break the neck of it. I do nothing for my subsistence —make no exertion. At the end of another year you shall applaud me,—not for verses, but for conduct." He was one, as he had said some years before, to "volunteer for uncomfortable hours." He had that in him "which will well bear the buffets of the world."

The remarkable statement to Fanny Brawne, "I cannot think of you without some sort of energy," tells us much. Energy is of his essence. It is the basis of his conception of morality, although it may transcend morality. "Though a quarrel in the Streets is a thing to be hated, the energies displayed in it are fine; the commonest Man shows a grace in his quarrel—By a superior being our reasonings may take the same tone—though erroneous they may be fine."

In his own life he recognizes two states of being which would seem equally opposed to energy. One is what he calls "agonie ennuiyeuse" or despair—"I must choose," he says, "between despair and Energy." The other is a happy passivity, what he calls indolence—"a sort of temper indolent and supremely careless"—or languor or laziness: "If I had teeth of pearl and the breath of lillies I should call it languor—but as I am [his own footnote here: "Especially as I have a black eye"] I must call it Laziness." And he goes on: "In this state of effeminacy the fibres of the brain are relaxed in common with the rest of the body, and to such a happy degree that pleasure has no show of enticement and pain no unbearable frown."

"Agonie ennuiyeuse" is, of course, spleen, or melancholy, or acedia: it is the very opposite of energy. But there is no real antagonism between Keats's "indolence" and his energy. Keats's great statement of the principle of passivity is contained in the marvelous letter to Reynolds of February 19, 1818. This letter, unpremeditated as it is, has the effect of a work of contrived art as it accumulates its similitudes and intensifies its meaning until at last it becomes incandescent in the lovely blank-verse sonnet of the thrush, with its reiterated "O fret not after knowledge—I have none." It is the exposition of the principle of the *power* of passivity, of what Keats calls "diligent Indolence." The passivity in question is of course related to Wordsworth's "wise passiveness," but it is far more richly characterized. Significantly enough, it is characterized in a sexual way: "Who shall say between Man and Woman which is the most delighted?"—that is, in the sexual act.[5] And he has in mind the power of conception, incubation, gestation. It is not the least remarkable thing about Keats that, for all his "tendency to class women in my books with roses and sweetmeats,—they never see themselves dominant," he had an awareness, rare in our culture, of the female principle as a power, an energy. He does not shrink from experiencing its manifestation in himself, believing it to be half of his power of creation. Yet bold as he is in this, he must still assert the virtue of the specifically "mascu-

[5] It is perhaps worth recalling that an answer to this question is given in the classical dictionary which Keats used—Lemprière's. Tiresias, who had been transformed into a woman and then, after some years, restored to his original sex, was asked to settle a dispute between Juno and Jupiter and gave it as his opinion that women have ten times the pleasure of men. This so angered Juno that she deprived Tiresias of his eyesight; in compensation Jupiter bestowed upon him the gift of prophecy.

line" energy: even the thrush assures him that "he's awake who thinks himself asleep," that by being conscious of his surrender to the passive, unconscious life he has affirmed the active principle.

V

The dialectic which Keats instituted between passivity and activity presents itself in another form, in the opposition between thought and sensation. The case against the notion that Keats was systematically anti-intellectual has been conclusively made by Professor Clarence Thorpe, but apparently for each new generation of readers the evidence of his hostility to intellect seems more dramatic and decisive than that of his almost extravagant respect for intellect. His having said, "O for a Life of Sensations rather than of Thoughts," his having with Lamb drunk confusion to Newton, his general concurrence in the antagonism to eighteenth-century rationalism which prevailed in his set, and perhaps especially what is usually understood to be the doctrine of "Lamia," are taken to lend sanction to the belief that Keats was uniformly hostile to the exercise of the conscious mind. But Keats is far less simple than this would make him out to be. The injunction of the thrush's song, "O fret not after knowledge," had great authority with him, yet he did fret after knowledge and thought it right to do so. When he speaks of applying himself energetically to poetry, he conceives of that application as being in part to reading and study. "I know nothing I have read nothing and I mean to follow Solomon's directions of 'get Wisdom—get understanding'—I find cavalier days are gone by. I find that I can have no enjoyment in the World but continual drinking of Knowledge— . . . there is but one way for me—the road lies through application study and thought."

The idea that Keats was anti-intellectual used to be easier to maintain when it was believed that, as one nineteenth-century critic put it, "Keats had no mind." To us the power of his mind is even more astonishing than the opinion that he had none, and we can scarcely be surprised that he should delight in its exercise. He did not think that difficult or abstract reading could corrupt his poetic impulse, and he was glad that he had kept his medical books; he found "every department of Knowledge . . . excellent and calculated towards a great whole." He conceived the emotional effect of knowledge to be analogous to that of poetry, which for him was successful when it led the reader to calmness. "An extensive knowledge is needful to thinking people—it takes away the heat and fever; and helps, by widening speculation, to ease the Burden of the Mystery." He said that "high Sensations" without knowledge induced anxiety—"horror"—but knowledge prevented fear. His judgment of his "Isabella" is that it has "too much inexperience of life and simplicity of knowledge in it."

He could, as we have seen, rate poetry inferior to action; he could also rate it inferior to philosophy. In the passage already referred to, in which he talks about how the charm of energy may be thought to redeem error, he says, "This is the very thing in which consists poetry; and if so it is not so fine a thing as philosophy— For the same reason that an eagle is not so fine a thing as a truth." He then goes on to say that he now understands from experience the force of Milton's line, "how charming is divine Philosophy." To Keats, ideas were what Milton said they were, "musical as is Apollo's lute," and he conceived that in heaven, where the potentiality of all things is realized, the nightingale will sing "not as a senseless tranced thing" but will utter philosophic truth.

If Keats did not accept the traditional antagonism between sensation and poetry on the one hand and intellect and knowledge on the other, it was because he understood intellect and knowledge in a certain way. He did not, that is, suppose that mind was an entity different in kind from and hostile to the sensations and emotions. Rather, mind came into being when the sensations and emotions were checked by external resistance or by conflict with each other, when, to use the language of Freud, the pleasure principle is confronted by the reality principle. Now, in Keats the reality principle

was very strong. Was it ever by anyone more starkly asserted than in
the phrase he used to Fanny Brawne: "I would mention that there
are impossibilities in the world"? And it was strong in proportion to
the strength of the pleasure principle. Philosophy and knowledge,
the matter of the intellect, were for him associated in their old traditional way with the burden of life: to be "philosophical" means to
acknowledge with the mind the pain of the world, and it means to
derive courage from taking thought. "Until we are sick, we understand not;—in fine, as Byron says, 'Knowledge is Sorrow'; and I go
on to say that 'Sorrow is Wisdom.' "[6]

But the sentence does not end here. It goes on: "—and further for
aught we can know for certainty 'Wisdom is folly'!" This is perhaps
a mere flourish to dismiss the subject. But it is also something more.
It is an instance of Keats's urge toward the dialectical view of any
large question, of his refusal to be fixed in a final judgment. As such
it points toward that faculty of the mind to which Keats gave the
name of "Negative Capability."

No one reading the letters of Keats can come on the phrase and its
definition without feeling that among the many impressive utterances of the letters this one is especially momentous. It is, indeed,
not too much to say that the power and quality of Keats's mind concentrate in this phrase, as does the energy of his heroism, for the
conception of Negative Capability leads us to Keats's transactions
with the problem of evil, and to know the high temper of his mind
we must follow where it leads.

VI

On the twenty-first of December, 1817, Keats wrote to his brothers,
telling them, among other things, of his having gone to the Christmas pantomime with his friends Brown and Dilke and that, while
walking home with them, he had what he called "not a dispute but
a disquisition" with Dilke. The disquisition touched on "various

[6] Byron actually said, "Sorrow is knowledge." (*Manfred* I. i. 10.)

subjects" which are not specified, and Keats says that as it proceeded "several things dovetailed in my mind, and at once it struck me what quality went to form a Man of Achievement especially in Literature. . . . I mean *Negative Capability,* that is when man is capable of being in uncertainties, Mysteries, doubts, without any irritable reaching after fact and reason."

In an ideological age such as ours the faculty of Negative Capability is a rare one, and Keats's naming and defining it attracts a good deal of notice either for praise or blame. It is often misunderstood. Thus, it is sometimes taken to mean that poetry should have no traffic with ideas, and that the creative writer is exempt from the judgment of intellectual validity. This is not in the least Keats's intention. Keats thinks of Negative Capability as, precisely, an element of intellectual power. At a later time, taking up the subject again,[7] he says, "the only means of strengthening one's intellect is to make up ones mind about nothing—to let the mind be a thoroughfare for all thoughts. Not a select party. . . ."

But this statement, although it clears away any doubts of the specifically intellectual nature of Negative Capability, is in itself very questionable. On its face it is obviously not true—it is certainly not true that "to make up one's mind about nothing" is the only means of strengthening one's intellect. Exclusion is quite as much a part of the intellectual process as inclusion, and making up one's mind is not only the end of intellection but one of the means of intellection. Yet Keats's statement may well be true in reference to a certain kind of person and to a certain kind of problem—to a certain kind of person dealing with a certain kind of problem. It is essential to an understanding of what Keats meant that we have in mind the kind of person who was Keats's interlocutor in the "disquisition" during which the idea came to him, and also the kind of problem that was at the moment preoccupying Keats's thought.

Charles Wentworth Dilke was a man whom Keats knew to be not only very good but very intelligent. But Keats was of the settled

---

[7] But he never uses the famous phrase again.

opinion that Dilke was far too doctrinaire in his intellect. He calls him a "Godwin perfectability Man," and because it is not only the doctrine of human perfectibility that is important in his judgment of Dilke—although it is *very* important—but also the over-systematic process of thought by which the doctrine is arrived at and maintained, he calls Dilke a "Godwin-methodist." And he says of his friend that he "will never come at a truth so long as he lives; because he is always trying at it." This is a habit of mind which Dilke shares with Coleridge—in the passage in which Keats formulates the idea of Negative Capability, he cites Coleridge as an example of "irritable reaching after fact and reason." Coleridge, he says, was incapable of "remaining Content with half knowledge."

We are aware of a simple paradox, for traditionally truth must be striven for—*ad astra per aspera*. And half-knowledge is a sciolist's knowledge and "a dangerous thing." But we must consider the particular kind of problem to which the exercise of Negative Capability is appropriate. It will not be a scientific problem (although more than one great discoverer in science has said that at times it is well to suspend the irritable reaching after fact and reason, to let the mind be a thoroughfare for all thoughts or no thoughts, that then the data often speak unbidden). It will be a human problem—Shakespeare is Keats's example of a mind content with half-knowledge, "capable of being in uncertainties, Mysteries, doubts." And in point of fact it is a particular and very large human problem, nothing less than the problem of evil.

This becomes apparent if we follow the line of thought that has been begun earlier in the letter. Before writing about the Christmas pantomime and Negative Capability, Keats tells his brothers that he has been to see Benjamin West's picture, "Death on the Pale Horse." He says that "it is a wonderful picture, when West's age is considered" (West was nearly eighty), but that he does not really admire it. One objection to it that he makes is that "there is nothing to be intense upon; no woman one feels mad to kiss; no face swelling into reality." Another objection is the artist's way of handling what Keats calls "disagreeables." "The excellence of every Art," he says, "is its intensity, capable of making all disagreeables evaporate, from their being in close relation with Beauty and Truth. Examine King Lear and you will find this exemplified throughout, but in this picture we have unpleasantness without any momentous depth of speculation excited, in which to bury its repulsiveness." And this theme is picked up again when Keats brings to an end his definition of Negative Capability: when he has made the famous remark about half-knowledge and remaining in "uncertainties, Mysteries, doubts," he says that the subject, if "pursued through Volumes would perhaps take us not further than this, that with a great poet the sense of Beauty overcomes every other consideration, or rather obliterates all consideration."

With this sentence we are at the very center of Keats's theory of art. It is a theory of extreme complexity and I shall not attempt to deal with it here. But the element of the theory that chiefly makes for its complexity—and its power—must at least be mentioned. Keats's theory of art is, among other things, an effort to deal with the problem of evil.

A contemporary literate mind is likely to be made uncomfortable by certain of the things that Keats says about the representation of evil in art, by the open resistance he makes to "disagreeables." We find him, for example, in "Sleep and Poetry," being very harsh with certain of his contemporaries, Byron in particular, over the subjects of their poetry. The themes, he says, are ugly clubs, the poets Polyphemes. And he quite shocks the modern literate mind by requiring of poetry that it should not feed "upon the burrs and thorns of life" and by judging those poets to be most worthy of respect "who simply tell the most heart-easing things." This is an opinion that will seem to us to have been dredged up from the depths of Philistinism. We can scarcely understand how a true poet, let alone a great poet, could have uttered it.

Similarly, when Keats concludes his remarks about Negative Capability with the observation that "with a great poet the sense of

Beauty overcomes every other consideration, or rather obliterates all consideration," meaning all considerations of what is disagreeable or painful, it may seem that he has evaded the issue, that, having raised the question of painful truth in art, he betrays it to beauty in a statement that really has no meaning. It is in this way that many readers understand the concluding aphorism, the "moral," of the "Ode to a Grecian Urn"—out of politeness to poetry they may consent to be teased, but they cannot suppose that they are enlightened by the statement, "Beauty is truth, truth beauty," for, as they say, beauty is not all of truth, and not all truth is beautiful. Nor will they be the more disposed to find meaning in the notorious aphorism by the poet's extravagant assertion that in it is to be found "all/Ye know on earth, and all ye need to know."

But the statement, "Beauty is truth, truth beauty," was not for Keats, and need not be for us, a "pseudo-statement," large, resonant, engaging, but without actual significance. Beauty was not for Keats, as it is for many, an inert thing, or a thing whose value lay in having no relevance to ordinary life: it was not a word by which he evaded, but a word by which he confronted, issues. What he is saying in his letter is that a great poet (e.g., Shakespeare) looks at human life, sees the terrible truth of its evil, but sees it so intensely that it becomes an element of the beauty which is created by his act of perception—in the phrase by which Keats describes his own experience as merely a reader of *King Lear,* he "burn[s] through" the evil. To say, as many do, that "truth is beauty" is a false statement is to ignore our experience of the tragic art. Keats's statement is an accurate description of the response to evil or ugliness which tragedy makes: the matter of tragedy is ugly or painful truth seen as beauty. To see life in this way, Keats believes, is to see life truly: that is, as it must be seen if we are to endure to live it. Beauty is thus a middle term which connects and reconciles two kinds of truth—through the mediation of beauty, truth of fact becomes truth of affirmation, truth of life. For we must understand about Keats that he sought strenuously to discover the reason why we should live, and that he called those things good, or beautiful, or true, which induced us to live or which conduced to our health. (He had not walked the hospital wards for nothing.)

This way of seeing life, the poet's way, characterized by "intensity," is obviously anything but a "negative" capability—it is the most *positive* capability imaginable. But Keats understood it to be protected and made possible by Negative Capability: the poet avoids making those doctrinal utterances about the nature of life, about life's goodness or badness or perfectibility, which, if he rests in them, will prevent his going on to his full poetic vision.

At this point Keats's opinion of Dilke becomes important again. Keats believed that the Negative Capability which made possible the poetic vision of life depended upon a certain personal quality which he thought Dilke lacked. Of that poor Dilke who will never come at a truth so long as he lives because he is always trying at it, Keats says that he is "a Man who cannot feel he has a personal identity unless he had made up his Mind about every thing." Negative Capability, the faculty of not having to make up one's mind about everything, depends upon the sense of one's personal identity and is the sign of personal identity. Only the self that is certain of its existence, of its identity, can do without the armor of systematic certainties.[8] To remain content with half-knowledge is to remain content with contradictory knowledges; it is to believe that "sorrow is wisdom" and also that "wisdom is folly." It is not all of truth that Keats is concerned with but rather that truth which is to be discovered between the contradiction of love and death, between the sense of personal identity and the certainty of pain and extinction.

Along with other of the English romantic poets, Keats is often said to have lacked an adequate awareness of evil and to have failed to see it as a condition of life and a problem of thought. I have indicated my belief that the contrary of this is true, that the problem

[8] This is only apparently contradicted by certain notable remarks which Keats made about men of genius in poetry *lacking* personal identity. (See the letter to Bailey of 22 November 1817 and the letter to Woodhouse of 27 October 1818.) In these passages he is speaking of the poet as poet, not of the poet as man.

of evil lies at the very heart of Keats's thought. But for Keats the awareness of evil exists side by side with a very strong sense of personal identity and is for that reason the less immediately apparent. To some contemporary readers it will seem for the same reason the less intense. In the same way it may seem to a contemporary reader that, if we compare Shakespeare and Kafka, leaving aside the degree of genius each has, and considering both only as expositors of man's suffering and cosmic alienation, it is Kafka who makes the more intense and complete exposition. And indeed the judgment may be correct, exactly because for Kafka the sense of evil is not contradicted by the sense of personal identity. Shakespeare's world, quite as much as Kafka's, is that prison cell which Pascal says the world is, from which daily the inmates are led forth to die; Shakespeare no less than Kafka forces upon us the cruel irrationality of the conditions of human life, the tale told by an idiot, the puerile gods who torture us not for punishment but for sport; and no less than Kafka, Shakespeare is revolted by the fetor of the prison of this world, nothing is more characteristic of him than his imagery of disgust. But in Shakespeare's cell the company is so much better than in Kafka's, the captains and kings and lovers and clowns of Shakespeare are alive and complete before they die. In Kafka, long before the sentence is executed, even long before the malign legal process is ever instituted, something terrible has been done to the accused. We all know what that is—he has been stripped of all that is becoming to a man except his abstract humanity, which, like his skeleton, never is quite becoming to a man. He is without parents, home, wife, child, commitment, or appetite; he has no connection with power, beauty, love, wit, courage, loyalty, or fame, and the pride that may be taken in these. So that we may say that Kafka's knowledge of evil exists without the contradictory knowledge of the self in its health and validity, that Shakespeare's knowledge of evil exists with that contradiction in its fullest possible force.[9] It is therefore not hard to

---

[9] It would, of course, be less than accurate and fair not to remark of Kafka that he had a very intense knowledge of the self through its negation, that his great and terrible point is exactly the horror of the loss of the Shakespearean knowledge of the self.

understand the virtually religious reverence in which Shakespeare began to be held in the nineteenth century, for when religion seemed no longer able to represent the actualities of life, it was likely to be Shakespeare who, to a thoughtful man, most fully confronted the truth of life's complex horror, while yet conveying the stubborn sense that life was partly blessed, not wholly cursed.

Now Keats's attachment to the principle of reality was, as I have said, a strong one. He perceived the fact of evil very clearly, and he put it at the very center of his mental life. He saw, as he said, "too far into the sea" and beheld there the "eternal fierce destruction" of the struggle for existence, and the shark and the hawk at prey taught him that the gentle and habitual robin was not less predatory, that life in its totality was cruel; he saw youth grow pale and specter-thin and die, saw life trod down by life, the hungry generations on the march. For all his partisanship with social amelioration, he had no hope whatever that life could be ordered in such a way that its condition might be anything but tragic. He was not a theological mind like Kafka—some other adjective of large import must be used to suggest the scope and dignity of the questions with which he was preoccupied—yet evil presented its problem to him in the theological or quasi-theological form in which alone it has any meaning. What is traditionally and technically called the problem of evil raises a question about the nature of God, who is said to be both benevolent and omnipotent, for man's experience of pain would seem to limit either God's benevolence or his power. And the evil which makes the problem truly a problem is neither that which is the natural outcome of man's wrong deeds, nor that which may be understood, by any human conception of justice, as divine punishment. In the Book of Job the problem of evil cannot be really stated until the ground has been cleared of the conventional apologetics which try to explain Job's suffering as punishment for his sins: the divine voice itself says that the suffering is not a punishment. For Dostoevski the problem of evil must be stated in terms of the suffering of children—of human creatures, that is, of whom we cannot say that their pain is the consequence of their guilt. And Keats, who thought of women as exempt from the moral life of men, and therefore not to be held responsible or guilty, conceives the problem of evil with particular reference to them. "Why," he asks, "should Woman suffer?" And that *women* should "have Cancers" is to him a conclusive instance of the unexplainable cruelty of the cosmos.

But at the same time that Keats had his clear knowledge of evil, he had his equally clear knowledge of the self. Most of us are conventional in our notions of reality and we suppose that what is grim and cruel is more real than what is pleasant. Like most conventionalities of thought, this one is a form of power-worship—evil and pain seem realer to us than the assertions of the self because we know that evil and pain always win in the end. But Keats did not share in our acquiescence. His attachment to reality was stronger and more complex than ours usually is, for to him the self was just as real as the evil that destroys it. The idea of reality and the idea of the self and its annihilation go together for him. "After all there is certainly something real in the World—. . . . Tom [his brother] has spit a leetle blood this afternoon, and that is rather a damper—but I know —the truth is there is something real in the World." He conceives of the energy of the self as at least one source of reality. "As Tradesmen say every thing is worth what it will fetch, so probably every mental pursuit takes its reality and worth from the ardour of the pursuer— being in itself a nothing." And again: "I am certain of nothing but of the holiness of the Heart's affections and the truth of the Imagination— What the imagination seizes as Beauty must be truth— whether it existed before or not—for I have the same Idea of all our Passions as of Love they are all in their sublime, creative of essential Beauty. . . . The Imagination may be compared to Adam's dream [in *Paradise Lost*]—he awoke and found it truth."

He affirms, that is, the creativity of the self that opposes circumstance, the self that is imagination and desire, that, like Adam, assigns names and values to things, and that can realize what it envisions.

Keats never deceives himself into believing that the power of the imagination is sovereign, that it can make the power of circumstance of no account. His sense of the stubborn actuality of the material world is as stalwart as Wordsworth's. It is, indeed, of the very nature of his whole intellectual and moral activity that he should hold in balance the reality of self and the reality of circumstance. In another letter to Bailey he makes the two realities confront each other in a very telling way. He is speaking of the malignity of society toward generous enthusiasm and, as he goes on, his thought moves from the life of society to touch upon the cosmos, whose cruelty, as he thinks of it, impels him to reject the life in poetry and the reward of fame he so dearly wants. "Were it in my choice," he says, "I would reject a petrarchal coronation—on account of my dying day, and because women have Cancers." But then in the next sentence but one: "Yet I am not old enough or magnanimous enough to annihilate self. . . ." He has brought his two knowledges face to face, the knowledge of the world of circumstance, of death and cancer, and the knowledge of the world of self, of spirit and creation, and the delight in them. Each seems a whole knowledge considered alone; each is but a half-knowledge when taken with the other; both together constitute a truth.

It is in terms of the self confronting hostile or painful circumstance that Keats makes his magnificent effort at the solution of the problem of evil, his heroic attempt to show how it is that life may be called blessed when its circumstances are cursed. This occurs in the course of his dazzling letter to George and Georgiana Keats in Kentucky which he began on February 14, 1819, and sealed on May 3. It is a massive journal-letter into which Keats copies, among lesser examples of his work, the sonnet "Why did I laugh to-night?," the two sonnets on fame, "La Belle Dame Sans Merci," the sonnet on sleep and the sonnet on rhyme, and the "Ode to Psyche." It is crammed full of gossip, personal, literary, and theatrical, and equally full of Keats's most serious and characteristic thought. The letter, indeed, is the quintessence of Keats's life-style, of his way of dealing with experience. It is one of the most remarkable documents of the culture of the century.

The climax of the letter occurs in the last full entry, that of April

15, in which Keats makes his dead-set at the problem of evil. This entry is the first after that of March 19, which in itself constitutes a very notable episode in Keats's intellectual life. The earlier entry is Keats's attempt to deal with the problem in aesthetic terms, as the later is his attempt to deal with it in moral terms. In the March 19 entry he writes that he is in a state of languorous relaxation in which "pleasure has no show of enticement and pain no unbearable frown," a condition which he calls "the only happiness." But at the moment of setting this down he receives a note from Haslam telling of the imminently expected death of his friend's father, and he is led to speak of the ironic mutability of life. "While we are laughing the seed of some trouble is put into the wide arable land of event— while we are laughing it sprouts it grows and suddenly bears a poison fruit which we must pluck." Then follows a meditation on our inability really to respond to the troubles of our friends and on the virtue of "disinterestedness." This leads to the thought that disinterestedness, so great a virtue in society, is not to be found in "wild nature," where its presence, indeed, would destroy the natural economy of tooth and claw. But from the spectacle of self-interested cruelty of wild nature he snatches the idea of the brilliance of the energies that are in play in the struggle for existence. "This it is that makes the Amusement of Life—to a speculative Mind. I go amongst the Fields and catch a glimpse of a Stoat or a fieldmouse peeping out of the withered grass—the creature hath a purpose and its eyes are bright with it. I go among the buildings of a city and I see a Man hurrying along—to what? the Creature has a purpose and his eyes are bright with it." He thinks of the disinterestedness of Jesus and of how little it has established itself as against the self-interest of men, and again he snatches at the idea that perhaps life may be justified by its sheer energy: "May there not be superior beings amused with any graceful, though instinctive attitude my mind may fall into, as I am entertained with the alertness of a Stoat or the anxiety of a Deer? Though a quarrel in the Streets is a thing to be hated, the energies displayed in it are fine; the commonest Man shows a grace in his quarrel— By a superior being our reasonings may take the same tone —though erroneous they may be fine— This is the very thing in which consists poetry—"

It is very brilliant, very fine, but it does not satisfy him; "amusement," "entertainment" are not enough. Even poetry is not enough. Energy is the very thing "in which consists poetry"—"and if so it is not so fine a thing as philosophy— For the same reason that an eagle is not so fine a thing as a truth."

"Give me this credit—" he cries across the broad Atlantic. "Do you not think I strive—to know myself? Give me this credit—" We cannot well refuse it.

The simple affirmation of the self in its vital energy means much to him, but it does not mean enough, and in the time intervening between the entry of March 19 and that of April 15 his mind has been moving toward a reconciliation of energy and truth, of passion and principle. He has been reading, he says, Robertson's *America* and Voltaire's *Siècle de Louis XIV* and his mind is full of the miseries of man in either a simple or a highly civilized state. He canvasses the possibilities of amelioration of the human fate and concludes that our life even at its conceivable best can be nothing but tragic, the very elements and laws of nature being hostile to man. Then, having stated as extremely as this the case of human misery, he breaks out with sudden contempt for those who call the world a vale of tears. "What a little circumscribed straightened notion!" he says. "Call the world if you Please 'The vale of Soul-making' . . . I say 'Soul making' Soul as distinguished from an Intelligence— There may be intelligences or sparks of the divinity in millions—but they are not Souls till they acquire identities, till each one is personally itself."

There follows a remarkable flight into a sort of transcendental psychology in the effort to suggest how intelligences become souls, and then: "Do you not see how necessary a World of Pains and troubles is to school an Intelligence and make it a Soul? A Place where the heart must feel and suffer in a thousand diverse ways."

And the heart is "the teat from which the Mind or intelligence sucks its identity."

He writes with an animus against Christian doctrine, but what he is giving, he says, is a sketch of *salvation*. And for the purpose of his argument he assumes immortality, he assumes a deity who makes beings in an infinite variety of identities, each identity being a "spark" of God's "essence"; he assumes that the soul may return to God enhanced by its acquisition of identity. This assumed, "I began by seeing how man was formed by circumstances—and what are circumstances?—but touchstones of his heart—? and what are touchstones? but proovings of his heart? and what are proovings of his heart but fortifiers or alterers of his nature? and what is his altered nature but his Soul?—and what was his Soul before it came into the world and had these provings and alterations and perfectionings?—An intelligence—without Identity—and how is this Identity to be made? Through the medium of the heart? And how is the heart to become this Medium but in a world of Circumstances?"

The faculty of Negative Capability has yielded doctrine—for the idea of soul-making, of souls creating themselves in their confrontation of circumstance, is available to Keats's conception only because he has remained with half-knowledge, with the double knowledge of the self and of the world's evil.

VII

So far as the idea of soul-making is doctrine—so far, that is, as it is something more than a moving rationale of heroism—it will probably not withstand the kind of scrutiny that today we are likely to give it. We have lost the *mystique* of the self. We cannot conceive of the self as having the same nature and the same value that Keats ascribed to it; we cannot respond to the justification of life by the heroic definition of self; and, having lost our knowledge of one term of Keats's equation, we are certain to find the reasons why his conclusion is wrong.

But when we deal adversely with Keats's notion of soul-making, we must at the same time deal with two greater poets than Keats. So far as Keats's resolution of the problem of evil is doctrinal, it leads us back to Milton. Here is Milton's characteristic doctrine of the conjoint nature of good and evil—"Good and evil we know in the field of this world grow up together almost inseparably. . . . Perhaps this is that doom which Adam fell into of knowing good and evil, that is to say, of knowing good by evil." Here is the Miltonic satisfaction at the expulsion from Eden, for from that great event all events follow, the life of "circumstances" has been instituted, history has been initiated, the human drama has begun, and now man may define his soul in the open and strenuous world of freedom as he never could in Eden—it is this, we feel, and not the great arguments of his theodicy that for Milton justify God's ways to man. And no one since Milton has put better and more feelingly the Miltonic doctrine of maturing freedom and responsibility in the field of this world than the young man who harked back incessantly to his Eden, to the primal bliss of satisfying the appetites without effort and without tears, who conceived the heroic vision of life because he first understood felicity.

Keats's doctrine of soul-making leads us not only to Milton, whose very theology was shaped by his love of the tragic poets, Shakespeare among them, but also to Shakespeare himself. What Keats calls "the bitter sweet of this Shakespearean fruit" is nothing else than the hard process of "provings and alterations and perfectionings" by which an "intelligence" acquires "identity" and becomes a "soul." The characterization of the "Shakespeareian fruit" appears in the sonnet "On Sitting Down to Read 'King Lear' Once Again," and *King Lear* is precisely the history of the definition of a soul by circumstance. The sonnet begins with a farewell to "golden tongued Romance with serene Lute"—Romance is precisely not "circumstances." And what Keats says he is leaving Romance for is "the fierce dispute, Betwixt Hell torment and impassion'd Clay"[10]—between, that is, the knowledge of evil and the knowledge of self. We

---

[10] The line appears so in the version of the sonnet in the Letters. Keats later revised "Hell torment" to "damnation."

can understand why Keats's admiration of Shakespeare was so much more than a literary admiration, why Shakespeare had for him something of the magnitude of a religious idea, figuring in his letters as a sort of patron saint or guardian angel, almost as a Good Shepherd. Shakespeare suggested the only salvation that Keats found it possible to conceive, the tragic salvation, the soul accepting the fate that defines it.

Whether his heroic resolution of the problem of evil means much or little to us, we cannot doubt that to Keats himself it was a felt reality. It was not a doctrine formulated to guide his life if it might —rather it is a statement, as accurate as such a statement can be, of the nature of his being. It is impossible not to be moved to extreme pity by Keats's last days, by the young man doomed to death at the very moment that his genius has come into the full power that it had promised, at the moment too when he was at last able to feel the long-awaited passion of love. Sometimes he is buoyed up by the euphoria which is characteristic of his disease, but more often he is bitter, jealous, and resentful; the cup is being taken from him, and he is in despair. And yet, however great our pity may be, we cannot miss, unless we willfully and perversely wish to miss, the hard core of self which remains in the man. "I know the color in that blood— it is arterial blood—I cannot be deceived in that color; that drop is my death warrant. I must die." These are the words that he is reported to have uttered on the occasion of his first hemorrhage, and they suggest the heroic quality of his last days. He permitted nothing to be falsified. There are impossibilities in this world, and he knew them. His tortured fancy sometimes overpowered him—he imagined that Fanny Brawne might be unchaste, that Brown was not faithful, that the Hunts spied on him: his self was nearly maddened by the certainty of its extinction. Yet the dominant note is of fortitude, of courage, and of heroic concern for those he loved. As he lay on his deathbed, he asked Severn, "Did you ever see anyone die?" Severn never had. "Well then I pity you, poor Severn. What trouble and danger you have got into for me. Now you must be firm for it will not last long. I shall soon be laid in the quiet grave. Thank God for the quiet grave. . . ." And at the end: "Severn, lift me up, for I am dying. I shall die easy. Don't be frightened! Thank God it has come."

The tone, we feel, is not ours. To identify it we go back in time, and say, perhaps, that it is of the Renaissance, of Shakespeare. We do not have what produces this tone, the implicit and explicit commitment to the self even in the moment of its extinction. Events, it would seem, have destroyed this commitment—and there are those who will rise to say that it was exactly the romantic commitment to the self that has produced the dire events of our day, that the responsibility for our present troubles, and for the denial of the self which our troubles entail, is to be laid to the great romantic creators. And even those who know better than this will yet find it all too easy to explain why Keats's heroic vision of the tragic life and the tragic salvation will not serve us now. They will tell us that we must, in our time, confront circumstances which are so terrible that the soul, far from being defined and developed by them, can only be destroyed by them. This may be so, and if it is so it makes the reason why Keats is not less but more relevant to our situation. As we see him in his letters he has for us a massive importance—he has, as we say, a historical importance. He stands as the last image of health at the very moment when the sickness of Europe began to be apparent— he with his intense naturalism that took so passionate an account of the mystery of man's nature, reckoning as boldly with pleasure as with pain, giving so generous a credence to growth, development, and possibility; he with his pride that so modestly, so warmly and delightedly, responded to the idea of community. The spiritual and moral health of which he seems the image we cannot now attain by wishing for it. But we cannot attain it without wishing for it, and clearly imagining it. "The Imagination may be compared to Adam's dream—he awoke and found it truth."

Little Dorrit

*L*ITTLE DORRIT is one of the three great novels of Dickens' great last period, but of the three it is perhaps the least established with modern readers. When it first appeared—in monthly parts from December 1855 to June 1857—its success was even more decisive than that of *Bleak House,* but the suffrage of later audiences has gone the other way, and of all Dickens' later works it is *Bleak House* that has come to be the best known. As for *Our Mutual Friend,* after having for some time met with adverse critical opinion among the enlightened—one recalls that the youthful Henry James attacked it for standing in the way of art and truth —it has of recent years been regarded with ever-growing admiration. But *Little Dorrit* seems to have retired to the background and shadow of our consciousness of Dickens.

This does not make an occasion for concern or indignation. With a body of work as large and as enduring as that of Dickens, taste and opinion will never be done. They will shift and veer as they have shifted and veered with the canon of Shakespeare, and each generation will have its special favorites and make its surprised discoveries. *Little Dorrit,* one of the most profound of Dickens' novels and one of the most significant works of the nineteenth century, will not fail to be thought of as speaking with a peculiar and passionate intimacy to our own time.

Little Dorrit is about society, which certainly does not distinguish it from the rest of Dickens' novels unless we go on to say, as we must, that it is *more* about society than any other of the novels, that it is about society in its very essence. This essential quality of the book has become apparent as many of the particular social conditions to which it refers have passed into history. Some of these conditions were already of the past when Dickens wrote, for although imprisonment for debt was indeed not wholly given up until 1869, yet imprisonment for small debts had been done away with in 1844, the prison of the Marshalsea had been abolished in 1842 and the Court of the Marshalsea in 1849. Bernard Shaw said of *Little Dorrit* that it converted him to socialism; it is not likely that any contemporary English reader would feel it appropriate to respond to its social message in the same way. The dead hand of outworn tradition no longer supports special privilege in England. For good or bad, in scarcely any country in the world can the whole art of government be said to be How Not To Do It. Mrs. General cannot impose the genteel discipline of Prunes and Prisms, and no prestige whatever attaches to "the truly refined mind" of her definition—"one that will seem to be ignorant of the existence of anything that is not perfectly proper, placid, and pleasant." At no point, perhaps, do the particular abuses and absurdities upon which Dickens directed his terrible cold anger represent the problems of social life as we now conceive them.

Yet this makes *Little Dorrit* not less but more relevant to our sense of things. As the particulars seem less immediate to our case, the general force of the novel becomes greater, and *Little Dorrit* is seen to be about a problem which does not yield easily to time. It is about society in relation to the individual human will. This is certainly a matter general enough—general to the point of tautology, were it not for the bitterness with which the tautology is articulated, were it not for the specificity and the subtlety and the boldness with which the human will is anatomized.

The subject of *Little Dorrit* is borne in upon us by the symbol, or emblem, of the book, which is the prison. The story opens in a prison in Marseilles. It goes on to the Marshalsea, which in effect it never leaves. The second of the two parts of the novel begins in what we are urged to think of as a sort of prison, the monastery of the Great St. Bernard. The Circumlocution Office is the prison of the creative mind of England. Mr. Merdle is shown habitually holding himself by the wrist, taking himself into custody, and in a score of ways the theme of incarceration is carried out, persons and classes being imprisoned by their notions of their predestined fate or their religious duty, or by their occupations, their life schemes, their ideas of themselves, their very habits of language.

Symbolic or emblematic devices are used by Dickens to one degree or another in several of the novels of his late period, but nowhere to such good effect as in *Little Dorrit.* The fog of *Bleak House,* the dust heap and the river of *Our Mutual Friend* are very striking, but they scarcely equal in force the prison image which dominates *Little Dorrit.* This is because the prison is an actuality before it is ever a symbol;[1] its connection with the will is real, it is the practical instrument for the negation of man's will which the will of society has contrived. As such, the prison haunted the mind of the nineteenth century, which may be said to have had its birth at the fall of the Bastille. The genius of the age, conceiving itself as creative will, naturally thought of the prisons from which it must be freed, and the trumpet call of the "Leonore" overture sounds through the century, the signal for the opening of the gates, for a general deliverance, although it grows fainter as men come to think of the prison not as a political instrument merely but as the ineluctable condition of life in society. "Most men in a brazen prison live"—the line in which Matthew Arnold echoes Wordsworth's "shades of the prison-house

---

[1] Since writing this, I have had to revise my idea of the actuality of the symbols of *Our Mutual Friend.* Professor Johnson's biography of Dickens has taught me much about the nature of dust heaps, including their monetary value, which was very large, quite large enough to represent a considerable fortune: I had never quite believed that Dickens was telling the literal truth about this. From Professor Dodd's *The Age of Paradox* I have learned to what an extent the Thames was visibly the sewer of London, of how pressing was the problem of the sewage in the city as Dickens knew it, of how present to the mind was the sensible and even the tangible evidence that the problem was not being solved. The moral *disgust* of the book is thus seen to be quite adequately comprehended by the symbols which are used to represent it.

begin to close/Upon the growing boy," might have served as the epigraph of *Little Dorrit*. In the mind of Dickens himself the idea of the prison was obsessive, not merely because of his own boyhood experience of prison life through his father's three months in the Marshalsea (although this must be given great weight in our under-standing of his intense preoccupation with the theme), but because of his own consciousness of the force and scope of his will.

If we speak of the place which the image of the prison occupied in the mind of the nineteenth century, we ought to recollect a certain German picture of the time, inconsiderable in itself but made sig-nificant by its use in a famous work of the early twentieth century. It represents a man lying in a medieval dungeon; he is asleep, his head pillowed on straw, and we know that he dreams of freedom because the bars on his window are shown being sawed by gnomes. This picture serves as the frontispiece of Freud's *Introductory Lectures on Psychoanalysis*—Freud uses it to make plain one of the more elementary ideas of his psychology, the idea of the fulfillment in dream or fantasy of impulses of the will that cannot be fulfilled in actuality. His choice of this particular picture is not fortuitous; other graphic representations of wish-fulfillment exist which might have served equally well his immediate didactic purpose, but Freud's general conception of the mind does indeed make the prison image peculiarly appropriate. And Freud is in point here because in a passage of *Little Dorrit* Dickens anticipates one of Freud's ideas, and not one of the simplest but nothing less bold and inclusive than the essential theory of the neurosis.

The brief passage to which I make reference occurs in the course of Arthur Clennam's pursuit of the obsessive notion that his family is in some way guilty, that its fortune, although now greatly di-minished, has been built on injury done to someone. And he con-jectures that the injured person is William Dorrit, who has been confined for debt in the Marshalsea for twenty years. Clennam is not wholly wrong in his supposition—there is indeed guilt in the family, incurred by Arthur's mother, and it consists in part of an injury done to a member of the Dorrit family. But he is not wholly right, for Mr. Dorrit has not been imprisoned through the wish or agency of Mrs. Clennam. The reasoning by which Arthur reaches his partly mistaken conclusion is of the greatest interest. It is based upon the fact that his mother, although mentally very vigorous, has lived as an invalid for many years. She has been imprisoned in a single room of her house, confined to her chair, which she leaves only for her bed. And her son conjectures that her imprisoning illness is the price she pays for the guilty gratification of keeping William Dorrit in *his* prison—that is, in order to have the right to injure another, she must unconsciously injure herself in an equivalent way: "A swift thought shot into [Arthur Clennam's] mind. In that long imprisonment here [i.e., Mr. Dorrit's] and in her long confinement to her room, did his mother find a balance to be struck? I admit that I was accessory to that man's captivity. I have suffered it in kind. He has decayed in his prison; I in mine. I have paid the penalty."

I have dwelt on this detail because it suggests, even more than the naked fact of the prison itself, the nature of the vision of society of *Little Dorrit*. One way of describing Freud's conception of the mind is to say that it is based upon the primacy of the will, and that the organization of the internal life is in the form, often fantastically parodic, of a criminal process in which the mind is at once the criminal, the victim, the police, the judge, and the executioner. And this is a fair description of Dickens' own view of the mind, as, having received the social impress, it becomes in turn the matrix of society.

In emphasizing the psychological aspects of the representation of society of *Little Dorrit* I do not wish to slight those more immediate institutional aspects of which earlier readers of the novel were chiefly aware. These are of as great importance now as they ever were in Dickens' career. Dickens is far from having lost his sense of the cruelty and stupidity of institutions and functionaries, his sense of the general rightness of the people as a whole and of the general wrongness of those who are put in authority over them. He certainly has not moved to the specious position in which all injustice is laid at the door of the original Old Adam in each of us, not to be done away with until we shall all, at the same moment, become the New Adam. The Circumlocution Office is a constraint upon the life of England which nothing can justify. Mr. Dorrit's sufferings and the injustice done to him are not denied or mitigated by his passionate commitment to some of the worst aspects of the society which deals with him so badly.

Yet the emphasis on the internal life and on personal responsibility is very strong in *Little Dorrit.* Thus, to take but one example, in the matter of the Circumlocution Office Dickens is at pains to remind us that the responsibility for its existence lies even with so good a man as Mr. Meagles. In the alliance against the torpor of the Office which he has made with Daniel Doyce, the engineer and inventor, Mr. Meagles has been undeviatingly faithful. Yet Clennam finds occasion to wonder whether there might not be "in the breast of this honest, affectionate, and cordial Mr. Meagles, any microscopic portion of the mustard-seed that had sprung up into the great tree of the Circumlocution Office." He is led to this speculation by his awareness that Mr. Meagles feels "a general superiority to Daniel Doyce, which seemed to be founded, not so much on anything in Doyce's personal character, as on the mere fact of [Doyce's] being an originator and a man out of the beaten track of other men."

Perhaps the single best index of the degree of complexity with which Dickens views society in *Little Dorrit* is afforded by the character of Blandois and his place in the novel. Blandois is wholly wicked, the embodiment of evil; he is, indeed, a devil. One of the effects of his presence in *Little Dorrit* is to complicate our response to the theme of the prison, to deprive us of the comfortable, philanthropic thought that prisons are nothing but instruments of injustice. Because Blandois exists, prisons are necessary. The generation of readers that preceded our own was inclined, I think, to withhold credence from Blandois—they did not believe in his aesthetic actuality because they did not believe in his moral actuality, the less so

because they could not account for his existence in specific terms
of social causation. But events have required us to believe that there
really are people who seem entirely wicked, and almost unaccount-
ably so; the social causes of their badness lie so far back that they
can scarcely be reached, and in any case causation pales into irrele-
vance before the effects of their actions; our effort to "understand"
them becomes a mere form of thought.

In this novel about the will and society, the devilish nature of
Blandois is confirmed by his maniac insistence upon his gentility, his
mad reiteration that it is the right and necessity of his existence to
be served by others. He is the exemplification of the line in *Lear*:
"The prince of darkness is a gentleman." The influence of Dickens
upon Dostoevski is perhaps nowhere exhibited in a more detailed
way than in the similarities between Blandois and the shabby-genteel
devil of *The Brothers Karamazov,* and also between him and Smerdyakov of the same novel. It is of consequence to Dickens as to
Dostoevski that the evil of the unmitigated social will should own
no country, yet that the flavor of its cosmopolitanism should be
"French"—that is, rationalistic and subversive of the very assumption of society. Blandois enfolds himself in the soiled tatters of the
revolutionary pathos. So long as he can play the game in his chosen
style, he is nature's gentleman dispossessed of his rightful place, he
is the natural genius against whom the philistine world closes its
dull ranks. And when the disguise, which deceives no one, is off, he
makes use of the classic social rationalization: Society has made him
what he is; he does in his own person only what society does in its
corporate form and with its corporate self-justification. "Society sells
itself and sells me: and I sell society."[2]

2 This is in effect the doctrine of Balzac's philosophical-anarchist criminal, Vautrin.
But in all other respects the difference between Blandois and Vautrin is extreme.
Vautrin is a "noble" and justified character; for all his cynicism, he is on the side
of virtue and innocence. He is not corrupted by the social injustices he has suffered
and perceived, by the self-pity to which they might have given rise; his wholesome-
ness may be said to be the result of his preference for *power* as against the *status*
which Blandois desires. The development of Blandois from Vautrin—I do not know
whether Dickens's creation was actually influenced by Balzac's—is a literary fact
which has considerable social import.

Around Blandois are grouped certain characters of the novel of whose manner of life he is the pure principle. In these people the social will, the will to status, is the ruling faculty. To be recognized, deferred to, and served—this is their master passion. Money is of course of great consequence in the exercise of this passion, yet in *Little Dorrit* the desire for money is subordinated to the desire for deference. The Midas figure of Mr. Merdle must not mislead us on this point—should, indeed, guide us aright, for Mr. Merdle, despite his destructive power, is an innocent and passive man among those who live by the social will. It is to be noted of all these people that they justify their insensate demand for status by some version of Blandois's pathos; they are confirmed in their lives by self-pity, they rely on the great modern strategy of being the insulted and injured. Mr. Dorrit is too soft a man for his gentility mania ever to be quite diabolical, but his younger daughter Fanny sells herself to the devil, damns herself entirely, in order to torture the woman who once questioned her social position. Henry Gowan, the cynical, incompetent gentleman-artist who associates himself with Blandois in order to *épater* society, is very nearly as diabolical as his companion. From his mother—who must dismiss once and for all any lingering doubt of Dickens' ability to portray what Chesterton calls the delicate or deadly in human character—he has learned to base his attack on society upon the unquestionable rightness of wronged gentility. Miss Wade lives a life of tortured self-commiseration which gives her license to turn her hatred and her hand against everyone, and she imposes her principle of judgment and conduct upon Tattycoram.

In short, it is part of the complexity of this novel which deals so bitterly with society that those of its characters who share its social bitterness are by that very fact condemned. And yet—so much further does the complexity extend—the subversive pathos of self-pity is by no means wholly dismissed, the devil has not wholly lied. No reader of *Little Dorrit* can possibly conclude that the rage of envy which Tattycoram feels is not justified in some degree, or that Miss Wade is wholly wrong in pointing out to her the insupportable ambiguity of her position as the daughter-servant of Mr. and Mrs. Meagles and the sister-servant of Pet Meagles. Nor is it possible to read Miss Wade's account of her life, "The History of a Self Tormentor," without an understanding that amounts to sympathy. We feel this the more—Dickens meant us to feel it the more—because the two young women have been orphaned from infancy, and are illegitimate. Their bitterness is seen to be the perversion of the desire for love. The self-torture of Miss Wade—who becomes the more interesting if we think of her as the exact inversion of Esther Summerson of *Bleak House*—is the classic maneuver of the child who is unloved, or believes herself to be unloved; she refuses to be lovable, she elects to be hateful. In all of us the sense of injustice precedes the sense of justice by many years. It haunts our infancy, and even the most dearly loved of children may conceive themselves to be oppressed. Such is the nature of the human will, so perplexed is it by the disparity between what it desires and what it is allowed to have. With Dickens as with Blake, the perfect image of injustice is the unhappy child, and, like the historian Burckhardt, he connects the fate of nations with the treatment of children. It is a commonplace of the biography and criticism of Dickens that this reflects his own sense of having been unjustly treated by his parents, specifically in ways which injured his own sense of social status, his own gentility; the general force of Dickens' social feelings derives from their being rooted in childhood experience, and something of the special force of *Little Dorrit* derives from Dickens' having discovered its matter in the depths of his own social will.

At this point we become aware of the remarkable number of false and inadequate parents in *Little Dorrit*. To what pains Dickens goes to represent delinquent parenthood, with what an elaboration of irony he sets it forth! "The Father of the Marshalsea"—this is the title borne by Mr. Dorrit, who, preoccupied by the gratification of being the First Gentleman of a prison, is unable to exercise the simplest paternal function; who corrupts two of his children by his dream of gentility; who will accept any sacrifice from his saintly daughter Amy, Little Dorrit, to whom he is the beloved child to be cherished and forgiven. "The Patriarch"—this is the name bestowed upon Mr. Casby, who stands as a parody of all Dickens' benevolent old gentlemen from Mr. Pickwick through the Cheerybles to John Jarndyce, an astounding unreality of a man who, living only to grip and grind, has convinced the world by the iconography of his dress and mien that he is the repository of all benevolence. The primitive appropriateness of the strange—the un-English!—punishment which Mr. Pancks metes out to this hollow paternity, the cutting off of his long hair and the broad brim of his hat, will be understood by any reader with the least tincture of psychoanalytical knowledge. Then the Meagles, however solicitous of their own daughter, are, as we have seen, but indifferent parents to Tattycoram. Mrs. Gowan's rearing of her son is the root of his corruption. It is Fanny Dorrit's complaint of her enemy, Mrs. Merdle, that she refuses to surrender the appearance of youth, as a mother should. And at the very center of the novel is Mrs. Clennam, a false mother in more ways than one; she does not deny love but she perverts and prevents it by denying all that love feeds on—liberty, demonstrative tenderness, joy, and, what for Dickens is the guardian of love in society, art. It is her harsh rearing of her son that has given him cause to say in his fortieth year, "I have no will."

Some grace—it is, of course, the secret of his birth, of his being really a child of love and art—has kept Arthur Clennam from responding to the will of his mother with a bitter, clenched will of his own. The alternative he has chosen has not, contrary to his declaration, left him no will at all. He has by no means been robbed of his ethical will, he can exert energy to help others, and for the sake of Mr. Dorrit or Daniel Doyce's invention he can haunt the Circumlocution Office with his mild, stubborn "I want to know. . . ." But the very accent of that phrase seems to forecast the terrible "I prefer not to" of Bartleby the Scrivener in Melville's great story of the will in its ultimate fatigue.

It is impossible, I think, not to find in Arthur Clennam the evidence of Dickens' deep personal involvement in *Little Dorrit*. If we ask what Charles Dickens has to do with poor Clennam, what The Inimitable has to do with this sad depleted failure, the answer must be: nothing, save what is implied by Clennam's consciousness that he has passed the summit of life and that the path from now on leads downward, by his belief that the pleasures of love are not for him, by his "I want to know . . . ," by his wish to negate the will in death. Arthur Clennam is that mode of Dickens' existence at the time of *Little Dorrit* which makes it possible for him to write to his friend Macready, "However strange it is never to be at rest, and never satisfied, and ever trying after something that is never reached, and to be always laden with plot and plan and care and worry, how clear it is that it must be, and that one is driven by an irresistible might until the journey is worked out." And somewhat earlier and with a yet more poignant relevance: "Why is it, that as with poor David, a sense always comes crushing upon me now, when I fall into low spirits, as of one happiness I have missed in life, and one friend and companion I have never made?"

If we become aware of an autobiographical element in *Little Dorrit*, we must of course take notice of the fact that the novel was conceived after the famous incident of Maria Beadnell, who, poor woman, was the original of Arthur Clennam's Flora Finching. She was the first love of Dickens' proud, unfledged youth; she had married what Dickens has taught us to call Another, and now, after twenty years, she had chosen to come back into his life. Familiarity with the story cannot diminish our amazement at it—Dickens was a subtle and worldly man, but his sophistication was not proof against against his passionate sentimentality, and he fully expected the past to come back to him, borne in the little hands of the adorable Maria. The actuality had a quite extreme effect upon him, and Flora, fat and foolish, is his monument to the discovered discontinuity between youth and middle age; she is the nonsensical spirit of the anticlimax of the years. And if she is in some degree forgiven, being represented as the kindest of foolish women, yet it is not without meaning that she is everywhere attended by Mr. F's Aunt, one of Dickens' most astonishing ideas, the embodiment of senile rage and spite, flinging to the world the crusts of her buttered toast. "He has proud stomach, this chap," she cries when poor Arthur hesitates over her dreadful gift. "Give him a meal of chaff!" It is the voice of one of the Parcae.

It did not, of course, need the sad comedy of Maria Beadnell for Dickens to conceive that something in his life had come to an end. It did not even need his growing certainty that, after so many years and so many children, his relations with his wife were insupportable—this realization was as much a consequence as it was a cause of the sense of termination. He was forty-three years old and at the pinnacle of a success unique in the history of letters. The wildest ambitions of his youth could not have comprehended the actuality of his fame. But the last infirmity of noble mind may lead to the first infirmity of noble will. Dickens, to be sure, never lost his love of fame, or of whatever of life's goods his miraculous powers might bring him, but there came a moment when the old primitive motive could no longer serve, when the joy of impressing his powers on the world no longer seemed delightful in itself, and when the first, simple, honest, vulgar energy of desire no longer seemed appropriate to his idea of himself.

We may say of Dickens that at the time of *Little Dorrit* he was at a crisis of the will which is expressed in the characters and forces of the novel, in the extremity of its bitterness against the social will, in its vision of peace and selflessness. This moral crisis is most immediately represented by the condition of Arthur Clennam's will, by his sense of guilt, by his belief that he is unloved and unlovable, by his retirement to the Marshalsea as by an act of choice, by his sickness unto death. We have here the analogy to the familiar elements of a religious crisis. This is not the place to raise the question of Dickens' relation to the Christian religion, which was a complicated one. But we cannot speak of *Little Dorrit* without taking notice of its reference to Christian feeling, if only because this is of considerable importance in its effect upon the aesthetic of the novel.

It has been observed of *Little Dorrit* that certain of Dickens' characteristic delights are not present in their usual force. Something of his gusto is diminished in at least one of its aspects. We do not have the amazing thickness of fact and incident that marks, say, *Bleak House* or *Our Mutual Friend*—not that we do not have sufficient thickness, but we do not have what Dickens usually gives us. We do not have the great population of characters from whom shines the freshness of their autonomous life. Mr. Pancks and Mrs. Plornish and Flora Finching and Flintwich are interesting and amusing, but they seem to be the fruit of conscious intention rather than of free creation. This is sometimes explained by saying that Dickens was fatigued. Perhaps so, but if we are aware that Dickens is here expending less of one kind of creative energy, we must at the same time be aware that he is expending more than ever before of another kind. The imagination of *Little Dorrit* is marked not so much by its powers of particularization as by its powers of generalization and abstraction. It is an imagination under the dominion of a great articulated idea, a moral idea which tends to find its full development in a religious experience. It is an imagination akin to that which created *Piers Plowman* and *Pilgrim's Progress*. And, indeed, it is akin to the imagination of *The Divine Comedy*. Never before has Dickens made so full, so Dantean, a claim for the virtue of the artist, and there is a Dantean pride and a Dantean reason in what he says of Daniel Doyce, who, although an engineer, stands for the creative mind in general and for its appropriate virtue: "His dismissal of himself [was] remarkable. He never said, I discovered this adaptation or invented that combination; but showed the whole thing as if the Divine artificer had made it, and he had happened to find it. So modest was he about it, such a pleasant touch of respect was mingled with his quiet admiration of it, and so calmly convinced was he that it was established on irrefragable laws." Like much else that might be pointed to, this confirms us in the sense that the whole energy of the imagination of *Little Dorrit* is directed to the transcending of the personal will, to the search for the Will in which shall be our peace.

We must accept—and we easily do accept, if we do not permit critical cliché to interfere—the aesthetic of such an imagination, which will inevitably tend toward a certain formality of pattern and toward the generalization and the abstraction we have remarked. In a novel in which a house falls physically to ruins from the moral collapse of its inhabitants, in which the heavens open over London to show a crown of thorns, in which the devil has something like an actual existence, we quite easily accept characters named nothing else than Bar, Bishop, Physician. And we do not reject, despite our inevitable first impulse to do so, the character of Little Dorrit herself. Her untinctured goodness does not appall us or make us misdoubt her, as we expect it to do. This novel at its best is only incidentally realistic; its finest power of imagination appears in the great general images whose abstractness is their actuality, like Mr. Merdle's dinner parties, or the Circumlocution Office itself, and in such a context we understand Little Dorrit to be the Beatrice of the *Comedy,* the Paraclete in female form. Even the physical littleness of this grown woman, an attribute which is insisted on and which seems likely to repel us, does not do so, for we perceive it to be the sign that she is not only the Child of the Marshalsea, as she is called, but also the Child of the Parable, the negation of the social will.

Anna Karenina

WHEN *Anna Karenina* first appeared, is was read with a special delight which had as its chief element an almost childlike wonder at recognizing in art what was familiar in life. This, people said, is the way things are, the way they really are, the way we have always known them to be, and no writer has ever represented them so before. The general feeling about the book was expressed by Matthew Arnold when he said in his essay on Tolstoi that *Anna Karenina* was not to be taken as a work of art but as a piece of life. In any strict sense, of course, Arnold's statement is quite illegitimate—art is art and life is life; we read novels and live life; and if we try to express the nature of our response to certain novels by saying that we "live" them, that is only a manner of speaking. But it is a manner of speaking which is necessary to suggest the character of Tolstoi's art.

The early response to *Anna Karenina* had in it, I have suggested, a certain naïvety. It was as if people up to then had had experience only of an art which was formal and conventional and were now for the first time confronting an example of naturalistic representation, as if they had never before had the opportunity to perceive what verisimilitude was. Yet of course this was not at all the case. Tolstoi originated no new genre. When *Anna Karenina* appeared—serially from 1875 to 1877 and as a volume in 1878—the novel as an art form had reached a very high point in its development and had made great conquests of that part of life with which the novel is pre-eminently concerned, the part of life which we call the *actual*. To mention only the novelists of France, where the theory of the actual had been more consciously formulated than anywhere else, Balzac had completed his great canon of French social history nearly three decades before, Flaubert had published both *Madame Bovary* and *L'Éducation sentimentale,* and Zola was in the full tide of his production. Yet with all these masters of actuality already on the scene —not to speak of his own *War and Peace,* which, although in the nineteenth century it did not have its modern reputation, was nevertheless much admired—Tolstoi still made with *Anna Karenina* the effect I have described.

And he continues to make it. In our time Proust and Joyce have greatly extended the dominion of the novel of actuality; our culture as a whole is obsessively committed to fact; we have removed virtually every taboo that once stood in the way of our grasp of the way things are and have evolved bold and elaborate sciences of human behavior which would have delighted Balzac and Zola. Yet still, when we read *Anna Karenina,* we exclaim in the old naïve wonder and surprise, Why *this* is the way it is, this is life itself! And a contemporary critic, Philip Rahv, in effect says for us today what Arnold said for the nineteenth-century readers of the book. In Tolstoi, Mr. Rahv says, "the cleavage between art and life is of a minimal nature. In a Tolstoian novel it is never the division but always the unity of art and life which makes the illumination. . . . One might say that in a sense there are no plots in Tolstoi but simply the unquestioned and unalterable process of life itself; such is the astonishing immediacy with which he possesses his characters that he can dispense with manipulative techniques, as he dispenses with the belletristic devices of exaggeration, distortion, and dissimulation."

This quality of lifelikeness, which, among all novelists, he possesses to the highest degree, does not make Tolstoi the greatest of novelists. Great as he is, there are effects which are to be gained by conscious manipulation and distortion, by plot and design, by sheer romancing, which he with his characteristic method cannot manage;

there are kinds of illumination and delight which Tolstoi cannot give us but which Dickens, Dostoevski, and James can. But if Tolstoi is not the greatest of novelists—and that particular superlative, in any case, stands stupidly in the way of our free response to literature—he can be called the most *central* of novelists. It is he who gives to the novel its norm and standard, the norm and standard not of art but of reality. It is against his work that we measure the degree of distortion, exaggeration, and understatement which other novelists use—and of course quite legitimately use—to gain their effects.

Only one other writer has ever seemed to his readers to have this normative quality—what we today are likely to feel about Tolstoi was felt during the eighteenth century in a more positive and formulated way about Homer. It was what Pope felt when he said that Nature and Homer were the same.

One of the ways of accounting for the normative quality of Homer is to speak of his objectivity. Homer gives us, we are told, the object itself without interposing his personality between it and us. He gives us the person or thing or event without judging it, as Nature itself gives it to us. And to the extent that this is true of Homer, it is true of Tolstoi. But again we are dealing with a manner of speaking. Homer and Nature are of course not the same, and Tolstoi and Nature are not the same. Indeed, what is called the objectivity of Homer or of Tolstoi is not objectivity at all. Quite to the contrary, it is the most lavish and prodigal subjectivity possible, for every object in the *Iliad* or in *Anna Karenina* exists in the medium of what we must call the author's love. But this love is so pervasive, it is so constant, and it is so equitable, that it creates the illusion of objectivity, for everything in the narrative, without exception, exists in it as everything in Nature, without exception, exists in time, space, and atmosphere.

To perceive the character of Tolstoi's objectivity, one has only to compare it with Flaubert's. As the word is used in literary criticism, Flaubert must be accounted just as objective as Tolstoi. Yet it is clear that Flaubert's objectivity is charged with irritability and Tolstoi's with affection. For Tolstoi everyone and everything has a saving grace. Like Homer, he scarcely permits us to choose between antagonists—just as we dare not give all our sympathy either to Hector or to Achilles, nor, in their great scene, either to Achilles or to Priam, so we cannot say, as between Anna and Alexei Karenin, or between Anna and Vronsky, who is right and who is wrong.

More than anything else, and certainly anterior to any specifically literary skill that we may isolate, it is this moral quality, this quality of affection, that accounts for the unique illusion of reality that Tolstoi creates. It is when the novelist really loves his characters that he can show them in their completeness and contradiction, in their failures as well as in their great moments, in their triviality as well as in their charm. And what other novelist than Tolstoi, without ever abating his almost sexual love for his heroine, can make us believe of her, as we believe of Anna, that she has become a difficult, almost an impossible, woman? Or what novelist can tell us, as Tolstoi tells us of Vronsky, that his romantic hero is becoming increasingly bald without using the fact to belittle him? What we call Tolstoi's objectivity is simply the power of his love to suffer no abatement from the notice and account it takes of the fact that life usually falls below its ideal of itself.

It is a subtle triumph of Tolstoi's art that it induces us to lend ourselves with enthusiasm to its representation of the way things are. We so happily give our assent to what Tolstoi shows us and so willingly call it reality because we have something to gain from its being reality. For it is the hope of every decent, reasonably honest person to be judged under the aspect of Tolstoi's representation of human nature. Perhaps, indeed, what Tolstoi has done is to constitute as reality the judgment which every decent, reasonably honest person is likely to make of himself—as someone not wholly good and not wholly bad, not heroic yet not without heroism, not splendid yet not without moments of light, not to be comprehended by any formula yet having his principle of being, and managing somehow, and despite conventional notions, to maintain an unexpected dignity.

This is, of course, another way of saying that Tolstoi's reality is not objective at all, that it is the product of his will and desire (and of ours). And when we have said this, we must say more—we must grant that to achieve this particular reality Tolstoi omitted from it what some other realities include. Most notably he omitted the evil which is at the center of the vision of his great contemporary, Dostoevski. Tolstoi, to be sure, was anything but unaware of man's suffering. Levin, who, in *Anna Karenina,* is Tolstoi's representation of himself, is brought to a crisis of the soul by the thought that "for every man, and himself too, there was nothing but suffering, death, and forgetfulness," and he reaches a point where he believes that he "must either interpret life so that it would not present itself to him as the evil jest of some devil, or shoot himself." This is in form the very same idea that tortures Ivan Karamazov. But how different it is in tone, how different in intensity. Levin's sense of negation, though painful, is vague and perhaps merely melancholy; it has nothing of the specific horror and hideousness of Ivan's. And Levin can bring his crisis to resolution with relative ease, for he has conveniently at hand the materials of peace that Ivan does not possess and probably would not have accepted—piety, work, tradition, and the continuity of the family.

Nowadays the sense of evil comes easily to all of us. We all share what Henry James called the "imagination of disaster," and with reason enough, the world being what it is. And it is with reason enough that we respond most directly to those writers in whom the imagination of disaster is highly developed, even extremely developed. To many of us the world today has the look and feel of a Dostoevski novel, every moment of it crisis, every detail of it the projection of exacerbated sensibility and blind, wounded will. It is comprehensible that, when the spell of Tolstoi is not immediately upon us, we might feel that he gives us, after all, not reality itself but a sort of idyl of reality.

No doubt the imagination of disaster was not particularly strong in Tolstoi.[1] But perhaps it is just here that his peculiar value for us

---

[1] Although strong enough to give us the character of Levin's brother Nicolai, whose despair of life is as entire and as deeply rooted as that of any of Dostoevski's characters.

lies. For the imagination of disaster is a bold and courageous function of the mind but it is also exclusive and jealous—it does not easily permit other imaginations to work beside it; it more readily
conceives evil than that to which the evil may befall; or, if it does
conceive the thing that may be harmed, it is likely to do so in a
merely abstract way. Our taste for the literature which arises from
this imagination is a natural one, yet it has in it this danger, that
we may come to assume that evil is equivalent to reality and may
even come, in some distant and unconscious way, to honor it as
such. Or it may happen that our preoccupation with evil will lead us
to lose our knowledge, or at least the literary confirmation of our
knowledge, of what goodness of life is. The literary production since
Tolstoi has been enormously brilliant and enormously relevant, yet
it is a striking fact that, although many writers have been able to
tell us of the pain of life, virtually no writer has been able to tell us
of pain in terms of life's possible joy, and although many have represented the attenuation or distortion of human relationships,
scarcely any have been able to make actual what the normalities of
relationships are. But in Tolstoi the family is an actuality; parenthood is a real and not a symbolic condition; the affections truly exist
and may be spoken of without embarrassment and as matters of
interest; love waxes and wanes, is tender or quarrelsome, but it is
always something more than a metaphor; the biological continuity
is a fact, not as in James Joyce's touchingly schematic affirmations,
but simply and inescapably. It is, we may say, by very reason of the
low pitch of his imagination of disaster that Tolstoi serves us, for
he reminds us of what life in its normal actuality is.

I have said that it is chiefly Tolstoi's moral vision that accounts for
the happiness with which we respond to *Anna Karenina*. That is
why criticism, so far as it is specifically literary criticism, must lay
down its arms before this novel. We live at a time when literary
criticism has made for itself very bold claims which are by no means
all extravagant. But the characteristic criticism of our time is the
psychological analysis of language. This is a technique of great usefulness, but there are moments in literature which do not yield the

secret of their power to any study of language, because the power does not depend on language but on the moral imagination. When we read how Hector in his farewell to Andromache picks up his infant son and the baby is frightened by the horsehair crest of his father's helmet and Hector takes it off and laughs and puts it on the ground, or how Priam goes to the tent of Achilles to beg back from the slayer the body of his son, and the old man and the young man, both bereaved and both under the shadow of death, talk about death and fate, nothing can explain the power of such moments over us—or nothing short of a recapitulation of the moral history of the race. And even when the charge of emotion is carried by our sense of the perfect appropriateness of the words that are used— Cordelia's "No cause. No cause"; or Ophelia's "I was the more deceived"; or Hamlet's "The rest is silence"—we are unable to deal analytically with the language, for it is not psychologically pregnant but only morally right; exactly in this way, we feel, should this person in this situation speak, and only our whole sense of life will explain our gratitude for the words being these and not some others.

In short, there are times when the literary critic can do nothing more than point, and *Anna Karenina* presents him with an occasion when his critical function is reduced to this primitive activity. Why is it a great novel? Only the finger of admiration can answer: because of this moment, or this, or this, mostly quiet moments, prosaic, circumstantial. Because of an observation of character: "Prince Kuzovlev sat with a white face on his thoroughbred mare from the Grabovsky stud, while an English groom led her by the bridle. Vronsky and his comrades knew Kuzovlev and his peculiarity of 'weak nerves' and terrible vanity. They knew he was afraid of everything, afraid of riding a spirited horse. But now, just because it was terrible, because people broke their necks, and there was a doctor standing at each obstacle, and an ambulance with a cross on it, and a sister of mercy, he had made up his mind to take part in the race." Or because of a fragment of social observation: "Vassenka Veslovsky had had no notion before that it was truly *chic* for a sportsman to be in tatters but to have his shooting outfit of the best quality. He saw it now as he looked at Stepan Arkadyevich, radiant in his rags, graceful, well-fed, and joyous, a typical Russian nobleman. And he made up his mind that the next time he went shooting he would certainly adopt the same get-up." Or because of Vronsky's unforgettable steeplechase and the almost tragic fall of the beautiful English mare; or Dolly's conversation with the peasant women about children and the business of being a woman; or Levin mowing with the peasants in the fields, the old peasant challenging him with "Once take hold of the rope, there's no letting it go!" and all the mowers watching for the master to break under the strain and on the whole glad that he does not; or the scene, taken from Tolstoi's own courtship of his wife, in which Levin and Kitty communicate by the initials of words written with chalk on a card table; or Alexei Karenin's determination to be a noble and Christian spirit and his inability to pursue his intention in the face of society's wish that he be ridiculous; or Anna's visit to her son on the morning of his birthday; or the passing of the moment in which Sergei, Levin's brother, might have proposed to Varenka, and the recognition by each of them that the moment had passed.

Part of the magic of the book is that it violates our notions of the ratio that should exist between the importance of an event and the amount of space that is given to it. Vronsky's sudden grasp of the fact that he is bound to Anna not by love but by the end of love, a perception which colors all our understanding of the relationship of the two lovers, is handled in a few lines; but pages are devoted to Levin's discovery that all his shirts have been packed and that he has no shirt to wear at his wedding. It was the amount of attention given to the shirts that led Matthew Arnold to exclaim that the book is not to be taken as art but as life itself, and perhaps as much as anything else this scene suggests the energy of animal intelligence that marks Tolstoi as a novelist. For here we have in sum his awareness that the spirit of man is always at the mercy of the actual and trivial, his passionate sense that the actual and trivial are of the greatest importance, his certainty that they are not of final importance. Does it sound like a modest sort of knowledge? Let us not deceive ourselves —to comprehend unconditioned spirit is not so very hard, but there is no knowledge rarer than the understanding of spirit as it exists in the inescapable conditions which the actual and the trivial make for it.

William Dean Howells and the Roots of Modern Taste

I

EVERY now and then in the past few years we have heard
that we might soon expect a revival of interest in the work
of William Dean Howells. And certainly, if this rumor
were substantiated, there would be a notable propriety in the event.
In the last two decades Henry James has become established as a
great magnetic figure in our higher culture. In the same period Mark
Twain has become as it were newly established—not indeed, like
James, as a source and object of intellectual energy, but at least as a
permanent focus of our admiring interest, as the representative of a
mode of the American mind and temperament which we are happy
to acknowledge. To say that Henry James and Mark Twain are
opposite poles of our national character would be excessive, yet it is
clear that they do suggest tendencies which are very far apart, so
that there is always refreshment and enlightenment in thinking of
them together. And when we do think of them together, diverse as
they are, indifferent to each other as they mostly were, deeply suspicious of each other as they were whenever they became aware of
each other, we naturally have in mind the man who stood between
them as the affectionate friend of both, the happy admirer of their
disparate powers, who saw so early the fullness of their virtues

which we now take for granted. It would make a pleasant symmetry if we could know that William Dean Howells has become the object of renewed admiration, that he is being regarded, like his two great friends, as a large, significant figure in our literature.

But the rumor of the revival is surely false. A certain number of people, but a very small number, do nowadays feel that they might find pleasure in Howells, their expectation being based, no doubt, on an analogy with the pleasure that is being found in Trollope. And the analogy is fair enough. Howells produced in the free Trollopian way, and with the same happy yielding of the rigorous artistic conscience in favor of the careless flow of life; and now and then, even in our exigent age, we are willing to find respite from the strict demands of conscious art, especially if we can do so without a great loss of other sanctions and integrities. Howells, it is thought, can give us the pleasures of our generic image of the Victorian novel. He was a man of principle without being a man of heroic moral intensity, and we expect of him that he will involve us in the enjoyment of moral activity through the medium of a lively awareness of manners, that he will delight us by touching on high matters in the natural course of gossip.

This is a very attractive expectation and Howells does not really disappoint it. He is not Trollope's equal, but at his best he is in his own right a very engaging novelist. Whether or not he deserves a stronger adjective than this may for the moment be left open to question, but engaging he undoubtedly is. And yet I think that he cannot now engage us, that we cannot expect a revival of interest in him—his stock is probably quite as high in the market as it will go. The excellent omnibus volume of Howells which Professor Commager recently brought out was piously reviewed but it was not bought. And when, in a course of lectures on American literature, I imagined that it might be useful to my students to have a notion of the cultural and social situation which Howells described, and therefore spent a considerable time talking about his books, I received the first anonymous letter I have ever had from a student—it warned me that the lapse of taste shown by my excessive interest in a dull writer was causing a scandal in the cafeterias.

As a historical figure, Howells must of course always make a strong claim upon our attention. His boyhood and youth, to which he so often returned in memory in his pleasant autobiographical books, were spent in circumstances of which everyone must be aware who wishes to understand the course of American culture. Howells' induction into the intellectual life gives us one of the points from which we can measure what has happened to the humanistic idea in the modern world. If we want to know what was the estate of literature a hundred years ago, if we want to be made aware of how the nineteenth century, for all its development of science and technology, was still essentially a humanistic period, we have only to take Howells' account of the intellectual life of the Ohio towns in which he lived—the lively concern with the more dramatic aspects of European politics, the circulation of the great English reviews, the fond knowledge of the English and American literature of the century, the adoration of Shakespeare, the general, if naïve, respect for learning. It was certainly not elaborate, this culture of little towns that were almost of the frontier, and we must not exaggerate the extent to which its most highly developed parts were shared, yet it *was* pervasive and its assumptions were general enough to support Howells in his literary commitment. In a log cabin he read to the bottom of that famous barrel of books, he struggled to learn four or five languages, he determined on a life of literature, and his community respected his enterprise and encouraged him in it. And it is worth observing that, as he himself says, he devoted himself to a literary career not so much out of disinterested love for literature as out of the sense that literature was an institutional activity by which he might make something of himself in the worldly way.

Howells' historical interest for us continues through all his developing career. His famous pilgrimage to New England, his round of visits to the great literary figures of Massachusetts, is a *locus classicus* of our literary history. It culminated, as everyone remembers, in that famous little dinner which Lowell gave for him at the Parker House; it was the first dinner that Howells had ever seen that was served in courses, in what was then called the Russian style, and it reached its significant climax when Holmes turned to Lowell and said, "Well, James, this is the apostolic succession, this is the laying on of hands." Much has been made of this story, and indeed much must be made of it, for although Holmes probably intended no more than an irony-lightened-kindliness to a very young man, his remark was previsionary, and the visit of Howells does mark a succession and an era, the beginning of an American literature where before, as Howells said, there had been only a New England literature. Then Howells' uprooting himself from Boston to settle in New York in 1888 marks, as Alfred Kazin observes, the shifting of the concentra- tions of literary capital from the one city to the other. And when, as old age came on and Howells was no longer a commanding figure with the New York publishers, when he suffered with characteristic mild fortitude the pain of having his work refused by a new gen- eration of editors, the culture of the American nineteenth century had at last come to its very end.

Howells' historical importance is further confirmed by the position he attained in the institutional life of American letters. Not long after Howells died, H. L. Mencken, who had been at pains to make Howells' name a byword of evasive gentility, wrote to regret his death, because, as he said, with irony enough but also with some seriousness, there was now no American writer who could serve as the representative of American letters, no figure who, by reason of age, length of service, bulk of work, and public respect, could stand as a literary patriarch. And since Mencken wrote, no such figure has arisen. Howells was indeed patriarchal as he grew older, large and most fatherly, and if he exercised his paternity only in the mild, puzzled American way, still he was the head of the family and he took his responsibility seriously. He asserted the dignity of the worker in literature at the same time that he defined the writer's place as being economically and socially with the manual worker rather than with the business man. He was receptive to the new and the strange; his defense of Emily Dickinson, for example, does him great credit. His personal and cultural timidity about sexual matters made him speak harshly of writers more daring in such things than himself, yet he fought effectively for the acceptance of contemporary European literature, and he was tireless in helping even those of the young men who did not share his reticences. Edmund Wilson once defined the literary character of Stephen Crane by differentiating him from "the comfortable family men of whom Howells was chief," yet Crane was in Howells' debt, as were Boyesen, Hamlin Garland, Norris, and Herrick.

He was not a man of great moral intensity, but he was stubborn. His comportment in the Haymarket affair marks, I think, the beginning in our life of the problem of what came to be called the writer's "integrity," and his novel *A Hazard of New Fortunes* is probably the first treatment of the theme which became almost obsessive in our fiction in the Thirties, the intellectual's risking his class position by opposing the prejudices of his class. Some years ago, it seemed appropriate for almost any academic writer on American literature to condescend to Howells' social views as being, in comparison with the tradition of revolutionary Marxism, all too "mild," and quite foolish in their mildness, another manifestation of his "genteel" quality. The fact is that Howells' sense of the anomalies and injustices of an expanding capitalism was very clear and strong. What is more, it was very *personal;* it became a part, and a bitter part, of his temperament. In his criticism of American life, he was not like Henry Adams or Henry James, who thought of America in reference to their own grand ambitions. Howells' ambitiousness reached its peak in youth and then compromised itself, or democratized itself, so that in much of his work he is only the journeyman, a craftsman quite without the artist's expectably aristocratic notions, and in his life, although he was a child of light and a son of the covenant, he also kept up his connections with the Philis-

tines—he was, we remember, the original of James's Strether; and
when such a man complains about America, we do not say that his
case is special, we do not discount and resist what he says, we listen
and are convinced. His literary criticism still has force and point
because it is so doggedly partisan with a certain kind of literature
and because it always had a social end in view.

It is of course in his novels that Howells is at his best as a social
witness, and he can be very good indeed. The reader who wants to
test for himself what were in actual fact Howells' powers of social
insight, which have for long been slighted in most accounts of them,
might best read *A Modern Instance,* and he would do well to read
it alongside so perceptive a work of modern sociology as David
Riesman's *The Lonely Crowd,* for the two books address themselves
to the same situation, a change in the American character, a debili-
tation of the American psychic tone, the diminution of moral tension. Nothing could be more telling than Howells' description of
the religious mood of the seventies and eighties, the movement from
the last vestiges of faith to a genteel plausibility, the displacement
of doctrine and moral strenuousness by a concern with "social adjustment" and the amelioration of boredom. And the chief figure of the
novel, Bartley Hubbard, is worthy to stand with Dickens' Bradley
Headstone, or James's Basil Ransom and Paul Muniment, or Flaubert's Sénécal, or Dostoevski's Smerdyakov and Shigalov, as one of a
class of fictional characters who foretell a large social actuality of the
future. Howells has caught in Hubbard the quintessence of the
average sensual man as the most sanguine of us have come to fear
our culture breeds him, a man somewhat gifted—and how right a
touch that Hubbard should be a writer of sorts, how deep in our
democratic culture is the need to claim some special undeveloped
gift of intellect or art!—a man trading upon sincerity and half-truth;
vain yet self-doubting; aggressive yet self-pitying; self-indulgent yet
with starts of conscience; friendly and helpful yet not loyal; impelled to the tender relationships yet wishing above all to live to
himself and by himself, essentially resenting all human ties. In the
seventy years since *A Modern Instance* appeared, no American

novelist has equaled Howells in the accuracy and cogency of his observation, nor in the seriousness with which he took the social and moral facts that forced themselves on his unhappy consciousness.

Yet if we praise Howells only as a man who is historically interesting, or if we praise him only as an observer who testifies truthfully about the American social fact of his time, we may be dealing as generously and as piously with his memory as the nature of his achievement permits, but we cannot be happy over having added to the number of American writers who must be praised thus circumspectly if they are to be praised at all. We have all too many American writers who live for us only because they can be so neatly "placed," whose life in literature consists in their being influences or precursors, or of being symbols of intellectual tendencies, which is to say that their life is not really in literature at all but in the history of culture.

Perhaps this is the fate to which we must abandon Howells. The comparison that is made between him and Trollope, while it suggests something of his quality, also proposes his limitations, which are considerable. As an American, and for reasons that Henry James made clear, he did not have Trollope's social advantages, he did not have at his disposal that thickness of the English scene and of the English character which were of such inestimable value to the English novelists as a standing invitation to energy, gusto, and happy excess. Nor did he have Trollope's assumption of a society essentially settled despite the changes that might be appearing; his consciousness of the past could not be of sufficient weight to balance the pull of the future, and so his present could never be as solid as Trollope's. "Life here," as he said, "is still for the future—it is a land of Emersons—and I like a little present moment in mine." He never got as much present moment as the novelist presumably needs, and his novels are likely to seem to most readers to be of the past because nothing in America is quite so dead as an American future of a few decades back, unless it be an American personage of the same time.

And yet it is still possible that Howells deserves something better

than a place in the mere background of American literature. It is
clear enough that he is not of a kind with Hawthorne, Melville,
James, and Whitman; nor of a kind with Emerson and Thoreau;
nor with Poe; nor with Mark Twain at his best. But neither is he of
a kind with H. B. Fuller and Robert Herrick, whose names are
usually mentioned with his as being in a line of descent from him.
If Howells is experienced not as he exists in the textbooks, but as he
really is on his own page, we have to see that there is something
indomitable about him; at least while we are reading him he does
not consent to being consigned to the half-life of the background of
literature. For one thing, his wit and humor save him. Much must
be granted to the man who created the wealthy, guilty, hypersensi-
tive Clara Kingsbury, called her "a large blonde mass of suffering,"
and conceived that she might say to poor Marcia Hubbard, "Why,
my child, you're a Roman matron!" and come away in agony that
Marcia would think she meant her nose. And the man is not easily
done with who at eighty-three, in the year of his death, wrote that
strange "realistic" idyl, *The Vacation of the Kelwyns,* with its paraphernalia of gypsies and dancing bears and its infinitely touching
impulse to speak out against the negation and repression of emotion,
its passionate wish to speak out for the benign relaxation of the
will, for goodness and gentleness, for "life," for the reservation of
moral judgment, for the charm of the mysterious, precarious little
flame that lies at the heart of the commonplace. No one since
Schiller has treated the genre of the idyl with the seriousness it
deserves, yet even without a standard of criticism the contemporary
reader will, I think, reach beyond the quaintness of the book to a
sense of its profundity, or at least of its near approach to profundity. It will put him in mind of the early novels of E. M. Forster,
and he will even be drawn to think of *The Tempest,* with which it
shares the theme of the need for general pardon and the irony of the
brave new world: Howells, setting his story in the year of the cen-
tennial of the Declaration of Independence, is explicit in his belief
that the brave newness of the world is all behind his young lovers.

When we praise Howells' social observation, we must see that it is of a precision and subtlety which carry it beyond sociology to literature. It is literature and not sociology to understand with Howells' innocent clarity the relationship of the American social classes, to know that a lady from Cambridge and the farmer's wife with whom she boards will have a natural antagonism which will be expressed in the great cultural issue of whether the breakfast steak should be fried or broiled. Again, when we have said all that there is to say about Howells' theory of character, have taken full account of its intentional lack of glory, we must see that in its reasoned neutrality, in its insistence on the virtual equality in any person of the good and the bad, or of the interesting and the dull, there is a kind of love, perhaps not so much of persons as of persons in society, of the social idea. At the heart of Herrick there is deadness and even a kind of malice. At the heart of Fuller there is a sort of moral inertness. But at the heart of Howells there is a loving wonder at the fact that persons of the most mediocre sort somehow manage to make a society.

I don't mean by this to define the whole quality and virtue of Howells but only to offer enough in his defense to make his case at least doubtful, because I want to ask the question, How much is our present friendly indifference to him of his making and how much is it of ours? It is a question which cannot be fully answered at this time but only in some later generation that is as remote from our assumptions as from Howells', yet it is worth attempting for what small self-knowledge the effort might bring.

II

Henry James's essay on Howells is well known, and in that essay there are three statements which by implication define the ground of our present indifference to Howells. They have the advantage for our inquiry of appearing in the friendliest possible context, and they are intended not as judgments, certainly not as adverse judgments, but only as descriptions.

This is the first statement: "He is animated by a love of the common, the immediate, the familiar, and the vulgar elements of life, and holds that in proportion as we move into the rare and strange we become vague and arbitrary; that truth of representation, in a word, can be achieved only so long as it is in our power to test and measure it."

Here is the second statement: "He hates a 'story,' and (this private feat is not impossible) has probably made up his mind very definitely as to what the pestilent thing consists of. Mr. Howells hates an artificial fable, a denouement that is pressed into service; he likes things to occur as in life, where the manner of a great many of them is not to occur at all."

And here is the third: "If American life is on the whole, as I make no doubt whatever, more innocent than that of any other country, nowhere is the fact more patent than in Mr. Howells' novels, which exhibit so constant a study of the actual and so small a perception of evil."

It will be immediately clear from these three statements how far from our modern taste Howells is likely to be. I have said they are objective statements, that they are descriptions and not judgments, yet we can hear in them some ambiguity of tone—some ambiguity of tone must inevitably be there, for James is defining not only his friend's work but, by inversion, his own. And almost in the degree that we admire James and defend his artistic practice, we are committed to resist Howells. But I think we must have the grace to see that in resisting Howells, in rejecting him, we are resisting and rejecting something more than a literary talent or temperament or method. There is in Howells, as I have tried to suggest, an odd kind of muted, stubborn passion which we have to take account of, and respect, and recognize for what it is, the sign of a commitment, of an involvement in very great matters—we are required to see that in making our judgment of him we are involved in considerations of way of life, of quality of being.

His passion and its meaning become apparent whenever he speaks of the commonplace, which was the almost obsessive object of his literary faith. "The commonplace? Commonplace? The common-place is just that light, impalpable, aerial essence which [the novel-ists] have never got into their confounded books yet. The novelist who could interpret the common feelings of commonplace people would have the answer to 'the riddle of the painful earth' on his tongue." We might go so far as to grant that the passion of this utterance has a kind of intellectual illumination in it which com-mands our respect, but we in our time cannot truly respond to it. We are lovers of what James calls the rare and strange, and in our litera-ture we are not responsive to the common, the immediate, the familiar, and the vulgar elements in life.

Or at least we have a most complicated relation to these elements. In our poetic language we do want something that has affinity with the common, the immediate, the familiar, and the vulgar. And we want a certain aspect or degree of these elements in all our literature —we want them in their extremity, especially the common and vul-gar. We find an interest in being threatened by them; we like them represented in their extremity to serve as a sort of outer limit of the possibility of our daily lives, as a kind of mundane hell. They figure for us in this way in *Ulysses*, in *The Waste Land*, in Kafka's novels and stories, even in Yeats, and they account, I believe, for the inter-est of comfortable middle-class readers in James Farrell's *Studs Lonigan*. In short, we consent to the commonplace as it verges upon and becomes the rare and strange. The commonplace of extreme poverty or ultimate boredom may even come to imply the demonic and be valued for that—let life be sufficiently depressing and suffi-ciently boring in its commonplaceness and we shall have been licensed to give up quiet desperation and to become desperately fierce. We are attracted by the idea of human life in, as it were, putrefaction, in stewing corruption—we sense the force gathering in the fermentation. But of course Howells' kind of commonness sug-gests nothing of this. The objection that many readers made to his early work was that it was drab and depressing, the point of com-parison being fiction of plot and melodramatic incident, what

Howells called the "romantic." But after a time the objection was to his tame gentility, the comparison being then with Zola. Howells admired Zola enormously and fought for his recognition, but he eventually thought that Zola failed in realism and surrendered to "romanticism." He meant that the matter of Zola's realism would lead his readers away from the facts of their middle-class lives. For Howells the center of reality was the family life of the middle class.

The feeling for the family with which Howells' theory of the commonplace was bound up was very strong in him, and Mr. Wilson is accurate when he makes it definitive of Howells' quality. His family piety seems to have amounted almost to a superstitiousness, for as such we must interpret his having said to Mark Twain, "I would rather see and talk with you than with any other man in the world," and then feeling it necessary to add, "outside my own family." His sorrows were family sorrows; after his marriage the direction of his life was given chiefly by the family necessities. All this, we may well feel, is excessive, and very likely it accounts for the insufficiency of personality, of self, in Howells that makes the chief trouble in our relation with him. He is too much the *pius Aeneas* without having Aeneas's sad saving grace of being the sire of an enormous destiny. Yet this must not lead us to lessen the credit we give to Howells for being the only nineteenth-century American writer of large reputation who deals directly and immediately with the family.

I do not know whether or not anyone has remarked the peculiar power the idea of the family has in literature—perhaps it has never been worth anyone's while to remark what is so simple and obvious, so easily to be observed from the time of the Greek epics and of the Greek drama down through the course of European literature. Even today, when our sense of family has become much attenuated, the familial theme shows its power in our most notable literature, in Joyce, in Proust, in Faulkner, in Kafka. But our present sense of the family is of the family in dissolution, and although of course the point of any family story has always been a threatened or an actual dissolution, this was once thought to be calamity where with us it is the natural course of things. We are sure that the nine-teenth-century family was an elaborate hoax and against nature. It is true that almost every second-rate novel will represent one of its good characters expressing the hope of a quiet home and charming and satisfying children; it is true that the family is at the center of the essential mythology of our social and economic life, the good and sufficient reason for accumulation and expenditure, and that the maintenance of the family in peace is the study of our psychological science, yet in our literature the family serves as but an ideality, a rather wistful symbol of peace, order, and continuity; it does not exist in anything like actuality.

This may explain our feeling of indifference to the realism of the commonplace. But our attitude toward the family must be understood in a very large context, as but one aspect of our attitude to the idea of *the conditioned,* of the material circumstances in which spirit exists. From one point of view, no people has ever had so intense an idea of the relationship of spirit to its material circumstances as we in America now have. Our very preoccupation with *things,* as Mary McCarthy once observed, is really a way of dealing with the life of spirit in the world of matter—our possessions, although they have reference to status and comfort, have a larger reference to the future of our souls, to energy and the sense of cleanliness and fitness and health; our materialism cannot be represented as the Roman *luxus* has been represented—its style is not meant to imply ease and rest and self-indulgence but rather an ideal of alertness and readiness of spirit. And this sense of the conditioned is carried out in our elaborate theories of child-rearing, and the extravagant store we set by education; and in our theories of morality and its relation to social circumstance.

Yet it is to be seen that those conditions to which we do respond are the ones which we ourselves make, or over which we have control, which is to say conditions as they are virtually spirit, as they deny the idea of *the conditioned.* Somewhere in our mental constitution is the demand for life as pure spirit.

The idea of unconditioned spirit is of course a very old one, but we are probably the first people to think of it as a realizable possibility and to make that possibility part of our secret assumption. It is this that explains the phenomenon of our growing disenchantment with the whole idea of the political life, the feeling that although we are willing, nay eager, to live in society, for we all piously know that man fulfills himself in society, yet we do not willingly consent to live in a particular society of the present, marked as it is bound to be by a particular economic system, by disorderly struggles for influence, by mere approximations and downright failures. Our aesthetic sense—I mean our deep comprehensive aesthetic sense, really our metaphysics—which is satisfied by the performance of a Bendix washing machine, is revolted by such a politically conditioned society. The wide disrepute into which capitalistic society has fallen all over the world is justified by the failures and injustices of capitalism; but if we want to understand the assumptions about politics of the world today, we have to consider the readiness of people to condemn the failures and injustices of that society as compared with their reluctance to condemn the failures and injustices of Communist society. The comparison will give us the measure of the modern preference for the unconditioned—to the modern more-or-less thinking man, Communist society is likely to seem a close approximation to the unconditioned, to spirit making its own terms.

The dislike of the conditioned is in part what makes so many of us dissatisfied with our class situation, and guilty about it, and unwilling to believe that it has any reality, or that what reality it may have is a possible basis of moral or spiritual prestige, the moral or spiritual prestige which is the most valuable thing in the world to those of us who think a little. By extension, we are very little satisfied with the idea of family life—for us it is part of the inadequate bourgeois reality. Not that we don't live good-naturedly enough with our families, but when we do, we know that we are "family men," by definition cut off from the true realities of the spirit. This, I venture to suppose, is why the family is excluded from American literature of any pretensions. Although not all families are thus excluded—for example, the family of Faulkner's *As I Lay Dying* is very happily welcomed. And on every account it should be, but probably one reason for our eager acceptance of it is that we find in that family's extremity of suffering a respite from the commonplace of the conditioned as we know it in our families, we actually find in it an intimation of liberty—when conditions become extreme enough there is sometimes a sense of deep relief, as if the conditioned had now been left quite behind, as if spirit were freed when the confining comforts and the oppressive assurances of civil life are destroyed.

But Howells was committed totally and without question to civil life, and when he wrote an essay called "Problems of Existence in Fiction," although he did include among the existential matters that the novelist might treat such grim, ultimate things as a lingering hopeless illness, it is but one item among such others as the family budget, nagging wives, daughters who want to marry fools, and the difficulties of deciding whom to invite to dinner.

In extenuation of Howells we remember that this is all the matter of Jane Austen, the high reverberations of whose touch upon the commonplace we have habituated ourselves to hear. But Howells does not permit us to defend him with the comparison; he is profligate in his dealings with the ordinary, and in *A Hazard of New Fortunes* he does not think twice about devoting the first six chapters to an account of the hero's search for an apartment. I have heard that someone has written to explicate the place of these chapters in the total scheme of the novel, and in perfect ignorance of this essay I hazard the guess that its intention is to rescue Howells from the appearance of an excess of literalness and ordinariness, and that, in the carrying out of this intention, Basil March's fruitless ringing of janitors' bells is shown to be a modern instance of the age-old theme of The Quest, or an analogue of the Twelve Tribes in the Wilderness, or of the flight into Egypt, or a symbol of the homelessness of the intellectual. But it is really just a house-hunt. Of course any house-hunt will inevitably produce lost and unhappy feelings, even a sense of cosmic alienation—so much in our dull daily lives really does make a significant part of man's tragic career on earth, which is what Howells meant by his passionate sentence about the charm and power of the commonplace. But when we yield to our contemporary impulse to enlarge all experience, to involve it as soon as possible in history, myth, and the oneness of spirit—an impulse with which, I ought to say, I have considerable sympathy—we are in danger of making experience merely typical, formal, and *representative,* and thus of losing one term of the dialectic that goes on between spirit and the conditioned, which is, I suppose, what we mean when we speak of man's tragic fate. We lose, that is to say, the actuality of the conditioned, the literality of matter, the peculiar authenticity and authority of the merely denotative.[1] To lose this is to lose not a material fact but a spiritual one, for it is a fact of spirit that it must exist in a world which requires it to engage in so dispiriting an occupation as hunting for a house. The knowledge of the antagonism between spirit and the conditioned—it is Donne's, it is Pascal's, it is Tolstoi's—may in literature be a cause of great delight because it is so rare and difficult; beside it the knowledge of pure spirit is comparatively easy.

III

To James's first statement about Howells, his second is clearly a corollary—"He hates a 'story' . . . [he] hates an artificial fable." We cannot nowadays be sure that all of our reading public loves a story in the way James did. Quite simple readers can be counted on to love a story, but there is a large, consciously intelligent middle part of our reading public that is inclined to suspect a story, in James's sense, as being a little dishonest. However, where theory of a certain complexity prevails, the implications of story, and even of

---

[1] Students have a trick of speaking of money in Dostoevski's novels as "symbolic," as if no one ever needed, or spent, or gambled, or squandered the stuff—and as if to think of it as an actuality were subliterary.

"artificial fable," are nowadays easily understood. In these uplands of taste we comprehend that artificial devices, such as manipulated plot, are a way not of escaping from reality but of representing it, and we speak with vivacity of "imaginary gardens with real toads in them." Indeed, we have come to believe that the toad is the less real when the garden is also real. Our metaphysical habits lead us to feel the deficiency of what we call literal reality and to prefer what we call essential reality. To be sure, when we speak of literal reality, we are aware that there is really no such thing—that everything that is *per*ceived is in some sense *con*ceived, or created; it is controlled by intention and indicates intention; and so on. Nevertheless, bound as we are by society and convention, as well as by certain necessities of the mind, there still is a thing that we persist in calling "literal reality," and we recognize in works of art a greater or less approximation to it. Having admitted the existence of literal reality, we give it a low status in our judgment of art. Naturalism, which is the form of art that makes its effects by the accumulation of the details of literal reality, is now in poor repute among us. We dismiss it as an analogue of an outmoded science and look to contemporary science to give authority to our preference for the abstract and conceptual; or we look to music to justify our impatience with the representational; and we derive a kind of political satisfaction from our taste, remembering that reactionary governments hate what we admire.

Our metaphysical and aesthetic prejudices even conspire to make us believe that our children have chiefly an "essential" sense of reality. We characterize the whole bent of their minds by their flights of fancy and by the extremity of distortion in their school paintings, preferring to forget that if they are in some degree and on some occasions essential realists, they are also passionately pedantic literalists—as they must be when their whole souls are so directed toward accommodation and control. The vogue of the "educational" toy with its merely essential representation is an adult vogue; the two-year-old wants the miniature Chevrolet with as many precise details as possible; it is not the gay chintz ball designed for the infant eye and grasp that delights him but rather the apple or the orange—its function, its use, its being valued by the family, give him his pleasure; and as he grows older his pedantry of literalism will increase, and he will scorn the adult world for the metaphysical vagaries of its absurd conduct—until he himself is seduced by them.

Now we must admit that Howells' extravagance of literalism, his downright, declared hatred of a story, was on the whole not very intelligent. He said of Zola that "the imperfection of his realism began with the perfection of his form." That is, just where Zola appeals to us, just where he disregards his own syllabus of the experimental novel to introduce dramatic extravagance, he is disappointing to Howells. And Howells, in his character of programmatic literalist, spoke disrespectfully of Scott (one of the founders of realism), of Dickens, and of Balzac, saying that the truth was not in them; and he went so far as to express impatience with the romancing of George Eliot, despite the clear affinity his realism has with hers. It is difficult to know what he made of his adored Jane Austen. Clearly it never occurred to him, as he sought to learn from her, that some of her finest effects are due to her carefully contrived stories. We, of course, find it natural to say that the perfection of her realism begins with the perfection of her form.

It is perhaps an expression of our desire for unconditioned spirit that we have of late years been so preoccupied with artifice and form. We feel that the shape which the mind gives to what the mind observes is more ideally characteristic of the mind than is the act of observation. Possibly it is, and if the last decades of criticism have insisted rather too much that this is so,[2] it is possible that a view of our historical situation might lead us to justify the overemphasis, for in the historical perspective we perceive such a depressing plethora of matter and so little form. Form suggests a

2 Who can imagine any of our critics saying with Ruskin that "No good work whatever can be perfect, and the demand for perfection is always a sign of a misunderstanding of the ends of art"; and ". . . No great man ever stops working till he has reached his point of failure . . ."?

principle of control—I can quite understand that group of my students who have become excited over their discovery of the old animosity which Ezra Pound and William Carlos Williams bear to the iamb, and have come to feel that could they but break the iambic shackles, the whole of modern culture could find a true expression.

The value of form must never be denigrated. But by a perversity of our minds, just as the commitment to a particular matter of literature is likely to be conceived in terms of hostility to form, so the devotion to the power of form is likely to be conceived in terms of hostility to matter, to matter in its sheer literalness, in its stubborn denotativeness. The claims of form to pre-eminence over matter always have a certain advantage because of the feeling to which I have just referred, that the mind's power of shaping is more characteristic of mind than its power of observation. Certainly the power of shaping is more intimately connected with what Plato called the "spirited" part of man, with the will, while observation may be thought of as springing from the merely "vegetative" part. The eye, it cannot choose but see, we cannot bid the ear be still; things impress themselves upon us against or with our will. But the plastic stress of spirit is of the will in the sense that it strives against resistance, against the stubbornness of what Shelley called the dull, dense world—it compels "all new successions to the forms they wear."

But Shelley's description of the act of creation suggests that the plastic will cannot possibly exercise itself without the recalcitrance of stupid literal matter. When we consider what is going on in painting at this moment, we perceive what may happen in an art when it frees itself entirely from the objective. No doubt the defense of the legitimacy of nonobjective art which is made by referring to the right of music to be unindentured to an objective reality is as convincing as it ever was. Yet do we not have the unhappy sense that sterility is overtaking the painters, that by totally freeing themselves from the objective reality which they believed extraneous to their art, they have provided the plastic will with no resisting object, or none except itself as expressed by other painters, and are therefore beginning to express themselves in mere competitive ingenuity? It is no accident of the *Zeitgeist* that the classic painting of our time is Cubism. The Cubists, bold as they were, accepted the conditioned, and kept in touch with a world of literality. And this is the opinion of one of the greatest of the Cubists, Juan Gris. "Those who believe in abstract painting," he wrote in a letter of 1919, "are like weavers who think they can produce material with only one set of threads and forget that there has to be another set to hold these together. Where there is no attempt at plasticity how can you control representational liberties? And where there is no concern for reality how can you limit and unite plastic liberties?"

What is true of the Cubists is also true of the great classic writers of our time—the sense of *things* is stronger in them than in their expositors. They grew in naturalism, in literalism, and they in their way insist on it as much as Flaubert, or the Goncourts, or Zola. The impulse of succeeding writers to build on Joyce is pretty sure to be frustrated, for it is all too likely to be an attempt to build on Joyce's notions of form, which have force only in relation to Joyce's superb sense of literal fact, his solid simple awareness that in the work of art some things are merely denotative and do not connote more than appears, that they are *data* and must be permitted to exist as data.

IV

The last of James's statements about Howells concerns his indifference to evil. For us today this constitutes a very severe indictment. We are all aware of evil; we began to be aware of it in certain quasi-religious senses a couple of decades or so ago; and as time passed we learned a great deal about the physical, political actuality of evil, saw it expressed in the political life in a kind of gratuitous devilishness which has always been in the world but which never before in Western Europe had been organized and, as it were, rationalized. A proper sense of evil is surely an attribute of a great writer, and nowadays we have been drawn to make it almost a touchstone of greatness, drawn to do so in part by our revived religious feelings or nostalgia for religious feelings, but of course also in part by our desire that literature should be in accord with reality as we now know it.

Our responsiveness to the idea of evil is legitimate enough, yet we ought to be aware that the management of the sense of evil is not an easy thing. Be careful, Nietzsche said, when you fight dragons, lest you become a dragon yourself. There is always the danger, when we have insisted upon the fact of evil with a certain intensity, that we will go on to cherish the virtue of our insistence, and then the very fact we insist upon. I would make a distinction between the relation to evil of the creator of the literary work and that of the reader, believing that the active confrontation of the fact of evil is likelier to be healthy than is the passive confrontation—there is something suspect in making evil the object of, as it were, aesthetic contemplation. But not even the creator is nowadays immune from all danger. Consider that the awareness of evil is held by us to confer a certain kind of spiritual status and prestige upon the person who exercises it, a status and prestige which are often quite out of proportion to his general spiritual gifts. Our time has a very quick sensitivity to what the sociologists call *charisma,* which, in the socio-political context, is the quality of power and leadership that seems to derive from a direct connection with great supernal forces, with godhead. This power we respond to when we find it in our literature in the form of alliances with the dark gods of sexuality, or the huge inscrutability of nature, or the church, or history; presumably we want it for ourselves. This is what accounts in our theory of literature for our preference for the hidden and ambiguous, for our demand for "tension" and "tragedy." And evil has for us its own *charisma.* Hannah Arendt, in *The Origins of Totalitarianism,* speaking of the modern disintegration, remarks that with us today "to yield to the mere process of disintegration has become an irresistible temptation, not only because it has assumed the spurious grandeur of 'historical necessity' but also because everything outside it has begun to appear lifeless, bloodless, meaningless, and unreal." Disintegration itself fascinates us because it is a power. Evil has always fascinated men, not only because it is opposed to good but also because it is, in its own right, a power.

Lifeless, bloodless, meaningless, and *unreal*—without stopping to estimate just how much life, blood, meaning, and reality Howells actually has, we must observe that the modern reader who judges him to have little is not exactly in a position to be objective, that he is likely to deal with Howells under the aspect of a universal judgment by which it is concluded that very little in our life has life, blood, meaning, and reality.

The sentence in which Howells invites American novelists to concern themselves with the "more smiling aspects" of life as being the "more American" is well known and has done much harm to his reputation. In fairness to Howells, we ought to be aware that the sentence may not be quite so dreadful as is generally supposed. For one thing, it is rather ambiguous—when Howells says "we invite," it is not clear whether "we" is the editorial pronoun referring to himself or is meant to stand for the American people: the phrase, that is, may be read as simply descriptive of a disposition of American culture. And even if we take the sentence in its worst construction, we ought to recall that it appears in an essay on Dostoevski in which Howells urges the reading of Dostoevski; that when he speaks of the more smiling aspects of life as being the more American it is in the course of a comparison of America with the Russia of Dostoevski; that he is careful to remark that America is not exempt from the sorrows of the natural course of life, only from those which are peculiar to the poverty and oppression of Dostoevski's land; and that he says he is not sure that America is in every way the gainer by being so thoroughly in material luck, so rich in the smiling aspects. But let us leave all extenuation aside and take the sentence only as it has established itself in the legendary way, as the clear sign of Howells' blindness to evil, his ignorance of the very essence of reality. Taken so, it perhaps cannot be thought a very wise statement, but our interpretation of it, the vehemence with which we are likely to press its meaning, tells us, I think, more about ourselves than about Howells. It raises the question of why we believe, as we do believe, that evil is of the very essence of reality.

The management of the sense of evil, I have said, is not easy. The sense of evil is properly managed only when it is not allowed to be preponderant over the sense of self. The reason Shakespeare holds his place in our imagination is that in him the sense of evil and the sense of self are in so delicate and continuous a reciprocation. And the ground of Keats's greatness, I have come to feel, is that precarious reciprocation of self and evil, similar to Shakespeare's. He maintained this reciprocation in a more conscious and explicit way than Shakespeare found necessary. He called to his aid in the affirmation of self against the knowledge of evil his intense imagination of pleasure—of pleasure of all kinds, the simplest and most primitive, such as eating and drinking, as well as the highest. He boldly put pleasure, even contentment, at the center of his theory of poetry, and at one point in the development of his theory he spoke of poetry as being most itself when it tells "heart-easing things." It is just for this reason that some readers denigrate him; they quite miss the intensity of his sense of reality, for where they make a duality of the principle of pleasure and the principle of reality, Keats made a unity—for him pleasure was a reality; it was, as Wordsworth had taught him, the grand principle of life, of mind, and of self. And it was this commitment to pleasure that made it possible for him to write the greatest exposition of the meaning of tragedy in our literature.

When we are so eager to say how wrong Howells was to invite the novelist to deal with the smiling aspects of life, we have to ask ourselves whether our quick antagonism to this mild recognition of pleasure does not imply an impatience with the self, a degree of yielding to what Hannah Arendt calls the irresistible temptation of disintegration, of identification by submission to the grandeur of historical necessity which is so much more powerful than the self. It is possible that our easily expressed contempt for the smiling aspects and our covert impulse to yield to the historical process are a way of acquiring charisma. It is that peculiar charisma which has always been inherent in death. It was neither a genteel novelist nor a romantic poet who most recently defended the necessity of the smiling aspects and the heart-easing things—Dr. Bruno Bettelheim was first known in this country for his study, made at first hand, of the psychology of the inmates of the German concentration camps. Dr. Bettelheim recently found occasion to remark that "a fight for the very survival of civilized mankind is actually a fight to restore man to a sensitivity toward the joys of life. Only in this way can man be liberated and the survival of civilized mankind be assured. Maybe a time has come in which our main efforts need no longer be directed toward modifying the pleasure principle. [Dr. Bettelheim is speaking of the practice of psychoanalysis.] Maybe it is time we became concerned with restoring pleasure gratification to its dominant role in the reality principle; maybe this society needs less a modification of the pleasure principle by reality, and more assertion of the pleasure principle against an overpowering pleasure-denying reality." It cannot be said of Howells' smiling aspects that they represent a very intense kind of pleasure; yet for most men they will at least serve, in Keats's phrase, to bind us to the earth, to prevent our being seduced by the godhead of disintegration.

V

"Your really beautiful time will come," wrote Henry James to Howells on the occasion of his seventy-fifth birthday—what James characteristically meant was the time when the critical intelligence would begin to render Howells its tribute. The really beautiful time has come to James, but it has not yet come to Howells, and probably it will be a very long time coming. We are not easy with the quiet men, the civil personalities—the very word *civil,* except as applied to disobedience or disorders, is uncomfortable in our ears. "Art inhabits temperate regions," said André Gide in 1940. Well, not always; but if the statement is perhaps a little inaccurate in the range of its generality, we can understand what led Gide to make it, for he goes on: "And doubtless the greatest harm this war is doing to culture is to create a profusion of extreme passions which, by a sort of inflation, brings about a devaluation of all moderate sentiments." And the devaluation of the moderate sentiments brings a concomitant devaluation of the extreme passions: "The dying anguish of Roland or the distress of a Lear stripped of power moves us by its exceptional quality but loses its special eloquence when reproduced simultaneously in several thousand copies." The extreme has become the commonplace of our day. This is not a situation which can be legislated or criticized out of existence, but while it endures we are not in a position to make a proper judgment of Howells, a man of moderate sentiments. It is a disqualification that we cannot regard with complacency, for if Gide is right, it implies that we are in a fair way of being disqualified from making any literary judgments at all.

The Bostonians

HE BOSTONIANS is one of a pair of novels, the other being *The Princess Casamassima,* which, in the family of Henry James's works, have a special connection with each other, a particular isolate relationship, as of twins. They were published in the same year, 1886, their previous serial appearances in magazines having been in part concurrent, and although *The Bostonians* was in point of fact the earlier conceived and the first written, they almost seem to have been composed simultaneously, in a single act of creation. They are set apart from James's other novels by having in common a quick responsiveness to the details of the outer world, an explicit awareness of history, of the grosser movements of society and civilization. They share a curious knowledge of the little groups of queer people who, in small dark rooms, agitate the foolish questions which will eventually be decided on the broad field of the future. Very likely it was because James was conscious of these characteristics of the two books—and, we feel, was pleased with them as the evidence of the enlargement of his social intelligence—that he had especially high hopes that the two novels would be happily received by the public.

The disappointment of these hopes is well known. With the exception of his later defeat in the theater, no check given to James's ambition was so disastrous. The English press treated *The Princess Casamassima* with an almost absolute contempt, and if it was more indulgent with *The Bostonians,* this was only because it found some satisfaction in an American's account of the eccentricity of American manners. The American reviewers were outraged by *The Bostonians;* their more lenient response to *The Princess Casamassima* was in part dictated by their settled opinion of the English social system, which the book might be thought to satirize. Both novels were called queer and foolish, and their failure caused a serious decline in their author's reputation and market.

When, in April of 1883, James had written out in his notebook the full scenario of *The Bostonians,* he had summarized his intention by saying, "I wished to write a very *American* tale."[1] It is possible to say of those of James's novels that are set in America—*The Bostonians* is the last until *The Ivory Tower* of some twenty years later—that they have a tone different from the novels which are set in Europe. I regard with suspicion my natural impulse to say that this is a specifically "American" tone, for I should not know how to explain with any confidence what that is. Yet it seems to me worth observing that, as against the heavy chiaroscuro which in *The Princess Casamassima* is appropriate to the rich clotted past of civilization as that novel evokes it, *The Bostonians* seems suffused by "the dry American light," and that it is marked by a comicality which has rather more kinship with American than with British humor, or with wit of any transatlantic kind. It is said of Miss Birdseye that "she was heroic, she was sublime, the whole moral history of Boston was reflect in her displaced spectacles"; it is said of Dr. Mary Prance that "it is true that if she had been a boy, she would have borne some relation to a girl," and also that "she was determined that she wouldn't be a patient, and it seemed that the only way not to be one was to be a doctor"—humor is latent in all James's writing, implicit in the nature of his prose, but I can bring to mind no other

[1] The tense of the predicate verb cannot pass without notice. James was not to compose the book until two years later, but when once he had completed the scenario, he felt that the main work was behind him, so natural to him was the act of writing, so little uncertainty intervened for him getween the intention and the act. Yet no one who has read both the scenario and the novel can fail to see how much was conceived in the actual writing that could never have been conceived in the scenario, however "divine" James thought "the principle of the scenario" to be.

of his novels in which it breaks so gaily out of latency and implicitness into the memorable free overtones of such sentences as these and of scenes analogous to these sentences.

As a representation of the American actuality, *The Bostonians* is in every way remarkable, and its originality is striking. James's Boston, Cambridge, and Cape Cod are superbly rendered, and these localities may still be known—for they have changed less than most American places—through his descriptions of them. No American writer before James had so fully realized the contemporary, physical scene of moral action and social existence. Nor had the nature of the American social existence ever been so brilliantly suggested. Manners have changed since James wrote, but not the peculiar tenuity of the fabric of American social life. The London of *The Princess Casamassima* is no doubt the city of dreadful loneliness, and the barriers of class which it represents are real enough, yet the story sees to it that people at opposite social poles from each other shall meet and become involved with each other. It is thus perfectly in the tradition of the English novel, which characteristically likes the social mixture to be thick and variously composed, and this is a literary preference which corresponds, at whatever distance, to an actuality of English life. But in the America of *The Bostonians,* as in the America that Tocqueville had observed some forty years before, society is but little organized to allow for variousness and complexity, and the social atoms seem to have a centrifugal tendency. Basil Ransom lives in New York with no other companion than his little variety actress. He makes every effort to avoid the company of his cousin, Mrs. Luna, and she, a lady of family and means, seems to have no social circle at all. Mrs. Burrage is by way of being a New York "hostess," but the guests at the party which she gives for Verena Tarrant seem all to have met each other for the first time. It is of the essence of Olive Chancellor's nature that she cannot endure social intercourse; a speech to a crowd is her notion of human communication, and she cannot laugh. Verena Tarrant has presumably never had a friend until Olive Chancellor institutes their ambiguous alliance. Dr.

Prance lives in virtual solitude. Miss Birdseye, having devoted a long life to humanity, becomes herself an object of devotion, but rather as if she were everyone's old school, or some dear outworn ideal. The character of Miss Birdseye scandalized Boston because it was thought to be a portrait of Elizabeth Peabody, Hawthorne's famous reforming sister-in-law, and William James—who had, in any case, a poor opinion of *The Bostonians*—undertook to rebuke his brother for his failure of taste. (Henry replied in a letter, a masterpiece of justifiable ambiguity, which has become the classic statement of the relation of the novelist's imagination to real persons.) Even with the most extravagant notions of the Boston genteel sensibility, it is difficult to understand what the ground of the offense was supposed to be, for if Miss Birdseye is indeed a portrait of Miss Peabody, it is the tenderest and most endearing imaginable. And perhaps that is what constituted the offense—for the law recognizes a certain wrong for which the novelist may be liable; it is called "invasion of privacy," and we may suppose that Boston was disturbed because James had committed this wrong, not in the mere legal meaning of the term but in a way far more disturbing: it was not Miss Peabody's privacy that he had invaded but rather the privacy of his readers. He had forced them into intimacy with a person whom they daily greeted, he had made her available to their understanding and to their conscious love, had terribly implied that the actual woman might be the object of the same emotions that they inevitably felt toward the image of her in the novel.

The Bostonians and *The Princess Casamassima* seem to be set apart from the rest of James's canon by the public and political matter with which they deal. But their representation of large, overt, opposed forces and principles does not, in point of fact, mark their inspiration as of an essentially different kind from that of James's other novels. It may be said of James—with, of course, some risk of excessive simplification—that virtually all his fiction represents the conflict of two principles, of which one is radical, the other conservative. The two principles are constant, although circumstances change their particular manifestations and the relative values which they are to be judged to have. They may be thought of as energy and inertia; or spirit and matter; or spirit and letter; or force and form; or creation and possession; or Libido and Thanatos. In their simpler manifestations the first term of the grandiose duality is generally regarded with unqualified sympathy and is identified with the ideality of youth, or with truth, or with art, or with America; the second term is regarded with hostility and represented as being one with age, or convention, or philistinism, or decadent Europe. But James's mind is nothing if not "dialectical"—the values assigned to each of the two opposing principles are not permitted to be fixed and constant. Daisy Miller's crude innocent defiance of European conventions is as right as rain, but *Madame de Mauves* suggests that only a small change in circumstance can make American innocence a downright malevolence. Art as against the philistine morality may not always be in the right—creation may corrupt itself into its opposite, possession, as in *The Author of Beltraffio*. Life may be seen to express itself in death and through death. And in *The Birth-place* James seems to be saying that truth can exist only in and through the life of institutions, or that it can be communicated only through sadly inadequate approximations of truth.

The nature of the terms of James's dialectic suggests why his fiction is always momentous. And it is quite within the scope of his genius to infer the political macrocosm from the personal microcosm, to write large and public the disorders of the personal life and to suppose, as he did in *The Bostonians* and *The Princess Casamassima,* that it is the most natural thing in the world that they should

> Divert and crack, rend and deracinate
> The unity and married calm of states. . . .

If we compare the two political movements which James undertook to represent, the revolutionary anarchism of *The Princess Casamassima* will perhaps on first inspection seem to promise more as a theme for a novel than the militant feminism of *The Bostonians*.

In a struggle for general social justice there is a natural force and dignity; and in a violent revolutionary intention there is the immediate possibility of high tragedy. But the doctrinaire demand for the equality of the sexes may well seem to promise but a wry and constricted story, a tale of mere eccentricity. The movement for female equality which became endemic in America and in the Protestant countries of Europe in the nineteenth century was predominantly social and legal in its program and even had—although not always—an outright anti-erotic bias which exposed it to the imputation of crankishness and morbidity. It would seem to be susceptible only of comic treatment, and the comedy it seems to propose is not of an attractive kind—it cannot, we know, have anything of the ancient bold freedom of *Lysistrata* or *The Thesmophoriazusae,* in which the women of Athens, in their very act of subverting the natural order of things, affirm the natural erotic community between men and women.

There is indeed some unpleasantness in the comedy of *The Bostonians,* yet exactly by risking this, by daring to seize on the qualities of the women's-rights movement which were "unnatural" and morbid, James possessed himself of a subject which was even larger in its significance than that of *The Princess Casamassima.* A movement of social revolution may question the culture in which it exists, or it may not—indeed we can say of social revolutions that they do not in fact question cultures as much as they seem to do and say they do. But a movement of sexual revolution is to be understood as a question which a culture puts to itself, and right down to its very roots. It is a question about what it means to be a man and what it means to be a woman—about the quality of being which people wish to have. James was interested in the thin vagaries of the female movement of reform only as they suggested a conflict between men and women that went far deeper than any quarrel over rights and equalities. And the conflict that he perceived was not the battle of the sexes which Meredith and Shaw delighted in, a fine formality of marching and countermarching and intricate maneuver on a com-

modious plain, chosen by mutual consent, the point of the engagement being to demonstrate that women have as bright a spiritedness, as firm a resolution, and as particular an intention of sexuality
as men. The opposing forces met on the field as if by appointment,
they were animated by the sense of adventure, and defeat brought
nothing much worse than honorable captivity on parole—no one in
the least believes that John Tanner regrets his surrender to Ann
Whitfield. The conflict which James described was very different
from this. It was the bitter total war of the sexes which Strindberg
conceived and which reached its fullest ideological and artistic expression in the works of D. H. Lawrence.

Tocqueville, whose great book figures in *The Bostonians* because
it is the favorite reading of the hero of the novel, had noted the
beginnings of sexual disorientation in America; and in James's own
time, American observers who were not bound by convention, men
so unlike as Walt Whitman and Henry Adams, were aware that
something had gone wrong with the sexual life of the nation. "The
men hate the women, and the women hate the men," Whitman had
said. Adams spoke of American men as having sacrificed their
sexuality to business and the machine, and as having induced in
American women an indifference even to maternity. And James,
when he had set down his intention of "writing a very *American*
tale," went on to say, "I asked myself what was the most salient
and peculiar point of our social life, the answer was: the situation of
women, the decline of the sentiment of sex. . . ."

No more than Tocqueville or Henry Adams or D. H. Lawrence
did James understand the sexual situation as an isolated fact, however momentous. For him, as for them, it was the sign of a general
diversion of the culture from the course of nature. He makes this
plain by his choice of a hero for *The Bostonians*. It was of course
essential to his plan that his hero be an outlander, alien to the culture
of Boston, and James at first thought that he should be a young man
from the West. But a Western hero, he soon saw, was not possible.
It must have occurred to him, for one thing, that in the West progressive social and political ideas had established themselves with

relative ease, feminism in particular having made far greater advances than in the East, so that he would scarcely be setting up a counterprinciple to Boston. And then the assumptions about a Western hero were inevitably that he was emancipated from tradition, optimistic, concerned with practice rather than with theory, and likely to be impatient of intellectual refinements, and, of course, that he was materially successful. Such a hero might indeed be used to make a cultural-sexual point—in 1906 the Western hero of William Vaughn Moody's *The Great Divide* was to rape the New England heroine for her own good; the audiences of Broadway were delighted with this show of benevolent violence which, as the play made clear, was symbolic of the energies of modern business enterprise and quite disposed of the decadent finickiness of the New England conscience. James had no desire for such an effect. He understood quite as well as Lawrence that the true masculine principle could not be affirmed by a hero who was energetic and successful in the material business of the modern world. In the dramatic nature of the case the spokesman for masculinity should be able to lay claim to none but personal powers; and he will be the better suited to his role if, like Basil Ransom, he has witnessed and participated in the defeat of his cultural tradition, if he has suffered the ruin of his fortunes, and is a stranger in the land of his conquerors.

By choosing a Southerner for his hero, James gained an immediate and immeasurable advantage. By this one stroke he set his story beyond any danger of seeming to be a mere bicker between morbid women and stupid men, the subject of dull, ill-natured jokes. When he involved the feminist movement with even a late adumbration of the immense tragic struggle between North and South, he made it plain that his story had to do with a cultural crisis. Nor could this crisis, if properly understood, seem particular to America, for North and South, as James understands them, represent the two opposing elements in that elaborate politics of culture which, all over the civilized world, has been the great essential subject of the literature of the nineteenth and twentieth centuries.

The South had never had a vigorous intellectual life, and of the systematic apologists for its customs and manners as against the customs and manners of an ever more powerful industrial capitalism, only a very few had been men of real intellectual authority. Yet with the strange previsionary courage which led him, in *The Princess Casamassima,* to imagine types of political character unknown to his own time but familiar to ours, James conceived Basil Ransom as if he were the leading, ideal intelligence of the group of gifted men who, a half-century later, were to rise in the South and to muster in its defense whatever force may be available to an intelligent romantic conservatism. Rejecting much of the sentimental legend of the South, admitting the Southern faults and falsities the more easily because they believed that no civilization can be anything but imperfect, the Southern Agrarians yet said that the South stood for a kind of realism which the North, with its abstract intellectuality, was forgetting to its cost. Like their imagined proto-martyr Ransom, they asserted a distrust of theory, an attachment to tradition, and above all, the tragic awareness of the intractability of the human circumstance.

But Basil Ransom is more daring than any of his intellectual descendants of the South. He has the courage of the collateral British line of romantic conservatives—he is akin to Yeats, Lawrence, and Eliot in that he experiences his cultural fears in the most personal way possible, translating them into sexual fear, the apprehension of the loss of manhood. "The whole generation is womanised," he says, "the masculine tone is passing out of the world; it's a feminine, a nervous, hysterical, chattering, canting age, an age of hollow phrases and false delicacy and exaggerated solicitudes and coddled sensibilities, which, if we don't soon look out, will usher in the reign of mediocrity, of the feeblest and flattest and the most pretentious that has ever been. The masculine character, the ability to dare and endure, to know and yet not to fear reality, to look the world in the face and take it for what it is—a very queer and partly very base mixture—this is what I want to preserve, or rather, as I may say, to recover; and I must say that I don't in the least care what becomes of you ladies while I make the attempt."

And the fear of the loss of manhood, which we are familiar with in Yeats, in Lawrence, and in *The Waste Land,* is given reason for its existence everywhere in *The Bostonians*. The book is full of malign, archaic influences; it is suffused with primitive fear. It is not for nothing that Olive Chancellor's sister is named Mrs. Luna— with her shallow, possessive sexuality, which has the effect of conjuring away all masculine potency, she might as well have been named Mrs. Hecate. The very name of Olive Chancellor might suggest a deteriorated Minerva, presiding in homosexual chastity over the Athens of the New World. The meeting of Olive's colleagues is referred to as a rendezvous of witches on the Brocken, a characterization which is supported throughout the book by James's rather unpleasant sense of the threatening sordidness of almost all women except those in their first youth. Verena Tarrant is conceived as a sort of Iphigenia in Tauris, forced to preside as the priestess of the sacrifice of male captives. Basil Ransom is explicit in his feeling that when he is with Olive Chancellor he is not "safe." And indeed his position is at all times a precarious one. We have the impression that he is the only man in Boston, among hordes of doctrinaire Bacchae, and certainly he is the only man in the book—Verena's poor young suitor, Burrage, lives under the shadow of his mother; Dr. Tarrant is a kind of shaman, gloomily doing sexual service of some dim, grim, shameful kind to deprived Boston ladies; and Matthias Pardon, the newspaper man, is represented as the castrate priest of the huge idol of publicity, which, in the dialectic of the book, stands in hateful opposition to the life of emotion and true sexuality. Perhaps the novel's crucial scene is that which takes place in Memorial Hall at Harvard, when Ransom finds it necessary to enforce upon Verena's imagination the pathos of the fate of the young men who had died in the recent war. These young men had been his enemies, but he feels bound to them by the ties of the sex they have in common, and the danger of battle had never been so great as the sexual danger of his present civil situation.

There is one biographical circumstance of the writing of *The Bostonians* which ought to be mentioned in any account of the novel. I have no doubt that it bears in an important way upon the personal problems of Henry James's own life which are implied, we must inevitably suppose, by Ransom's fears. But the investigation of these problems lies outside my competence and my purpose, and I mention the circumstance only for reasons that are purely literary, only, that is, because an awareness of it is likely to make for a warmer understanding of the book.

In 1881 James visited his country and his family for the first time since 1876, the year in which he had made his decision to establish his home in England. From the beginning the visit was not a happy one. James disliked Boston, where he lived to be near his parents in Cambridge, and he was bored and restless. In January he went to stay with Henry Adams in Washington, and there, on the thirtieth of the month, he received the telegram announcing his mother's serious illness which was intended to prepare him for her death.

It was James's first familial loss and it shocked and saddened him deeply. Yet it also, as he writes of it in his notebook, moved him to a kind of joy. He had always known that he loved his mother, but not until he saw her in her shroud did he know how tender his love was. Mrs. James had been a quiet woman, with none of the spirited quality of her husband, the elder Henry James. But her son wrote of her, "She was our life, she was the house, she was the keystone of the arch. She held us all together, and without her we are scattered reeds. She was patience, she was wisdom, she was exquisite maternity." And as his impassioned memorial of her draws to its close, he says, "It was the perfect mother's life—the life of a perfect wife. To bring her children into the world—to expend herself, for years, for their happiness and welfare—then, when they had reached a full maturity and were absorbed in the world and their own interests—to lay herself down in her ebbing strength and yield up her pure soul to the celestial power that had given her this divine commission." Perhaps nothing that Henry James ever wrote approaches this passage in the explicit cognizance it takes of the biological nature of moral fact.

James stayed with his father and his sister Alice until May, when, at his father's insistence, he returned to England and his work. But in December came the news of his father's imminent death. The elder Henry James, it was said, had no wish to survive his wife; in his last illness he refused food and gently faded away. The younger Henry arrived too late to see his father for the last time, too late even for the funeral. William James's famous letter of farewell to their "sacred old Father" also arrived too late, but Henry took it to the Cambridge cemetery and read it aloud over the grave, sure, as he wrote to William, that "somewhere out of the depths of the still bright winter air" the father heard.

His mother was the strength that is not power as the world knows power, the strength of conservation, the unseen, unregarded, seemingly unexerted force that holds things to their center. She had lived the ancient elemental course of life, which is without theory or formulation, too certain of itself and too much at one with itself even to aspire. His father, according to his particular lights, had had the masculine power, "the ability to dare and endure, to know and yet not to fear reality." During his sad visit to his parental land in 1883, the last for twenty years, when the parental family had come to an end, Henry James wrote out the scenario of *The Bostonians,* which is a story of the parental house divided against itself, of the keystone falling from the arch, of the sacred mothers refusing their commission and the sacred fathers endangered.

Wordsworth and the Rabbis

OUR commemoration of the hundredth anniversary of Wordsworth's death must inevitably be charged with the consciousness that if Wordsworth were not kept in mind by the universities he would scarcely be remembered at all.[1] In our culture it is not the common habit to read the books of a century ago, and very likely all that we can mean when we say that a writer of the past is "alive" in people's minds is that, to those who once read him as a college assignment or who have formed an image of him from what they have heard about him, he exists as an attractive idea, as an intellectual possibility. And if we think of the three poets whom Matthew Arnold celebrated in his "Memorial Verses," we know that Byron is still attractive and possible, and so is Goethe. But Wordsworth is not attractive and not an intellectual possibility. He was once the great, the speaking poet for all who read English. He spoke both to the ordinary reader and to the literary man. But now the literary man outside the university will scarcely think of referring to Wordsworth as one of the important events of modern literature; and to the ordinary reader he is likely to exist as the very type of the poet whom life has passed by, presumably for the good reason that he passed life by.

If we ask why Wordsworth is no longer the loved poet he once was, why, indeed, he is often thought to be rather absurd and even

[1] The Centenary was celebrated in America at Cornell and Princeton Universities on April 21 and 22, 1950.

a little despicable, one answer that suggests itself is that for modern taste he is too Christian a poet. He is certainly not to be wholly characterized by the Christian element of his poetry. Nor can we say of him that he is a Christian poet in the same sense that Dante is, or Donne, or Hopkins. With them the specific Christian feeling and doctrine is of the essence of their matter and their conscious intention, as it is not with Wordsworth. Yet at the present time, the doctrinal tendency of the world at large being what it is, that which *is* Christian in Wordsworth may well seem to be more prominent than it ever was before, and more decisive. I have in mind his concern for the life of humbleness and quiet, his search for peace, his sense of the burdens of this life, those which are inherent in the flesh and spirit of man. Then there is his belief that the bonds of society ought to be inner and habitual, not merely external and formal, and that the strengthening of these bonds by the acts and attitudes of charity is a great and charming duty. Christian too seems his responsiveness to the idea that there is virtue in the discharge of duties which are of the great world and therefore dangerous to simple peace—his sense of affinity with Milton was as much with Milton's political as with his poetical career, and the Happy Warrior is the man who has, as it were, sacrificed the virtuous peace of the poet to the necessities of public life. There is his impulse to submit to the conditions of life under a guidance that is at once certain and mysterious; his sense of the possibility and actuality of enlightenment, it need scarcely be said, is one of the characteristic things about him. It was not he who said that the world was a vale of soul-making, but the poet who did make this striking paraphrase of the Christian sentiment could not have uttered it had not Wordsworth made it possible for him to do so.[2] And then, above all, there is his consciousness of the *neighbor,* his impulse to bring into the circle of significant life those of the neighbors who are simple and outside the circle of social pride, and also those who in the judgment of the world are

[2] It is of some relevance to our argument that when Keats wrote the famous phrase he believed that he was controverting, not affirming, a tendency of Christian thought.

queer and strange and useless: faith and hope were to him very great virtues, but he conceived that they rested upon the still greater virtue, charity.

Certainly what I have called Christian in Wordsworth scarcely approaches, let alone makes up, the sum of Christianity. But then no personal document or canon can do that, not even the work of a poet who is specifically Christian in the way of Dante, or of Donne, or of Hopkins. When we speak of a poet as being of a particular religion, we do not imply in him completeness or orthodoxy, or even explicitness of doctrine, but only that his secular utterance has the decisive mark of the religion upon it. And if a religion is manifold in its aspects and extensive in time, the marks that are to be found on the poets who are in a relation to it will be various in kind. It seems to me that the marks of Christianity on Wordsworth are clear and indelible. It is therefore worth trying the hypothesis that the world today does not like him because it does not like the Christian quality and virtues.

But the question at once arises whether this hypothesis is actually available to us. Professor Hoxie Neal Fairchild says that it is not. In the chapter on Wordsworth in the third volume of his *Religious Trends in English Poetry,* he tells us that Wordsworth was *not* a Christian poet and goes on to express his doubt that Wordsworth was ever properly to be called a Christian person even when he became a communicant of the Church and its defender. And Professor Fairchild goes so far as to tell us that as a poet Wordsworth is actually dangerous to the Christian faith. He is dangerous in the degree that he may be called religious at all, for his religion is said to be mere religiosity, the religion of nothing more than the religious emotion, beginning and ending in the mere sense of transcendence. Naked of dogma, bare of precise predication of God and the nature of man, this religiosity of Wordsworth's is to be understood as a pretentious and seductive rival of Christianity. It is the more dangerous because it gives license to man's pretensions—Professor Fairchild subscribes to the belief that romanticism must bear a large part of the responsibility for our present ills, especially for those which involve man's direct and conscious inhumanity to man.

We can surely admit the cogency of Professor Fairchild's argument within the terms of its intention. The nineteenth century was in many respects a very Christian century, but in the aspect of it which bulks largest in our minds it developed chiefly the ethical and social aspects of Christian belief, no doubt at the cost of the dogmatic aspect, which had already been weakened by the latitudinarian tendency of the eighteenth century. And it is probably true that when the dogmatic principle in religion is slighted, religion goes along for a while on generalized emotion and ethical intention— "morality touched by emotion"—and then loses the force of its impulse, even the essence of its being. In this sort of attenuation of religion, romanticism in general, and Wordsworth in particular, did indeed play a part by making the sense of transcendence and immanence so real and so attractive. During the most interesting and important period of his career, Wordsworth seems to have been scarcely aware of the doctrines of the Church in which he had been reared. He spoke of faith, hope, and charity without reference to the specifically Christian source and end of these virtues. His sense of the need for salvation did not take the least account of the Christian means of salvation. Of evil in the Christian sense of the word, of sins as an element of the nature of man, he also took no account.

And yet, all this being true, as we look at Wordsworth in the context of his own time and in the context of our time, what may properly be called the Christian element of his poetry can be made to speak to us, as it spoke to so many Christians in the nineteenth century, as it spoke to so many who were not Christians and made them in one degree or another accessible to Christianity.

"Any religious movement," says Christopher Dawson, an orthodox Christian scholar, "which adopts a purely critical and negative attitude to culture is . . . a force of destruction and disintegration which mobilizes against it the healthiest and most constructive elements in society—elements which can by no means be dismissed as worthless from the religious point of view." Romanticism in general was far from worthless to Christianity, far from worthless to that very Anglo-Catholicism which inclines to be so strict with it. And this is true of Wordsworth in particular. He certainly did not in his great period accept as adequate what the Church taught about the nature of man. But he was one of the few poets who really discovered something about the nature of man. What he discovered can perhaps be shown, if the argument be conducted by a comparison of formulas and doctrine, to be at variance with the teachings of Christianity. Yet I think it can also be shown that Wordsworth discovered much that a strong Christianity must take account of, and be easy with, and make use of. It can be shown too, I believe, that the Church has found advantage in what Wordsworth has told us of the nature of man.

Professor Fairchild, I need scarcely say, understands Christianity far better than I do, through his having studied it ever so much more than I have; and of course he understands it far better than I might ever hope to, because he has experienced it as a communicant. He has also, I am sure, tested his conclusions by the whole tendency of the Church to which he gives so strong and thoughtful an allegiance. My own reading of this tendency, at least as it appears in literature and in literary criticism, where it has been so influential, is that it is not inclined to accept Wordsworth as a Christian poet. And still, even against the force of Professor Fairchild's judgment, I cannot help feeling that there is an important element of Christianity with which Wordsworth has a significant affinity, even though this element is not at the present time of chief importance to Christian intellectuals.

But this is not an occasion for anything like contentiousness, and I ought not to seem to be forcing even a great poet into a faith whose members do not want him there. I am not, in any case, so much concerned to prove that Wordsworth is a Christian poet as to account for a certain quality in him which makes him unacceptable to the modern world. And so, without repudiating my first hypothesis, I shall abandon it for this fresh one: that the quality in Wordsworth that now makes him unacceptable is a Judaic quality.

My knowledge of the Jewish tradition is, I fear, all too slight to permit me to hope that I can develop this new hypothesis in any very enlightening way. Yet there is one Jewish work of traditional importance which I happen to know with some intimacy, and it lends a certain color of accuracy to my notion. This is the work called *Pirke Aboth,* that is, the sayings, the *sententiae,* of the Fathers. It was edited in the second century of the present era by the scholar and teacher who bore the magnificent name of Rabbi Jehudah the Prince, and who is traditionally referred to by the even more magnificent name of *Rabbi*—that is to say, *the* rabbi, the master teacher, the greatest of all. In its first intention *Pirke Aboth,* under the name *Aboth,* "Fathers," was one of the tractates of the Mishnah, which is the traditional Jewish doctrine represented chiefly by rabbinical decisions. But *Aboth* itself, the last of the tractates, does not deal with decisions; nor is it what a common English rendering of the longer title, "Ethics of the Fathers," would seem to imply, for it is not a system of ethics at all but simply a collection of maxims and *pensées,* some of them very fine and some of them very dull, which praise the life of study and give advice on how to live it.

In speaking of Wordsworth a recollection of boyhood cannot be amiss—my intimacy with *Pirke Aboth* comes from my having read it many times in boyhood. It certainly is not the kind of book a boy is easily drawn to read, and certainly I did not read it out of piety. On the contrary, indeed: for when I was supposed to be reading my prayers—very long, and in the Hebrew language, which I never mastered— I spent the required time and made it seem that I was doing my duty by reading the English translation of the *Pirke Aboth,* which, although it is not a devotional work, had long ago been thought of as an aid to devotion and included in the prayer book. It was more attractive to me than psalms, meditations, and supplications; it seemed more humane, and the Fathers had a curious substantiality. Just where they lived I did not know, nor just when, and certainly the rule of life they recommended had a very quaint difference from the life I knew, or, indeed, from any life that I wanted to know. Yet they were real, their way of life had the charm of coherence. And when I went back to them, using R. Travers Herford's scholarly edition and translation of their sayings,[3] I could entertain the notion that my early illicit intimacy with them had had its part in preparing the way for my responsiveness to Wordsworth, that between the Rabbis and Wordsworth an affinity existed.

But I must at once admit that a large difficulty stands in the way of the affinity I suggest. The *Aboth* is a collection of the sayings of masters of the written word. The ethical life it recommends has study as both its means and its end, the study of Torah, of the Law, which alone can give blessedness. So that from the start I am at the disadvantage of trying to make a conjunction between scholars living for the perpetual interpretation of a text and a poet for whom the natural world was at the heart of his doctrine and for whom books were barren leaves. The Rabbis expressed a suspiciousness of the natural world which was as extreme as Wordsworth's suspiciousness of study. That the warning was given at all seems to hint that it was possible for the Rabbis to experience the natural world as a charm and a temptation: still, the *Aboth* does warn us that whoever interrupts his study to observe the beauty of a fine tree or a fine meadow is guilty of sin. And yet I think it can be said without more extravagance than marks my whole comparison that it is precisely here, where they seem most to differ, that the Rabbis and Wordsworth are most at one. For between the Law as the Rabbis understood it and Nature as Wordsworth understood that, there is a pregnant similarity.

The Rabbis of the *Aboth* were Pharisees. I shall assume that the long scholarly efforts of Mr. Herford, as well as those of George Foot

---

[3] *Pirke Aboth,* edited with introduction, translation and commentary, third edition (New York: 1945). I have also consulted the edition and translation of the Very Rev. Dr. Joseph H. Hertz, Chief Rabbi of the British Empire, and in my quotations I have drawn upon both versions, and sometimes, when it suited my point, I have combined two versions in a single quotation.

Moore, have by now made it generally known that the Pharisees were not in actual fact what tradition represents them to have been. They were anything but mere formalists, and of course they were not the hypocrites of popular conception. Here is Mr. Herford's statement of the defining principle of Pharisaism: "The central conception of Pharisaism is Torah, the divine Teaching, the full and inexhaustible revelation which God had made. The knowledge of what was revealed was to be sought, and would be found, in the first instance in the written text of the Pentateuch; but the revelation, the real Torah, was the meaning of what was there written, the meaning as interpreted by all the recognized and accepted methods of the schools, and unfolded in ever greater fullness of detail by successive generations of devoted teachers. The written text of the Pentateuch might be compared to the mouth of a well; the Torah was the water which was drawn from it. He who wished to draw the water must needs go to the well, but there was no limit to the water which was there for him to draw. . . . The study of Torah . . . means therefore much more than the study of the Pentateuch, or even of the whole Scripture, regarded as mere literature, written documents. It means the study of the revelation made through those documents, the divine teaching therein imparted, the divine thought therein disclosed. Apart from the direct intercourse of prayer, the study of Torah was the way of closest approach to God; it might be called the Pharisaic form of the Beatific Vision. To study Torah was, to the devout Pharisee, to 'think God's thoughts after him,' as Kepler said." The Rabbis, that is, found sermons in texts, tongues in the running commentary.

And Mr. Herford goes on to say that it might be observed of the *Aboth* that it makes very few direct references to God. "This is true," he says, "but it is beside the mark. Wherever Torah is mentioned, there God is implied. He is behind the Torah, the Revealer of what is Revealed."

What I am trying to suggest is that, different as the immediately present objects were in each case, Torah for the Rabbis, Nature for

Wordsworth, there existed for the Rabbis and for Wordsworth a great object, which is from God and might be said to represent Him as a sort of surrogate, a divine object to which one can be in an intimate passionate relationship, an active relationship—for Wordsworth's "wise passiveness" is of course an activity—which one can, as it were, handle, and in a sense create, drawing from it inexhaustible meaning by desire, intuition, and attention.

And when we turn to the particulars of the *Aboth* we see that the affinity continues. In Jewish tradition the great Hillel has a peculiarly Wordsworthian personality, being the type of gentleness and peace, and having about him a kind of *joy* which has always been found wonderfully attractive; and Hillel said—was, indeed, in the habit of saying: he "used to say"—"If I am not for myself, who, then, is for me? And if I am for myself, what then am I?" Mr. Herford implies that this is a difficult utterance. But it is not difficult for the reader of Wordsworth, who finds the Wordsworthian moral essence here, the interplay between individualism and the sense of community, between an awareness of the self that must be saved and developed, and an awareness that the self is yet fulfilled only in community.

Then there is this saying of Akiba's: "All is foreseen, and yet free will is given; and the world is judged by grace, and yet all is according to the work." With how handsome a boldness it handles the problem of fate and free will, or "grace" and "works," handles the problem by stating it as an antinomy, escaping the woeful claustral preoccupation with the alternatives, but not their grandeur. This refusal to be fixed either in fate or in free will, either in grace or in works, and the recognition of both, are characteristic of Wordsworth.

There are other parallels to be drawn. For example, one finds in the *Aboth* certain remarks which have a notable wit and daring because they go against the whole tendency of the work in telling us that the multiplication of words is an occasion for sin, and the chief thing is not study but action. One finds the injunction to the scholar to divide his time between study and a trade, presumably in the interest of humility. And the scholar is warned that the world must not be too much with him, that, getting and spending, he lays waste his powers. There is the concern, so typical of Wordsworth, with the "ages of man," with the right time in the individual's development for each of life's activities. But it is needless to multiply the details of the affinity, which in any case must not be insisted on too far. All that I want to suggest is the community of ideal and sensibility between the *Aboth* and the canon of Wordsworth's work—the passionate contemplation and experience of the great object which is proximate to Deity; then the plain living that goes with the high thinking, the desire for the humble life and the discharge of duty; and last, but not least important, a certain insouciant acquiescence in the anomalies of the moral order of the universe, a respectful indifference to, or graceful surrender before, the mysteries of the moral relation of God to man.

This last element, as it is expressed in the *pensée* of Akiba which I have quoted, has its connection with something in the *Aboth* which for me is definitive of its quality. Actually it is something not in the *Aboth* but left out—we find in the tractate no implication of moral struggle. We find the energy of assiduity but not the energy of resistance. We hear about sin, but we do not hear of the sinful nature of man. Man in the *Aboth* guards against sin but he does not struggle against it, and of evil we hear nothing at all.

When we have observed this, it is natural to observe next that there is no mention in the *Aboth* of courage or heroism. In our culture we connect the notion of courage or heroism with the religious life. We conceive of the perpetual enemy within and the perpetual enemy without, which must be "withstood," "overcome," "conquered"—the language of religion and the language of fighting are in our culture assimilated to each other. Not so in the *Aboth*. The enemy within seems not to be conceived of at all. The enemy without is never mentioned, although the *Aboth* was compiled after the Dispersion, after the Temple and the nation had been destroyed—

with what heroism in the face of suffering we know from Josephus. Of the men whose words are cited in the *Aboth,* many met martyrdom for their religion, and the martyrology records their calm and fortitude in torture and death; of Akiba it records his heroic joy. And yet in their maxims they never speak of courage. There is not a word to suggest that the life of virtue and religious devotion requires the heroic quality.

As much as anything else in my boyhood experience of the *Aboth* it was this that fascinated me. It also repelled me. It had this double effect because it went so clearly against the militancy of spirit which in our culture is normally assumed. And even now, as I consider this indifference to heroism of the *Aboth,* I have the old ambiguous response to it, so that I think I can understand the feelings that readers have when they encounter something similar in Wordsworth. It is what Matthew Arnold noted when in the "Memorial Verses" he compared Wordsworth with Byron, who was for Arnold the embodiment of militancy of spirit. Arnold said of Wordsworth that part of his peculiar value to us arose from his indifference to "man's fiery might," to the Byronic courage in fronting human destiny.

> The cloud of mortal destiny,
> Others will front it fearlessly—
> But who, like him, will put it by?

Arnold certainly did not mean that Wordsworth lacked courage or took no account of it. Wordsworth liked nothing better, indeed, than to recite examples of courage, but the Wordsworthian courage is different in kind from the Byronic. For one thing, it is never aware of itself, it is scarcely personal. It is the courage of mute, insensate things, and it is often associated with such things, "with rocks, and stones, and trees," or with stars. Michael on his hilltop, whose character is defined by the light of his cottage, which was called "The Evening Star," and by the stones of his sheepfold; or the Leech Gatherer, who is like some old, great rock; or Margaret, who, like a tree, endured as long as she might after she was blasted—of the Lesser Celandine it is said that its fortitude in meeting the rage of the storm is neither its courage nor its choice but "its necessity in being old," and the same thing is to be said of all Wordsworth's exemplars of courage: they endure because they are what they are, and we might almost say that they survive out of a kind of biological faith, which is not the less human because it is nearly an animal or vegetable faith; and, indeed, as I have suggested, it is sometimes nearly mineral. Even the Happy Warrior, the man in arms, derives his courage not from his militancy of spirit but from his calm submission to the law of things.

In Wordsworth's vision of life, then, the element of quietude approaches passivity, even insentience, and the dizzy raptures of youth have their issue in the elemental existence of which I have spoken. The scholars of the *Aboth* certainly had no such notion; they lived for intellectual sentience. But where the scholars and Wordsworth are at one is in the quietism, which is not in the least a negation of life, but, on the contrary, an affirmation of life so complete that it needed no saying. To the Rabbis, as I read them, there life was, unquestionable because committed to a divine object. There life was —in our view rather stuffy and airless, or circumscribed and thin, but very intense and absolutely and utterly real, not needing to be affirmed by force or assertion, real because the object of its regard was unquestioned, and because the object was unquestionably more important than the individual person who regarded it and lived by it. To Wordsworth, as I read him, a similar thing was true in its own way. Much as he loved to affirm the dizzy raptures of sentience, of the ear and the eye and the mind, he also loved to move down the scale of being, to say that when the sentient spirit was sealed by slumber, when it was without motion and force, when it was like a rock or a stone or a tree, not hearing or seeing, and passive in the cosmic motion—that even then, perhaps especially then, existence was blessed.

Nothing could be further from the tendency of our Western culture, which is committed to an idea of consciousness and activity, of motion and force. With us the basis of spiritual prestige is some form of aggressive action directed outward upon the world, or inward upon ourselves. During the last century and a half this ideal has been especially strong in literature. If the religious personality of preceding times took to itself certain of the marks of military prestige, the literary personality now takes to itself certain of the marks of religious prestige, in particular the capacity for militant suffering.

A peculiarly relevant example of this lies to hand in T. S. Eliot's explanation of the decline of Wordsworth's genius from its greatness to what Mr. Eliot calls the "still sad music of infirmity." The small joke, so little characteristic of Mr. Eliot's humor, suggests something of the hostile uneasiness that Wordsworth can arouse in us. And Mr. Eliot's theory of the decline suggests the depth of our belief in the value of militancy, of militant suffering, for Mr. Eliot tells us that the trouble with Wordsworth was that he didn't have an eagle: it is that eagle which André Gide's Prometheus said was necessary for success in the spiritual or poetic life—*"Il faut avoir un aigle."* As an explanation of Wordsworth's poetic career this is, we perceive, merely a change rung on the weary idea that Wordsworth destroyed his poetic genius by reversing his position on the French Revolution or by terminating his connection with Annette Vallon. Wordsworth had no need of an eagle for his greatness, and its presence or absence had nothing to do with the decline of his genius. His pain, when he suffered, was not of the kind that eagles inflict, and his power did not have its source in his pain. But we are disturbed by the absence of the validating, the poetically respectable bird, that *aigle obligatoire.* We like the fiercer animals. Nothing is better established in our literary life than the knowledge that the tigers of wrath are to be preferred to the horses of instruction, a striking remark which is indeed sometimes very true, although not always. We know that we ought to prefer the bulls in the ring to the horses, and when we choose between the two kinds of horses of Plato's chariot we all know that Plato was wrong, that it is the blacks, not the whites, which are to be preferred. We do not, to be sure, live in the fashion of the beasts we admire in our literary lives, but we cherish them as representing something that we all seek. They are the emblems of the *charisma*—to borrow from the sociologists a word they have borrowed from the theologians—which is the hot, direct relationship with Godhead, or with the sources of life, upon which depend our notions of what I have called spiritual prestige.

The predilection for the powerful, the fierce, the assertive, the personally militant, is very strong in our culture. We find it in the liberal-bourgeois admiration of the novels of Thomas Wolfe and Theodore Dreiser. On a lower intellectual level we find it in the long popularity of that curious underground work *The Fountainhead*. On a higher intellectual level we find it in certain aspects of the work of Yeats and Lawrence. We find it too, if not in our religion itself, then at least in one of our dominant conceptions of religion—to many intellectuals the violence of Dostoevski represents the natural form of the religious life, to many gentle spirits the ferocity of Léon Bloy seems quite appropriate to the way of faith; and although some years ago Mr. Eliot reprobated D. H. Lawrence, in the name of religion, for his addiction to this characteristic violence, yet for Mr. Eliot the equally violent Baudelaire is pre-eminently a Christian poet.[4]

I cannot give a better description of the quality of our literature with which I am concerned than by quoting the characterization of it which Richard Chase found occasion to make in the course of a review of a work on the nineteenth century by a notable English scholar, Professor Basil Willey. It is relevant to remark that Professor Willey deals with the nineteenth century from the point of view of the Anglican form of Christianity, and Mr. Chase is commenting on Professor Willey's hostility to a certain Victorian figure who, in any discussion of Wordsworth, must inevitably be in our minds—

---

[4] In his brief introduction to Father Tiverton's *D. H. Lawrence and Human Existence,* Mr. Eliot has indicated that he has changed his mind about Lawrence's relation to the religious life. I think he was right to do so. The revision of his opinion confirms, if anything, what I say of the place of violence in our conception of the religious life.

John Stuart Mill. His name seems very queer and shocking when it is spoken together with the names of the great figures of modern literature. Yet Mr. Chase is right when he says that "among the Victorians, it is Mill who tests the modern mind," and goes on to say that "in relation to him at least two of its weaknesses come quickly to light. The first is its morose desire for dogmatic certainty. The second is its hyperaesthesia: its feeling that no thought is permissible except an extreme thought: that every idea must be directly emblematic of concentration camps, alienation, madness, hell, history, and God; that every word must bristle and explode with the magic potency of our plight."

I must be careful not to seem to speak, as certainly Mr. Chase is not speaking, against the sense of urgency or immediacy, or against power or passion. Nor would I be taken to mean that the Wordsworthian quietism I have described is the whole desideratum of the emotional life. It obviously wasn't that for Wordsworth himself— he may be said to be the first poet who praised movement and speed for their own sakes, and dizziness and danger; he is the poet of rapture. No one can read Book Five of *The Prelude* and remain unaware of Wordsworth's conception of literature as urgency and immediacy, as power and passion. Book Five, which is about literature and the place of reading in our spiritual development, opens with an impressive eschatological vision, a vision of final events— Wordsworth shared in his own way our present sense of the possible end of man and of all the works of man's spirit, and it is important to observe that in the great dream of the Arab who hastens before the advancing flood to rescue Science and Poetry, represented by the Stone and the Shell he carries, the prophecy of the world destroyed is made to seem the expression of the very essence of literature. It is in this book that Wordsworth defends the violence and fearfulness of literature from the "progressive" ideas of his day; it is here that he speaks of the poet as "crazed/By love and feeling, and internal thought/Protracted among endless solitude," and of the "reason" that lies couched "in the blind and awful lair" of the poet's madness; and it is here that he defends the "maniac's" dedication at the cost of the domestic affections:

> Enow there are on earth to take in charge
> Their wives, their chidren, and their virgin loves,
> Or whatsoever else the heart holds dear;
> Enow to stir for these. . . .

As we speak of Wordsworth's quietism this opposite element of his poetry must be borne in mind. Then too, if we speak in anything like praise of his quietism, we must be conscious of the connection of his quietism with an aspect of his poetry that we rightly dread. When, in *The Excursion,* the Wanderer and the Poet and the Pastor sit upon the gravestones and tell sad stories of the deaths of other mild old men, for the benefit of the Solitary, who has had his fling at life and is understandably a little bitter, we know that something wrong is being done to us; we long for the winding of a horn or the drawing of a sword; we want someone to dash in on a horse —I think we want exactly a stallion, St. Mawr or another; for there can be no doubt about it, Wordsworth, at the extreme or perversion of himself, carries the element of quietude to the point of the denial of sexuality. And this is what makes the *Aboth* eventually seem to us quaint and oppressive, what, I suppose, makes a modern reader uneasy under any of the philosophies which urge us to the contemplative accord with a unitary reality and warn us that the accord will infallibly be disturbed and destroyed by the desires. Whether it be the Torah of the Rabbis, or the Cosmos of Marcus Aurelius, or the Nature of Spinoza or of Wordsworth, the accord with the unitary reality seems to depend upon the suppression not only of the sexual emotions but also of the qualities that are associated with sexuality: high-heartedness, wit, creative innovation, will.

But now, when we have touched upon the Wordsworthian quality that is very close to the Stoic *apatheia,* to not-feeling, let us remember what great particular thing Wordsworth is said to have accomplished. Matthew Arnold said that in a wintry clime, in an iron time, Wordsworth taught us to *feel*. This statement, extreme as it is, will be seen to be not inaccurate if we bring to mind the many instances of spiritual and psychological crisis in the nineteenth century in which affectlessness, the loss of the power to feel, played an important part. *Ennui, noia*—how often we meet with them in nineteenth-century biography; and the *acedia* which was once a disorder of the specifically religious life becomes now a commonplace of secular spirituality. Arnold, when he wrote the "Memorial Verses," could not, of course, have read Mill's autobiography, which so specifically and eloquently confirms Arnold's attribution to Wordsworth of a "healing power" through an ability to make us feel. And yet, although Arnold's statement is accurate so far as it goes, and is supported by Wordsworth's own sense of the overarching intention of his poetic enterprise, it does not go far enough. Wordsworth did, or tried to do, more than make us feel: he undertook to teach us how to *be*.

In *The Prelude,* in Book Two, Wordsworth speaks of a particular emotion which he calls "the sentiment of Being." The "sentiment" has been described in this way: "There is, in sanest hours, a consciousness, a thought that arises, independent, lifted out from all else, calm, like the stars, shining eternal. This is the thought of identity—yours for you, whoever you are, as mine for me. Miracle of miracles, beyond statement, most spiritual and vaguest of earth's dreams, yet hardest basic fact, and only entrance to all facts." This, of course, is not Wordsworth, it is Walt Whitman, but I quote Whitman's statement in exposition of Wordsworth's "sentiment of Being" because it is in some respects rather more boldly explicit, although not necessarily better, than anything that Wordsworth himself wrote about the sentiment, and because Whitman goes on to speak of his "hardest basic fact" as a political fact, as the basis, and the criterion, of democracy.

Through all his poetic life Wordsworth was preoccupied by the idea, by the sentiment, by the problem, of being. All experience, all emotions lead to it. He was haunted by the mysterious fact that he existed. He could discover in himself different intensities and qualities of being—"Tintern Abbey" is the attempt to distinguish these intensities and qualities. Being is sometimes animal; sometimes it is an "appetite and a passion"; sometimes it is almost a suspension of the movement of the breath and blood. The *Lyrical Ballads* have many intentions, but one of the chief of them is the investigation of the problems of being. "We are Seven," which is always under the imputation of bathos, is established in its true nature when we read it as an ontological poem; its subject is the question, What does it mean when we say a person *is*? "The Idiot Boy," which I believe to be a great and not a foolish poem, is a kind of comic assertion of the actuality—and, indeed, the peculiar intensity—of being in a person who is outside the range of anything but our merely mechanical understanding. Johnny on the little horse, flourishing his branch of holly under the moon, is a creature of rapture, who, if he is not quite "human," is certainly elemental, magical, perhaps a little divine—"It was Johnny, Johnny everywhere." As much as anyone, and more than many—more than most —he *is,* and feels that he is.

From even the little I have said, it will be seen that as soon as the "sentiment of Being" is named, or represented, there arises a question of its degree of actuality or of its survival. "The glad animal movements" of the boy, the "appetite" and the "passion" of the young man's response to Nature easily confirm the sense of being. So do those experiences which are represented as a "sleep" or "slumber," when the bodily senses are in abeyance. But as the man grows older the stimuli to the experience of the sentiment of being grow fewer or grow less intense—it is this fact rather than any question of poetic creation (such as troubled Coleridge) that makes the matter of the Immortality Ode. Wordsworth, as it were, puts the awareness of being to the test in situations where its presence may perhaps most easily be questioned—in very old people. Other kinds of people also serve for the test, such as idiots, the insane, children, the dead, but I emphasize the very old because Wordsworth gave particular attention to them, and because we can all be aware from our own experience what a strain very old people put upon our powers of attributing to them personal being, "identity." Wordsworth's usual way is to represent the old man as being below the human condition, apparently scarcely able to communicate, and then suddenly, startlingly, in what we have learned to call an "epiphany," to show forth the intensity of his human existence. The old man in "Animal Tranquillity and Decay" is described as being so old and so nearly inanimate that the birds regard him as little as if he were a stone or a tree; for this, indeed, he is admired, and the poem says that his unfelt peace is so perfect that it is envied by the very young. He is questioned about his destination on the road—

> I asked him whither he was bound, and what
> The object of his journey; he replied,
> "Sir! I am going many miles to take
> A last leave of my son, a mariner,
> Who from a sea-fight has been brought to Falmouth,
> And there is dying in an hospital."

The revelation of the actuality of his being, of his humanness, quite dazzles us.[5]

The social and political implication of Wordsworth's preoccupation with ontology is obvious enough. It is not, however, quite what Wordsworth sometimes says it is. The direct political lesson that the poet draws from the Old Cumberland Beggar is interesting, but it is beside his real, his essential, point. "Deem not this man useless," he says in his apostrophe to the political theorists who have it in mind to put the Beggar into a workhouse, and he represents the usefulness of the Beggar as consisting in his serving as the object of a habitual charity and thus as a kind of communal institution, a communal bond. But this demonstrated utility of the Beggar is really secondary to the fact that he *is*—he is a person, he takes a pleasure, even though a minimal one, in his being, and therefore he may not in conscience be dealt with as a mere social unit. So with all the

---

[5] The concluding lines of the poem as originally printed in *Lyrical Ballads,* where the poem bears the title "Old Man Travelling," were deleted by Wordsworth in subsequent editions, which is a misfortune.

dramatis personae of the *Lyrical Ballads*—the intention of the poet is to require us to acknowledge their being and thus to bring them within the range of conscience, and of something more immediate than conscience, natural sympathy. It is an attractive thing about Wordsworth, and it should be a reassuring thing, that his acute sense of the being of others derives from, and serves to affirm and heighten, his acute sense of his own being.

I have spoken of Wordsworth's preoccupation with being as if it were unique, and as if it accounted for, or led to what accounts for, the contemporary alienation from his work and his personality. In some ways his preoccupation *is* unique, and certain aspects of it do lead to the present alienation from him. Yet from what I have said about him, it must be clear that between Wordsworth and the great figures of our literature there is a very close affinity indeed, if only in the one regard of the preoccupation with being. There is scarcely a great writer of our own day who has not addressed himself to the ontological crisis, who has not conceived of life as a struggle to be— not to live, but to be. They do so, to be sure, under a necessity rather different from Wordsworth's, and this necessity makes it seem appropriate that, with Byron, they assert "man's fiery might." (Blake suggests more aptly than Byron the quality of the militancy of most modern writers, but I stay with the terms of the opposition as Arnold gives them to us.) They feel the necessity to affirm the personal qualities that are associated with a former time, presumably a freer and more personally privileged time—they wish, as a character in one of Yeats's plays says, "to bring back the old disturbed exalted life, the old splendor." Their image of freedom and personal privilege is often associated with violence, sometimes of a kind that does not always command the ready assent we are habituated to give to violence when it appears in moral or spiritual contexts. A tenant's sliced-off ear, which is an object of at least momentary pleasure to Yeats, a kick given by an employer to his employee, which wins the approval of Lawrence—these are all too accurately representative of the nature of the political fantasies that Yeats and Lawrence built upon the perception of the loss of freedom and privilege, the loss of the sense of being. Yet we know that this violence stands against an extreme fate of which we are all conscious. We really know in our time what the death of the word can be—for that knowledge we have only to read an account of contemporary Russian literature. We really know what the death of the spirit means—we have seen it overtake whole peoples. Nor do we need to go beyond our own daily lives to become aware, if we dare to, of how we have conspired, in our very virtues, to bring about the devaluation of whatever is bold and assertive and free, replacing it by the bland, the covert, the manipulative. If we wish to understand the violence, the impulse toward charismatic power, of so much of our literature, we have but to consider that we must endure not only the threat to being which comes from without but also the seduction to non-being which establishes itself within. We need, in Coleridge's words, something to "startle this dull pain, and make it move and live." Violence is a means of self-definition; the bad conscience, Nietzsche says, assures us of our existence.

Wordsworth, then, is not separated from us by his preoccupation with being, for it is our preoccupation. Yet he is separated from us. His conception of being seems different from ours.

In Book Five of *The Prelude* Wordsworth gives us a satiric picture of the boy educated according to the "progressive" ideas of his day, and on the whole we follow him readily enough in the objections he makes to these ideas—this can be said even though it often happens that readers, misled by their preconceptions of Wordsworth, take his sarcasm seriously and suppose that he is actually praising "this model of a child." And we follow him when he speaks of the presumptuousness of pedagogical theorists. denouncing them as, in effect, engineers of the spirit: he flatters at least one element of our ambivalence toward the psychological expert. We are responsive to his notion of what a boy should be: "not . . . too good," "not unresentful where self-justified." Possibly we are not in perfect agreement with him on all points—perhaps we will feel that he has dealt rather too harshly with the alert political and social consciousness of the progressive child, or that he goes too far in thinking that a child's imagination should be fed on fanciful books; perhaps, too, the equalities of the boys he really admires would not be precisely the qualities we would specify—"Fierce, moody, patient, venturous, modest, shy." But on the whole his discussion of pedagogics appeals to the enlightened muddled concern with "adjustment" and "aggression" which occupies the P.T.A. segment of our minds, and if we have our reservation about details we can at least, as I say, follow Wordsworth through most of his argument. But I think we cease to follow him when, in the course of the argument, he rises to one of his great poetical moments. This is the passage "There was a Boy. . . ." It was perhaps rather finer when it stood alone as a poem in itself in *Lyrical Ballads,* but it is still very fine in its place in *The Prelude,* where it follows the description of the model child. The Boy is described as having had a trick of imitating the hooting of owls, and at night he would call across Windermere, trying to get the owls to answer; and often they did answer, but sometimes they did not, and then the silence would be strange and significant.

> . . . In that silence, while he hung
> Listening, a gentle shock of mild surprise
> Has carried far into his heart the voice
> Of mountain torrents; or the visible scene
> Would enter unawares into his mind,
> With all its solemn imagery, its rocks,
> Its woods, and that uncertain heaven, received
> Into the bosom of the steady lake.

We may be ready enough to acknowledge the "beauty" of the poem, but the chances are that we will be rather baffled by its intention. We perceive that the Boy is obviously intended to represent something very good and right, meant to be an example of very full being. But what baffles us, what makes us wonder what the poem has to do with education and the development of personality, is that the Boy exercises no will, or at least, when his playful will is frustrated, is at once content with the pleasures that follow upon the suspended will. And as likely as not we will be impelled to refer the poem to that "mysticism" which is supposed to be an element of Wordsworth's mind. Now Wordsworth's mind does have an element of mysticism—it is that "normal mysticism" which, according to a recent writer on the Rabbis, marked the Rabbinical mind.[6] Wordsworth's mysticism, if we wish to call it that, consists of two elements, his conception of the world as being semantic, and his capacity for intense pleasure. When we speak of him as a mystic in any other sense, we are pretty sure to be expressing our incomprehension of the intensity with which he experienced his own being, and our incomprehension of the relation which his sentiment of being bore to his will. Thus, we have no trouble understanding him when, in Book Six of *The Prelude,* in the remarkable episode of the crossing of the Alps, he speaks of the glory of the will.

> . . . Whither we be young or old,
> Our destiny, our being's heart and home,
> Is with infinitude, and only there;
> With hope it is, hope that can never die,
> Effort, and expectation, and desire,
> And something evermore about to be.

The note on which the will is affirmed is high, Miltonic—it echoes the accents of Satan's speech in the Council of Hell; and the passage resumes its movement with a line the martial tenor of which we happily respond to: "Under such banners militant, the soul . . . ." But we are checked by what ensues:

[6] Max Kadushin, *The Rabbinical Mind* (New York: 1951). This impressive work of scholarship has received far less general notice than it deserves. I read it after I had written this essay—read it not only with admiration for its intellectual achievement but also with a peculiar personal pleasure, because its author, in his seminary days, had been one of the long-suffering men who tried to teach me Hebrew, with what success I have indicated; yet he did teach me—it was no small thing for a boy of twelve to be in relation with a serious scholar. Dr. Kadushin has been kind enough to tell me that what I have said about the Rabbis is not wrong. In revising my essay I have not tried to amend my primitive account by what is to be learned from Dr. Kadushin's presentation of the Rabbis in all their great complexity of thought. But the phrase, "normal mysticism," seemed too apt not to quote.

Under such banners militant, the soul
Seeks for no trophies, struggles for no spoils
That may attest her prowess, blest in thoughts
That are their own perfection and reward,
Strong in herself and in beatitude. . . .

The soul's energy is directed to the delight of the soul in itself.

Wordsworth is describing the action of what, at a later time, a man of very different mind, Hegel, was to call a new human faculty, the faculty of *Gemüt*. The word, I gather, is not entirely susceptible of translation—"heart," with the implication of responsiveness, and of high-heartedness and large-heartedness, is an approximation. Hegel defines his faculty of *Gemüt* as expressing itself as a desire, a will, which has "no particular aims, such as riches, honors, and the like; in fact, it does not concern itself with any worldly condition of wealth, prestige, etc., but with the entire condition of the soul—a general sense of enjoyment."

Much that I have said about the tendency of our culture would seem to deny the truth of Hegel's statement that *Gemüt* is one of the characteristics of our time, and much more evidence might be adduced to confirm the impression that nothing could be less characteristic of our time than the faculty of *Gemüt*, that we scarcely conceive of it, let alone exercise it. Yet at the same time I think it is true to say that it plays in our culture a covert but very important part.

Of our negative response to *Gemüt,* to the "sentiment of Being," Mr. Eliot provides an instance—again, for it is Mr. Eliot's high gift to be as pertinent when we think him wrong as when we think him right. In *The Cocktail Party* there is a description of the two virtuous ways of life, that of "the common routine" and that of the spiritual heroism of the saint and martyr. The two ways, Mr. Eliot tells us, are of equal value; the way of the saint is not better than that of the householder. Yet when it comes to describing the life of the common routine, Mr. Eliot says of those who elect it that they

> Learn to avoid excessive expectation,
> Become tolerant of themselves and others,
> Giving and taking in the usual actions
> What there is to give and take. They do not repine;
> And are contented with the morning that separates
> And with the evening that brings together
> For casual talk before the fire
> Two people who know that they do not understand each other,
> Breeding children whom they do not understand
> And who will never understand them.

Well, few of us will want to say much for the life of the common routine, and no doubt, under the aspect of modern life with its terrible fatigues, and in the consciousness of its gross threats, the sort of thing that Mr. Eliot says here will be pretty nearly all that any of us will want to say. Yet if we think of the description of the common routine as being not merely the expression of one possible mood among many—and it is not merely that: it is what it says it is, the description of a "way"—we must find it very strange. There is in it no reference to the pain which is an essential and not an accidental part of the life of the common routine. There is no reference to the principles, the ethical discipline, by which the ordinary life is governed—all is habit. There is no reference to the possibility of either joy or glory—I use the Wordsworthian words by intention. The possibility of *Gemüt* does not appear. Mr. Eliot does not say that his couples are in Limbo, that they are in a condition of not-being, which would of course be a true thing to say of many householding couples: he is describing the virtuous way of life that is alternative to the way of the saint. This failure to conceive the actuality of the life of common routine is typical of modern literature since, say, Tolstoi. I do not say this in order to suggest that domestic life, the common routine, in itself makes an especially appropriate subject for literature—I don't think it does—but in order to suggest a limitation of our conception of the spiritual life. Mr. Eliot's representation of the two "ways" exemplifies how we are drawn to the violence of extremity. We imagine, with nothing in between, the dull not-being of life, the intense not-being of death; but we do not imagine being—we do not imagine that it can be a joy. We are in love, at least in our literature, with the fantasy of death. Death and suffering, when we read, are our only means of conceiving the actuality of life.

Perhaps this is not new and we but intensify what is indigenous in our culture. Perhaps this is in the nature of life as Western culture has long been fated to see it. Perhaps it is inescapable for us that the word "tragic" should be used as an ultimate recommendation of a sense of life. Yet we, when we use the word, do not really mean it in its old, complex, mysterious sense—we mean something like "violent" or "conclusive": we mean death. And just here lies a paradox and our point. For it is precisely what Wordsworth implies by his passionate insistence on being, even at a very low level of consciousness, pride, and assertiveness, as well as at the highest level of quasi-mystic intensity, that validates a conception of tragedy, and a conception of heroism. The saintly martyrdom which Mr. Eliot represents in his play is of course not intended to be taken as tragic: the idea of martyrdom precludes the idea of tragedy. But if we ask why the martyrdom seems as factitious as it does, must we not answer that this is because it is presented in a system of feeling which sets very little store by— which, indeed, denies the possibility of—the "beatitude" which Wordsworth thought was the birthright of every human soul? And this seems to be borne out by the emphasis which Mr. Eliot puts on the peculiar horror of the mode of the martyr's death, as if only by an extremity of pain could we be made to realize that a *being* was actually involved, that a life has been sacrificed—or, indeed, has been lived.

Wordsworth's incapacity for tragedy has often been remarked on, and accurately enough. Yet we cannot conclude that Wordsworth's relation to tragedy is wholly negative. The possibility of tragic art depends primarily upon the worth we ascribe not to dying but to living, and to living in "the common routine." The power of the Homeric tragedy, for example, derives from the pathos, which the poet is at pains to bring before us repeatedly, of young men dying, of not seeing ever again the trees of their native farmsteads, of their parents never again admiring and indulging them, of the cessation of their being in the common routine. The tragic hero, Achilles, becomes a tragic hero exactly because he has made choice to give up the life of the common routine, which all his comrades desire, in favor of a briefer but more intense quality of being of transcendent glory. The pathos of his particular situation becomes the great thing it is because of the respondent pathos of Hector and Priam, which is the pathos of the family and the common routine, which we understand less and less and find ourselves more and more uncomfortable with. And I think it can be shown that every tragic literature owes its power to the high esteem in which it holds the common routine, and the sentiment of being which arises from it, the elemental *given* of biology. And that is what Wordsworth had in mind when, in the "Preface" of 1800, defending the idea that poetry should give "immediate pleasure," he said that this idea was "a homage paid to the native and naked dignity of man, to the grand elementary principle of pleasure, by which he knows, and feels, and lives, and moves."

Yet if we are aware of the tendency of our literature I have exemplified by the passage from Mr. Eliot's play, we must at the same time be aware of the equally strong counter-tendency. In speaking of our alienation from Wordsworth, it has not been my intention to make a separation between Wordsworth and the litera-ture of our time. The separation cannot be made. Wordsworth and the great writers of our time stand, as I have said, on the common ground of the concern with being and its problems—Wordsworth, indeed, may be said to have discovered and first explored the ground upon which our literature has established itself. Our hyper-aesthesia, our preference for the apocalyptic subject and the charis-matic style, do indeed constitute a taste which alienates many readers from Wordsworth, and no doubt the more if we believe, as some do, that it is a taste wholly appropriate to the actualities of our historical situation. Yet we can without too much difficulty become aware of how much of the Wordsworthian "mildness," which so readily irritates us, and how much of the Wordsworthian quietism (as I have called it), which dismays us, are in the grain of our literature, expressed through the very intensities which seem to deny them. Thus, to bring Wordsworth and James Joyce into conjunction might at first seem a joke or a paradox, or an excess of historicism, at best a mere device of criticism. We will at once be conscious of the calculated hauteur of Joyce's implied personality, the elaborations of his irony, the uncompromising challenge of his style and his manner, and by the association of contrast we will remember that horrendous moment in *The Prelude* when Wordsworth says, "My drift I fear/Is scarcely obvious." How can we fail to think only of the abysses of personality, theory, and culture that separate the two men? And yet when we have become acclimated to Joyce, when the charismatic legend becomes with familiarity not so fierce and the vatic paraphernalia of the style and method less intimidating, do we not find that we are involved in a conception of life that reiterates, in however different a tonality, the Wordsworthian vision? One of the striking things about *Ulysses* (to speak only of that work) is that the idea of evil plays so small a part in it. One hears a good deal about the essential Christian orthodoxy of Joyce, and perhaps this is an accurate opinion, but his orthodoxy, if he has it, takes no account of the evil which is so commonly affirmed by the literary expressions of orthodoxy; the conception of sin has but a tangential relevance to the book. The element of sexuality which plays so large a part in the story does not raise considerations of sin and evil; it is dealt with in the way of poetic naturalism. The character of Leopold Bloom, who figures in the life of Joyce's Poet much as the old men in Wordsworth figure in his life—met by chance and giving help of some transcendent yet essentially human kind—is conceived in Wordsworthian terms: in terms, that is, of his humbleness of spirit. If we speak of Wordsworth in reference to the Rabbis and their non-militancy, their indifference to the idea of evil, their acceptance of cosmic contradiction, are we not to say that Bloom is a Rabbinical character? It is exactly his non-militancy that makes him the object of general contempt and, on one occasion, of rage. It is just this that has captivated his author, as the contrast with the armed pride, the jealousy and desire for prestige, the bitter militancy of Stephen Dedalus. Leopold Bloom is deprived of every shred of dignity except the dignity of that innocence which for Joyce, as for Wordsworth, goes with the "sentiment of Being."

Again and again in our literature, at its most apocalyptic and intense, we find the impulse to create figures who are intended to suggest that life is justified in its elemental biological simplicity, and, in the manner of Wordsworth, these figures are conceived of as being of humble status and humble heart: Lawrence's simpler people or primitive people whose pride is only that of plants or animals; Dreiser's Jennie Gerhardt and Mrs. Griffiths, who stand as oases in the wide waste of their creator's dull representation of energy; Hemingway's waiters with their curious silent dignity; Faulkner's Negroes, of whom it is said, as so often it is said in effect of Wordsworth's people, *they endured;* and Faulkner's idiot boys, of whom it is to be said, *they are*—the list could be extended to suggest how great is the affinity of our literature with Wordsworth. And these figures express an intention which is to be discerned through all our literature—the intention to imagine, and to reach, a condition of the soul in which the will is freed from "particular aims," in which it is "strong in itself and in beatitude." At least as early as Balzac our literature has shown the will seeking its own negation—or, rather, seeking its own affirmation by its rejection of the aims which the world sets before it and by turning its energies upon itself in self-realization. Of this particular affirmation of the will Wordsworth is the proponent and the poet.

George Orwell
and the Politics of Truth

GEORGE ORWELL'S *Homage to Catalonia* is one of the important documents of our time. It is a very modest book —it seems to say the least that can be said on a subject of great magnitude. But in saying the least it says the most. Its manifest subject is a period of the Spanish Civil War, in which, for some months, until he was almost mortally wounded, its author fought as a soldier in the trenches. Everyone knows that the Spanish war was a decisive event of our epoch, everyone said so when it was being fought, and everyone was right. But the Spanish war lies a decade and a half behind us, and nowadays our sense of history is being destroyed by the nature of our history—our memory is short and it grows shorter under the rapidity of the assault of events. What once occupied all our minds and filled the musty meeting halls with the awareness of heroism and destiny has now become chiefly a matter for the historical scholar. George Orwell's book would make only a limited claim upon our attention if it were nothing more than a record of personal experiences in the Spanish war. But it is much more than this. It is a testimony to the nature of modern political life. It is also a demonstration on the part of its author of one of the right ways of confronting that life. Its importance is therefore of the present moment and for years to come.

A politics which is presumed to be available to everyone is a relatively new thing in the world. We do not yet know very much about it. Nor have most of us been especially eager to learn. In a politics presumed to be available to everyone, ideas and ideals play a great part. And those of us who set store by ideas and ideals have never been quite able to learn that, just because they do have power nowadays, there is a direct connection between their power and another kind of power, the old, unabashed, cynical power of force. We are always being surprised by this. The extent to which Communism made use of unregenerate force was perfectly clear years ago, but many of us found it impossible to acknowledge this fact because Communism spoke boldly to our love of ideas and ideals. We tried as hard as we could to believe that politics might be an idyl, only to discover that what we took to be a political pastoral was really a grim military campaign or a murderous betrayal of political allies, or that what we insisted on calling agrarianism was in actuality a new imperialism. And in the personal life what was undertaken by many good people as a moral commitment of the most disinterested kind turned out to be an engagement to an ultimate immorality. The evidence of this is to be found in a whole literary genre with which we have become familiar in the last decade, the personal confession of involvement and then of disillusionment with Communism.

Orwell's book, in one of its most significant aspects, is about disillusionment with Communism, but it is not a confession. I say this because it is one of the important positive things to say about *Homage to Catalonia,* but my saying it does not imply that I share the *a priori* antagonistic feelings of many people toward those books which, on the basis of experience, expose and denounce the Communist party. About such books people of liberal inclination often make uneasy and rather vindictive jokes. The jokes seem to me unfair and in bad taste. There is nothing shameful in the nature of these books. There is a good chance that the commitment to Communism was made in the first place for generous reasons, and it is certain that the revulsion was brought about by more than sufficient causes. And clearly there is nothing wrong in wishing to record the painful experience and to draw conclusions from it. Nevertheless, human nature being what it is—and in the uneasy readers of such books as well as in the unhappy writers of them—it is a fact that public confession does often appear in an unfortunate light, that its moral tone is less simple and true than we might wish it to be. But the moral tone of Orwell's book is uniquely simple and true. Orwell's ascertaining of certain political facts was not the occasion for a change of heart, or for a crisis of the soul. What he learned from his experiences in Spain of course pained him very much, and it led him to change his course of conduct. But it did not destroy him; it did not, as people say, cut the ground from under him. It did not shatter his faith in what he had previously believed, nor weaken his political impulse, nor even change its direction. It produced not a moment of guilt or self-recrimination.

Perhaps this should not seem so very remarkable. Yet who can doubt that it constitutes in our time a genuine moral triumph? It suggests that Orwell was an unusual kind of man, that he had a temper of mind and heart which is now rare, although we still respond to it when we see it.

It happened by a curious chance that on the day I agreed to write this essay as the introduction to the new edition of *Homage to Catalonia,* and indeed at the very moment that I was reaching for the telephone to tell the publisher that I would write it, a young man, a graduate student of mine, came in to see me, the purpose of his visit being to ask what I thought about his doing on essay on George Orwell. My answer, naturally, was ready, and when I had given it and we had been amused and pleased by the coincidence, he settled down for a chat about our common subject. But I asked him not to talk about Orwell. I didn't want to dissipate in talk what ideas I had, and also I didn't want my ideas crossed with his, which were sure to be very good. So for a while we merely exchanged bibliographical information, asking each other which of

Orwell's books we had read and which we owned. But then, as if he could not resist making at least one remark about Orwell himself, he said suddenly in a very simple and matter-of-fact way, "He was a virtuous man." And we sat there, agreeing at length about this statement, finding pleasure in talking about it.

It was an odd statement for a young man to make nowadays, and I suppose that what we found so interesting about it was just this oddity—its point was in its being an old-fashioned thing to say. It was archaic in its bold commitment of sentiment, and it used an archaic word with an archaic simplicity. Our pleasure was not merely literary, not just a response to the remark's being so appropriate to Orwell, in whom there was indeed a quality of an earlier and simpler day. We were glad to be able to say it about anybody. One doesn't have the opportunity very often. Not that there are not many men who are good, but there are few men who, in addition to being good, have the simplicity and sturdiness and activity which allow us to say of them that they are virtuous men, for somehow to say that a man "is good," or even to speak of a man who "is virtuous," is not the same thing as saying, "He is a virtuous man." By some quirk of the spirit of the language, the form of that sentence brings out the primitive meaning of the word virtuous, which is not merely moral goodness, but also fortitude and strength in goodness.

Orwell, by reason of the quality that permits us to say of him that he was a virtuous man, is a figure in our lives. He was not a genius, and this is one of the remarkable things about him. His not being a genius is an element of the quality that makes him what I am calling a figure.

It has been some time since we in America have had literary figures—that is, men who live their visions as well as write them, who *are* what they write, whom we think of as standing for something as men because of what they have written in their books. They preside, as it were, over certain ideas and attitudes. Mark Twain was in this sense a figure for us, and so was William James.

So too were Thoreau, and Whitman, and Henry Adams, and Henry James, although posthumously and rather uncertainly. But when in our more recent literature the writer is anything but anonymous, he is likely to be ambiguous and unsatisfactory as a figure, like Sherwood Anderson, or Mencken, or Wolfe, or Dreiser. There is something about the American character that does not take to the idea of the figure as the English character does. In this regard, the English are closer to the French than to us. Whatever the legend to the contrary, the English character is more strongly marked than ours, less reserved, less ironic, more open in its expression of willfulness and eccentricity and cantankerousness. Its manners are cruder and bolder. It is a demonstrative character—it shows itself, even shows off. Santayana, when he visited England, quite gave up the common notion that Dickens' characters are caricatures. One can still meet an English snob so thunderingly shameless in his worship of the aristocracy, so explicit and demonstrative in his adoration, that a careful, modest, ironic American snob would be quite bewildered by him. And in modern English literature there have been many writers whose lives were demonstrations of the principles which shaped their writing. They lead us to be aware of the moral personalities that stand behind the work. The two Lawrences, different as they were, were alike in this: that they assumed the roles of their belief and acted them out on the stage of the world. In different ways this was true of Yeats, and of Shaw, and even of Wells. It is true of T. S. Eliot, for all that he has spoken against the claims of personality in literature. Even E. M. Forster, who makes so much of privacy, acts out in public the role of the private man, becoming for us the very spirit of the private life. He is not merely a writer, he is a figure.

Orwell takes his place with these men as a figure. In one degree or another they are geniuses, and he is not; if we ask what it is he stands for, what he is the figure of, the answer is: the virtue of not being a genius, of fronting the world with nothing more than one's simple, direct, undeceived intelligence, and a respect for the powers one does have, and the work one undertakes to do. We admire geniuses, we love them, but they discourage us. They are great concentrations of intellect and emotion, we feel that they have soaked up all the available power, monopolizing it and leaving none for us. We feel that if we cannot be as they, we can be nothing. Beside them we are so plain, so hopelessly threadbare. How they glitter, and with what an imperious way they seem to deal with circumstances, even when they are wrong! Lacking their patents of nobility, we might as well quit. This is what democracy has done to us, alas—told us that genius is available to anyone, that the grace of ultimate prestige may be had by anyone, that we may all be princes and potentates, or saints and visionaries and holy martyrs, of the heart and mind. And then when it turns out that we are no such thing, it permits us to think that we aren't much of anything at all. In contrast with this cozening trick of democracy, how pleasant seems the old, reactionary Anglican phrase that used to drive people of democratic leanings quite wild with rage—"my station and its duties."

Orwell would very likely have loathed that phrase, but in a way he exemplifies its meaning. And it is a great relief, a fine sight, to see him doing this. His novels are good, quite good, some better than others, some of them surprising us by being so very much better than their modesty leads us to suppose they can be, all of them worth reading; but they are clearly not the work of a great or even of a "born" novelist. In my opinion, his satire on Stalinism, *Animal Farm,* was overrated—I think people were carried away by someone's reviving systematic satire for serious political purposes. His critical essays are almost always very fine, but sometimes they do not fully meet the demands of their subject—as, for example, the essay on Dickens. And even when they are at their best, they seem to have become what they are chiefly by reason of the very plainness of Orwell's mind, his simple ability to look at things in a downright, undeceived way. He seems to be serving not some dashing daimon but the plain, solid Gods of the Copybook Maxims. He is not a genius—what a relief! What an encouragement. For he communicates to us the sense that what he has done any one of us could do.

Or could do if we but made up our mind to do it, if we but surrendered a little of the cant that comforts us, if for a few weeks we paid no attention to the little group with which we habitually exchange opinions, if we took our chance of being wrong or inadequate, if we looked at things simply and directly, having in mind only our intention of finding out what they really are, not the prestige of our great intellectual act of looking at them. He liberates us. He tells us that we can understand our political and social life merely by looking around us; he frees us from the need for the inside dope. He implies that our job is not to be intellectual, certainly not to be intellectual in this fashion or that, but merely to be intelligent according to our lights—he restores the old sense of the democracy of the mind, releasing us from the belief that the mind can work only in a technical, professional way and that it must work competitively. He has the effect of making us believe that we may become full members of the society of thinking men. That is why he is a figure for us.

In speaking thus of Orwell, I do not mean to imply that his birth was presided over only by the Gods of the Copybook Maxims and not at all by the good fairies, or that he had no daimon. The good fairies gave him very fine free gifts indeed. And he had a strong daimon, but it was of an old-fashioned kind and it constrained him to the paradox—for such it is in our time—of taking seriously the Gods of the Copybook Maxims and putting his gifts at their service. Orwell responded to truths of more than one kind, to the bitter, erudite truths of the modern time as well as to the older and simpler truths. He would have quite understood what Karl Jaspers means when he recommends the "decision to renounce the absolute claims of the European humanistic spirit, to think of it as a stage of development rather than the living content of faith." But he was not interested in this development. What concerned him was survival, which he connected with the old simple ideas that are often not ideas at all but beliefs, preferences, and prejudices. In the modern world these had for him the charm and audacity of newly discovered truths. Involved as so many of us are, at least in our literary lives, in a bitter metaphysics of human nature, it shocks and dismays us when Orwell speaks in praise of such things as responsibility, and orderliness in the personal life, and fair play, and physical courage—even of snobbery and hypocrisy because they sometimes help to shore up the crumbling ramparts of the moral life.

It is hard to find personalities in the contemporary world who are analogous to Orwell. We have to look for men who have considerable intellectual power but who are not happy in the institutionalized life of intellectuality; who have a feeling for an older and simpler time, and a guiding awareness of the ordinary life of the people, yet without any touch of the sentimental malice of populism; and a strong feeling for the commonplace; and a direct, unabashed sense of the nation, even a conscious love of it. This brings Péguy to mind, and also Chesterton, and I think that Orwell does have an affinity with these men—he was probably unaware of it—which tells us something about him. But Péguy has been dead for quite forty years, and Chesterton (it is a pity) is at the moment rather dim for us, even for those of us who are Catholics. And of course Orwell's affinity with these men is limited by their Catholicism, for although Orwell admired some of the effects and attitudes of religion, he seems to have had no religious tendency in his nature, or none that went beyond what used to be called natural piety.

In some ways he seems more the contemporary of William Cobbett and William Hazlitt than of any man of our own century. Orwell's radicalism, like Cobbett's, refers to the past and to the soil. This is not uncommon nowadays in the social theory of literary men, but in Orwell's attitude there is none of the implied aspiration to aristocracy which so often marks literary agrarian ideas; his feeling for the land and the past simply served to give his radicalism a conservative—a conserving—cast, which is in itself attractive, and to protect his politics from the ravages of ideology. Like Cobbett, he does not dream of a new kind of man, he is content with the old kind, and what moves him is the desire that this old kind of man should have freedom, bacon, and proper work. He had the passion for the literal actuality of life as it is really lived which makes Cobbett's *Rural Rides* a classic, although a forgotten one; his own *The Road to Wigan Pier* and *Down and Out in Paris and London* are in its direct line. And it is not the least interesting detail in the similarity of the two men that both had a love affair with the English language. Cobbett, the self-educated agricultural laborer and sergeant major, was said by one of his enemies to handle the language better than anyone of his time, and he wrote a first-rate handbook of grammar and rhetoric; Orwell was obsessed by the deterioration of the English language in the hands of the journalists and pundits, and nothing in *Nineteen Eighty-Four* is more memorable than his creation of Newspeak.

Orwell's affinity with Hazlitt is, I suspect, of a more intimate temperamental kind, although I cannot go beyond the suspicion, for I know much less about Orwell as a person than about Hazlitt. But there is an unquestionable similarity in their intellectual temper which leads them to handle their political and literary opinions in much the same way. Hazlitt remained a Jacobin all his life, but his unshakable opinions never kept him from giving credit when it was deserved by a writer of the opposite persuasion, not merely out of chivalrous generosity but out of respect for the truth. He was the kind of passionate democrat who could question whether democracy could possibly produce great poetry, and his essays in praise of Scott and Coleridge, with whom he was in intense political disagreement, prepare us for Orwell on Yeats and Kipling.

The old-fashionedness of Orwell's temperament can be partly explained by the nature of his relation to his class. This was by no means simple. He came from that part of the middle class whose sense of its status is disproportionate to its income, his father having been a subordinate officer in the Civil Service of India, where Orwell was born. (The family name was Blair, and Orwell was christened Eric Hugh; he changed his name, for rather complicated reasons, when he began to write.) As a scholarship boy he attended the expensive preparatory school of which Cyril Connolly has given an account in *Enemies of Promise*. Orwell appears there as a school "rebel" and "intellectual." He was later to write of the absolute misery of the poor boy at a snobbish school. He went to Eton on a scholarship, and from Eton to Burma, where he served in the police. He has spoken with singular honesty of the ambiguousness of his attitude in the imperialist situation. He disliked authority and the manner of its use, and he sympathized with the Burmese; yet at the same time he saw the need for authority and he used it, and he was often exasperated by the natives. When he returned to England on leave after five years of service, he could not bring himself to go back to Burma. It was at this time that, half voluntarily, he sank to the lower depths of poverty. This adventure in extreme privation was partly forced upon him, but partly it was undertaken to expiate the social guilt which he felt he had incurred in Burma. The experience seems to have done what was required of it. A year as a casual worker and vagrant had the effect of discharging Orwell's guilt, leaving him with an attitude toward the working class that was entirely affectionate and perfectly without sentimentality.

His experience of being declassed, and the effect which it had upon him, go far toward defining the intellectual quality of Orwell and the particular work he was to do. In the thirties the middle-class intellectuals made it a moral fashion to avow their guilt toward the lower classes and to repudiate their own class tradition. So far as this was nothing more than a moral fashion, it was a moral anomaly. And although no one can read history without being made aware of what were the grounds of this attitude, yet the personal claim to a historical guilt yields but an ambiguous principle of personal behavior, a still more ambiguous basis of thought. Orwell broke with much of what the English upper middle class was and admired. But his clear, uncanting mind saw that, although the morality of history might come to harsh conclusions about the middle class and although the practicality of history might say that its day was over, there yet remained the considerable residue of its genuine virtues. The love of personal privacy, of order, of manners, the ideal of fairness and responsibility—these are very simple virtues indeed and they scarcely constitute perfection of either the personal or the social life. Yet they still might serve to judge the present and to control the future.

Orwell could even admire the virtues of the lower middle class, which an intelligentsia always finds it easiest to despise. His remarkable novel, *Keep the Aspidistra Flying,* is a *summa* of all the criticisms of a commercial civilization that have ever been made, and it is a detailed demonstration of the bitter and virtually hopeless plight of the lower-middle-class man. Yet it insists that to live even in this plight is not without its stubborn joy. Péguy spoke of "fathers of families, those heroes of modern life"—Orwell's novel celebrates this biological-social heroism by leading its mediocre, middle-aging poet from the depths of splenetic negation to the acknowledgment of the happiness of fatherhood, thence to an awareness of the pleasures of marriage, and of an existence which, while it does not gratify his ideal conception of himself, is nevertheless his own. There is a dim, elegiac echo of Defoe and of the early days of the middle-class ascendancy as Orwell's sad young man learns to cherish the small personal gear of life, his own bed and chairs and saucepans— his own aspidistra, the ugly, stubborn, organic emblem of survival.

We may say that it was on his affirmation of the middle-class virtues that Orwell based his criticism of the liberal intelligentsia. The characteristic error of the middle-class intellectual of modern times is his tendency to abstractness and absoluteness, his reluctance to connect idea with fact, especially with personal fact. I cannot recall that Orwell ever related his criticism of the intelligentsia to the implications of *Keep the Aspidistra Flying,* but he might have done so, for the prototypical act of the modern intellectual is his abstracting himself from the life of the family. It is an act that has something about it of ritual thaumaturgy—at the beginning of our intellectual careers we are like nothing so much as those young members of Indian tribes who have had a vision or a dream which gives them power on condition that they withdraw from the ordinary life of the tribe. By intellectuality we are freed from the thralldom to the familial commonplace, from the materiality and concreteness by which it exists, the hardness of the cash and the hardness of getting it, the inelegance and intractability of family things. It gives us power over intangibles and imponderables, such as Beauty and Justice, and it permits us to escape the cosmic ridicule which in our youth we suppose is inevitably directed at those who take seriously the small concerns of the material quotidian world, which we know to be inadequate and doomed by the very fact that it is so absurdly *conditioned*—by things, habits, local and temporary customs, and the foolish errors and solemn absurdities of the men of the past.

The gist of Orwell's criticism of the liberal intelligentsia was that they refused to understand the conditioned nature of life. He never quite puts it in this way but this is what he means. He himself knew what war and revolution were really like, what government and administration were really like. From first-hand experience he knew what communism was. He could truly imagine what nazism was. At a time when most intellectuals still thought of politics as a nightmare abstraction, pointing to the fearfulness of the nightmare as evidence of their sense of reality, Orwell was using the imagination of a man whose hands and eyes and whole body were part of his thinking apparatus. Shaw had insisted upon remaining sublimely unaware of the Russian actuality; Wells had pooh-poohed the threat of Hitler and had written off as anachronisms the very forces that were at the moment shaping the world—racial pride, leader-worship, religious belief, patriotism, love of war. These men had trained the political intelligence of the intelligentsia, who now, in their love of abstractions, in their wish to repudiate the anachronisms of their own emotions, could not conceive of directing upon Russia anything like the same stringency of criticism they used upon their own nation. Orwell observed of them that their zeal for internationalism had led them to constitute Russia their new fatherland. And he had the simple courage to point out that the pacifists preached their doctrine under condition of the protection of the British navy, and that, against Germany and Russia, Gandhi's passive resistance would have been of no avail.

He never abated his anger against the established order. But a paradox of history had made the old British order one of the still beneficent things in the world, and it licensed the possibility of a social hope that was being frustrated and betrayed almost everywhere else. And so Orwell clung with a kind of wry, grim pride to the old ways of the last class that had ruled the old order. He must sometimes have wondered how it came about that he should be praising sportsmanship and gentlemanliness and dutifulness and physical courage. He seems to have thought, and very likely he was right, that they might come in handy as revolutionary virtues—he remarks of Rubashov, the central character of Arthur Koestler's novel *Darkness at Noon,* that he was firmer in loyalty to the revolution than certain of his comrades because he had, and they had not, a bourgeois past. Certainly the virtues he praised were those of survival, and they had fallen into disrepute in a disordered world.

Sometimes in his quarrel with the intelligentsia Orwell seems to sound like a leader-writer for the *Times* in a routine wartime attack on the highbrows.

. . . The general weakening of imperialism, and to some extent of the whole British morale, that took place during the nineteen thirties, was partly the work of the left-wing intelligentsia, itself a kind of growth that sprouted from the stagnation of the Empire.

The mentality of the English left-wing intelligentsia can be studied in half a dozen weekly and monthly papers. The immediately striking thing about all these papers is their generally negative querulous attitude, their complete lack at all times of any constructive suggestion.

There is little in them except the irresponsible carping of people who have never been and never expect to be in a position of power.

During the past twenty years the negative faineant outlook which has been fashionable among the English left-wingers, the sniggering of the intellectuals at patriotism and physical courage, the persistent effort to chip away at English morale and spread a hedonistic, what-do-I-get-out-of-it attitude to life, has done nothing but harm.

But he was not a leader-writer for the *Times*. He had fought in Spain and nearly died there, and on Spanish affairs his position had been the truly revolutionary one. The passages I have quoted are from his pamphlet, *The Lion and the Unicorn*, a persuasive statement of the case for socialism in Britain.

Toward the end of his life Orwell discovered another reason for his admiration of the old middle-class virtues and his criticism of the intelligentsia. Walter Bagehot used to speak of the political advantages of *stupidity,* meaning by the word a concern for one's own private material interests as a political motive which was preferable to an intellectual, theoretical interest. Orwell, it may be said, came to respect the old bourgeois virtues because they were stupid—that is, because they resisted the power of abstract ideas. And he came to love things, material possessions, for the same reason. He did not in the least become what is called "anti-intellectual"—this was simply not within the range of possibility for him—but he began to fear that the commitment to abstract ideas could be far more maleficent than the commitment to the gross materiality of property had ever been. The very stupidity of things has something human about it, something meliorative, something even liberating. Together with the stupidity of the old unthinking virtues it stands against the ultimate and absolute power which the unconditioned idea can develop. The essential point of *Nineteen Eighty-Four* is just this, the danger of the ultimate and absolute power which mind can develop when it frees itself from conditions, from the bondage of things and history.

But this, as I say, is a late aspect of Orwell's criticism of intellectuality. Through the greater part of his literary career his criticism was simpler and less extreme. It was as simple as this: that the contemporary intellectual class did not think and did not really love the truth.

In 1937 Orwell went to Spain to observe the civil war and to write about it. He stayed to take part in it, joining the militia as a private. At that time each of the parties still had its own militia units, although these were in process of being absorbed into the People's Army. Because his letters of introduction were from people of a certain political group in England, the ILP,[1] which had connections with the POUM,[2] Orwell joined a unit of that party in Barcelona. He was not at the time sympathetic to the views of his comrades and their leaders. During the days of interparty strife, the POUM was represented in Spain and abroad as being a Trotskyist party. In point of fact it was not, although it did join with the small Trotskyist party to oppose certain of the policies of the dominant Communist party. Orwell's own preference, at the time of his enlistment, was for the Communist party line, and because of this he looked forward to an eventual transfer to a Communist unit.

It was natural, I think, for Orwell to have been a partisan of the Communist program for the war. It recommended itself to most people on inspection by its apparent simple common sense. It proposed to fight the war without any reference to any particular political idea beyond a defense of democracy from a fascist enemy. When the war was won, the political and social problems would be solved, but until the war should be won, any debate over these problems was to be avoided as leading only to the weakening of the united front against Franco.

Eventually Orwell came to understand that this was not the practical policy he had at first thought it to be. His reasons need not be reiterated here—he gives them with characteristic cogency and modesty in the course of this book, and under the gloomy but probably

---

[1] Independent Labour Party.
[2] *Partido Obrero de Unificación Marxista*—Party of Marxist Unification.

correct awareness that, the economic and social condition of Spain being what it was, even the best policies must issue in some form of dictatorship. In sum, he believed that the war was revolutionary or nothing, and that the people of Spain would not fight and die for a democracy which was admittedly to be a bourgeois democracy.

But Orwell's disaffection from the Communist party was not the result of a difference of opinion over whether the revolution should be instituted during the war or after it. It was the result of his discovery that the Communist party's real intention was to prevent the revolution from ever being instituted at all—"The thing for which the Communists were working was not to postpone the Spanish revolution till a more suitable time, but to make sure it never happened." The movement of events, led by the Communists, who had the prestige and the supplies of Russia, was always to the right, and all protest was quieted by the threat that the war would be lost if the ranks were broken, which in effect meant that Russian supplies would be withheld if the Communist lead was not followed. Meanwhile the war was being lost because the government more and more distrusted the non-Communist militia units, particularly those of the Anarchists. "I have described," Orwell writes, "how we were armed, or not armed, on the Aragon front. There is very little doubt that arms were deliberately withheld lest too many of them should get into the hands of the Anarchists, who would afterwards use them for a revolutionary purpose; consequently, the big Aragon offensive which would have made Franco draw back from Bilbao and possibly from Madrid, never happened."

At the end of April, after three months on the Aragon front, Orwell was sent to Barcelona on furlough. He observed the change in morale that had taken place since the days of his enlistment—Barcelona was no longer the revolutionary city it had been. The heroic days were over. The militia, which had done such splendid service at the beginning of the war, was now being denigrated in favor of the People's Army, and its members were being snubbed as seeming rather queer in their revolutionary ardor, not to say dangerous. The tone of the black market and of privilege had replaced the old idealistic puritanism of even three months earlier. Orwell observed this but drew no conclusions from it. He wanted to go to the front at Madrid, and in order to do so he would have to be transferred to the International Column, which was under the control of the Communists. He had no objection to serving in a Communist command and, indeed, had resolved to make the transfer. But he was tired and in poor health and he waited to conclude the matter until another week of his leave should be up. While he delayed, the fighting broke out in Barcelona.

In New York and in London the intelligentsia had no slightest doubt of what had happened—could not, indeed, have conceived that anything might have happened other than what they had been led to believe had actually happened. The Anarchists, together with the "Trotskyist" POUM—so it was said—had been secreting great stores of arms with a view to an uprising that would force upon the government their premature desire for collectivization. And on the third of May their plans were realized when they came out into the streets and captured the Telephone Exchange, plus breaking the united front in an extreme manner and endangering the progress of the war. But Orwell in Barcelona saw nothing like this. He was under the orders of the POUM, but he was not committed to its lines, and certainly not to the Anarchist line, and he was sufficiently sympathetic to the Communists to wish to join one of their units. What he saw he saw as objectively as a man might ever see anything. And what he records is now, I believe, accepted as the essential truth by everyone whose judgment is worth regarding. There were no great stores of arms cached by the Anarchists and the POUM—there was an actual shortage of arms in their ranks. But the Communist-controlled government had been building up the strength of the Civil Guard, a gendarmerie which was called "nonpolitical" and from which workers were excluded. That there had indeed been mounting tension between the government and the dissident forces is beyond question, but the actual fighting was touched off by acts of provocation committed by the government itself—shows of military strength, the call to all private persons to give up arms, attacks on Anarchist centers, and, as a climax, the attempt to take over the Telephone Exchange, which since the beginning of the war had been run by the Anarchists.

It would have been very difficult to learn anything of this in New York or London. The periodicals that guided the thought of left-liberal intellectuals knew nothing of it, and had no wish to learn. As for the aftermath of the unhappy uprising, they appeared to have no knowledge of that at all. When Barcelona was again quiet—some six thousand Assault Guards were imported to quell the disturbance —Orwell returned to his old front. There he was severely wounded, shot through the neck; the bullet just missed the windpipe. After his grim hospitalization, of which he writes so lightly, he was invalided to Barcelona. He returned to find the city in process of being purged. The POUM and the Anarchists had been suppressed; the power of the workers had been broken and the police hunt was on. The jails were already full and daily becoming fuller—the most devoted fighters for Spanish freedom, men who had given up everything for the cause, were being imprisoned under the most dreadful conditions, often held incommunicado, often never to be heard of again. Orwell himself was suspect and in danger because he had belonged to a POUM regiment, and he stayed in hiding until, with the help of the British consul, he was able to escape to France. But if one searches the liberal periodicals, which have made the cause of civil liberties their own, one can find no mention of this terror. Those members of the intellectual class who prided themselves upon their political commitment were committed not to the fact but to the abstraction.[3]

[3] In looking through the files of *The Nation* and the *New Republic* for the period of the Barcelona fighting, I have come upon only one serious contradiction of the interpretation of events that constituted the editorial position of both periodicals. This was a long letter contributed by Bertram Wolfe to the correspondence columns of *The Nation*. When this essay first appeared, some of my friends took me to task for seeming to imply that there were no liberal or radical intellectuals who did not accept the interpretations of *The Nation* and the *New Republic*. There were indeed

And to the abstraction they remained committed for a long time to come. Many are still committed to it, or nostalgically wish they could be. If only life were not so tangible, so concrete, so made up of facts that are at variance with each other; if only the things that people say are good things were really good; if only the things that are pretty good were entirely good and we were not put to the everlasting necessity of qualifying and discriminating; if only politics were not a matter of power—*then* we should be happy to put our minds to politics, *then* we should consent to think!

But Orwell had never believed that the political life could be an intellectual idyl. He immediately put his mind to the politics he had experienced. He told the truth, and told it in an exemplary way, quietly, simply, with due warning to the reader that it was only one man's truth. He used no political jargon, and he made no recriminations. He made no effort to show that his heart was in the right place, or the left place. He was not interested in where his heart might be thought to be, since he knew where it was. He was interested only in telling the truth. Not very much attention was paid to his truth—*Homage to Catalonia* sold poorly in England, it had to be remaindered, it was not published in America, and the people to whom it should have said most responded to it not at all.

Its particular truth refers to events now far in the past, as in these days we reckon our past. It does not matter the less for that—this particular truth implies a general truth which, as now we cannot fail to understand, must matter for a long time to come. And what matters most of all is our sense of the man who tells the truth.

---

such liberal or radical intellectuals. But they were relatively few in number and they were treated with great suspiciousness and even hostility by the liberal and radical intellectuals as a class. It is as a class that Orwell speaks of the intellectuals of the left in the thirties, and I follow him in this.

Flaubert's Last Testament

FLAUBERT died suddenly in 1880, having brought close to its
end but leaving unfinished and unrevised the novel that had
occupied his thought for eight years. The entire dedication
of himself with which Flaubert responded to the claims of art is of
course the very essence of his legend, but to *Bouvard and Pécuchet*
he gave a special and savage devotion which went beyond the call
of literary duty as even he understood it. The book was to him more
than a work of art; it was a deed. At the moment of what he conceived to be the ultimate defeat of true culture, it was an act of
defiance and revenge. Flaubert was not unique in nineteenth-century
France for his belief that bourgeois democracy was bringing about
the death of mind, beauty, literature, and greatness; this opinion,
among the distinguished writers of the century, was virtually a
commonplace. But he was unique in the immediacy and simplicity
with which he experienced the debacle—"I can no longer talk with
anyone without growing angry; and whenever I read anything by
one of my contemporaries I rage."[1] He was unique too in the
necessity he felt to see the crisis in all its possible specificity of
detail. For him the modern barbarism was not merely a large
general tendency which could be comprehended by a large general

---

[1] The quotations from Flaubert's letters are from the admirable *Selected Letters of
Gustave Flaubert* edited and translated by Francis Steegmuller. The quotations from
Bouvard and Pécuchet are from the version of E. W. Stonier and T. W. Earp.

emotion; he was constrained to watch it with a compulsive and obsessive awareness of its painful particularities. He was made rabid, to use his own word, by *this* book, *this* phrase, *this* solecism, *this* grossness of shape or form, *this* debasement of manners, *this* hollow imitation of thought. He was beyond believing that he could do anything to stem or divert the flood of swinishness, as he called it, that was sweeping away every hope of the good life—*Bouvard and Pécuchet* is a triumph of the critical mind, but if we suppose criticism to be characterized by the intention to correct and reform, the book cannot be called a work of criticism. In its intention it is to be compared not with any other literary work but with the stand of Roland at Roncesvalles. No less beset than the hero, no less hopeless, no less grim, and no less grimly glad, Flaubert resolves that while the breath of life is in him he will give blow for blow and pile up the corpses of his enemies as a monument to the virtues they despise and he adores.

His long fierce passion for the book was not matched by the expectation of certain of his friends who were most competent to estimate the chances of its success. "I am preparing a book," he wrote to Turgenev in November of 1872, "in which I shall spit out my bile." But Turgenev grew troubled, and so did Taine and Zola, because Flaubert was precisely not spitting out his bile. The new novel, as Flaubert said of it, was to be "a kind of encyclopedia made into farce," and he devoured libraries, his notebooks grew ever more numerous, and his pride in them grew with their number; he was to brag that he had read fifteen hundred books in preparation for the novel. Anyone who loved Flaubert must have been dismayed as he gave year after year of his life to gathering the materials for a massive joke which was no doubt very funny but surely not so funny as to need this sacrificial attention from a man of genius. His love of research, his insatiable craving for particularity, was said to have spoiled *Salammbô* by overloading it with antiquarian lumber. Now it threatened to defeat the new work. Turgenev and Taine believed that an intellectual satire such as Flaubert planned must be short if it was to be read; Turgenev pointed to Swift and Voltaire in support of his opinion that *Bouvard and Pécuchet* must be treated *presto*. But Flaubert persisted in his extravagance. What he wanted to do, he said, was nothing less than to take account of the whole intellectual life of France. "If it were treated briefly, made concise and light, it would be a fantasy—more or less witty, but without weight or plausibility; whereas if I give it detail and development I will seem to be believing my own story, and it can be made into something serious and even frightening." And he believed that it was exactly by an excess of evidence that he would avoid pedantry.

The misgivings of his friends seemed in part justified by the public response to the book when it was published in the year after Flaubert's death. At first it was accepted merely as a "document," that is, its interest seemed to derive less from itself than from its connection with its author. But as the years passed, the first impression was corrected. With due allowance made for its unfinished, unrevised state, but quite in its own right, *Bouvard and Pécuchet* was given its place beside the great works of Flaubert's canon. Its pleasures are granted to be very different from those of *Madame Bovary* and *A Sentimental Education,* but French readers find in it a peculiar interest and charm consonant with its nature.

Its nature is singular. We cannot go so far as to say with Ezra Pound that the novel "can be regarded as the inauguration of a new form which has no precedents," and in any case, Mr. Pound, after having said that "neither *Gargantua,* nor *Don Quixote,* nor Sterne's *Tristram Shandy* had furnished the archetype," goes on to show its clear connection with at least the first-named book. And if it can be argued that *Bouvard and Pécuchet,* in its character of "a kind of encyclopedia made into farce," has no specific literary genre except perhaps that which is comprised by *Gargantua,* it is still true that there are a sufficient number of works sufficiently analogous with it in one respect or another to constitute, if not a genre, then at least a tradition in which it may be placed. Yet its singularity must not be slighted.

If we try to say what was the characteristic accomplishment of the

French novelists of the nineteenth century, we can scarcely help concluding that it was the full, explicit realization of the idea of society as a definitive external circumstance, the main *condition,* of the individual life. American literature of the great age was, as D. H. Lawrence was the first to see, more profound in this respect than the French, in that it went deeper into the unconscious life of society; and in England, Dickens in his way and the later Trollope in his were more truly perceptive of social motives and movements. But the French achievement was more explicit than either the American or the English; it made itself available to more people. Almost, we might be moved to say, it made itself too available: it is the rare person who can receive the full news of the inherent social immorality without injury to his own morality, without injury, indeed, to his own intellect—nothing can be so stultifying as the simple, unelaborated belief that society is a fraud. Yet with the explicit social intelligence of the great French novels we dare not quarrel—it is a *given* of our culture, it is one of the ineluctable elements of our modern fate, and on the whole one of the nobler elements. What *Bouvard and Pécuchet* adds to this general fund of social intelligence is the awareness of the part that is played in our modern life by ideas—not merely by assumptions, which of course have always played their part in every society, but by ideas as they are formulated and developed in books. The originality of Flaubert's perception lies in its intensity; other novelists before Flaubert had been aware of the importance of ideas in shaping the lives of their heroes, and Flaubert himself, in *A Sentimental Education,* had shown Frédéric Moreau living in a kind of ideological zoo—Sénécal, Regimbart, Deslauriers, Pellerin, all have learned from books the roar or squeal or grunt by which they identify themselves. But in *Bouvard and Pécuchet* the books themselves are virtually the *dramatis personae;* it is they, even more than the actual people of the Norman village, that constitute reality for the two comic heroes. Through this extravagance Flaubert signalizes the ideological nature of modern life.

No one has followed Flaubert in his enterprise. In the essay to which I have referred, Mr. Pound was bringing, in 1922, the first news of Joyce's *Ulysses* to the readers of the *Mercure de France,* and he spoke at some length of the connection that is to be found between *Ulysses* and *Bouvard and Pécuchet.* "Between 1880 and the year *Ulysses* was begun," he says, "no one had the courage to make a gigantic collection of absurdities, nor the patience to seek out the man-type, the most general generalization"—and he goes on to speak of Leopold Bloom as being, like Bouvard and Pécuchet, "the basis of democracy, the man who believes what he reads in the papers." The connection between the two novels is certainly worth remarking, but although *Ulysses* does indeed resemble *Bouvard and Pécuchet* in its encyclopedic effect, the use made of the absurdities they collect is very different in the one novel and in the other. The difference is defined by the dissimilar intellectual lives of Leopold Bloom and Bouvard and Pécuchet. To Bloom, ideas are the furniture or landscape of his mind, while to Bouvard and Pécuchet they exist, as I have suggested, as characters in the actual world. Bloom's ideas are notions; they are bits and pieces of fact and approximations and adumbrations of thought pieced together from newspapers and books carelessly read; Bloom means to look them up and get them straight but he never does. They are subordinate to his emotions, to which they lend substance and color. If a judgment is passed upon them by the author, it is of an oblique sort and has to do with their tone, with their degree of vulgarity, not with their inner consistency or cogency. But Bouvard and Pécuchet are committed to ideas and confront them fully. They amass books and study them. Ideas are life and death to them.

There is no necessity to choose between the two conceptions of what Mr. Pound called "the man-type, the most general generalization." Leopold Bloom represents much of the modern mind from the lowest to the highest. His representativeness probably needs less to be insisted on that that of Bouvard and Pécuchet, who stand for the condition of life of any reader of this book, of any person who must decide by means of some sort of intellectual process what is the correct *theory* of raising his children, or what is the right *principle* of education; or whom he shall be psychoanalyzed by—a Freudian, a Reichian, a Washingtonian; whether he "needs" religion, and if so, which confession is most appropriate to his temperament and cultural background; what kind of architecture he shall adopt for his house, and what the true theory of the modern is; what kind of heating is best suited to his life-style; how he shall feel about the State; about the Church; about Labor; about China; about Russia; about India. If we try to say how the world has changed from, say, two hundred years ago, we must see that it is in the respect that the conscious mind has been brought to bear upon almost every aspect of life; that ideas, good, bad, indifferent, are of the essence of our existence. That is why Flaubert was made "rabid" by his perception of stupidity. And if we look to see if anyone has matched Flaubert in the passion of his response to ideas, I think we find that Nietzsche alone saw the modern world as Flaubert did, and with Flaubert's intensity of passion.

But when we have become aware of the singularity of *Bouvard and Pécuchet,* we must be no less aware of the tradition in which its singularity exists. As for the novel's connection with Rabelais, this may be observed even in certain aspects of the prose, not necessarily as a result of influence, perhaps only because of the effect of an analogous subject matter. "He planted passion-flowers in the shade, pansies in the sun, covered hyacinths with manure, watered the lilies after they had flowered, destroyed the rhododendrons by cutting them back, stimulated the fuchsias with glue, and roasted the pomegranate tree by exposing it to the kitchen fire"—the errors of this catalogue are committed not by the infant Gargantua but by Pécuchet. Rabelais knew nothing of encyclopedias but he too wrote "a sort of encyclopedia made into farce." His intention was in part that of Flaubert—it was the intention of burlesque, the mockery of learning. But only in part: Rabelais had also the intention of which Flaubert's is the exact inversion. It is no doubt all too easy to reduce Rabelais to a classroom example of the high optimism of the early

Renaissance, and to make more naïve than it really is his humanistic delight in the arts, sciences, crafts, and exercises which are available to man. Yet the optimism and the humanistic delight are certainly of the essence of Rabelais and they are specifically controverted in *Bouvard and Pécuchet*. We have but to look at the respective treatments of gymnastics to see how Flaubert stands Rabelais on his head—Gargantua's friend Gymnast can make any demand upon his agility and strength, to Rabelais' great delight, but nothing is sadder than the middle-aged Bouvard and Pécuchet putting themselves to school to the regimen and apparatus of Amoros's manual of physical culture, which, absurd as it is, descends in a direct line from the Renaissance idea of the Whole Man, the vaunting mind in the vaulting body.

If we speak of encyclopedias, there is one actual encyclopedia which we must have in recollection—the great *Encyclopédie* itself. Flaubert never makes Diderot the object of his satire—one may well suppose that the author of *Rameau's Nephew* was the last man in the world with whom Flaubert would have sought a quarrel—but Diderot's great enterprise of the *Encyclopédie,* which derived its impulse as much from the spirit of Rabelais as from the spirit of Bacon, is the heroic and optimistic enterprise of which the researches of *Bouvard and Pécuchet* are the comic and pessimistic counterpart. To have thought of Diderot busily running about France, taking notes on this trade or that process, learning how spinning or weaving or smelting or brewing was done, so that all the world might have a healthy knowledge of the practical arts, would be to have the inspiration for those scenes in which Bouvard and Pécuchet undertake to deal with practical life, to grow their own food and to preserve it, to make their own cordial ("Bouvarine," it is to be called!). *Bouvard and Pécuchet* in its despair that anything at all can be done is the negation of the morning confidence and hope of the *Encyclopédie*.

Which brings us to the third book of *Gulliver's Travels*. The Voyage to Laputa, in which Swift satirizes the scientific theories of his day, may be thought of as the ambivalent prolegomenon to the *Encyclopédie*—ambivalent because Swift was Baconian in his conception of the practical aim of science but anti-Baconian in his contempt for any kind of scientific method he knew of, even Bacon's positivism. In the expression of his scorn he provides a striking precedent for *Bouvard and Pécuchet,* which had for its explanatory subtitle, "The failings of the methods of science." The analogy that may be drawn between Flaubert's book and Swift's goes considerably beyond what is suggested merely by the Voyage to Laputa—it leads us, indeed, to the personal similarity of Flaubert and Swift. But this may better be observed in another place.

Mr. Pound, having particularly in mind the encyclopedic nature of *Bouvard and Pécuchet,* finds *Don Quixote* to be a very different kind of thing—"Cervantes parodied but a single literary folly, the chivalric folly." Yet it is not the parody of the chivalric idea that in itself makes *Don Quixote* what it is, but rather the complex drama that results from putting an elaborate idea to the test in the world of actuality. Flaubert said of Madame Bovary that she was the sister of Don Quixote; Bouvard and Pécuchet are at least consanguineous enough to be cousins. And their idea, despite its encyclopedic mutations, is, after all, as much a unity as Don Quixote's: they believe that the world yields to mind. And if *Don Quixote,* then certainly *Candide,* which also tests an idea in the laboratory of the world. The conclusion of *Bouvard and Pécuchet,* "Let us return to copying," has not become proverbial only because its proverbial possibilities have been pre-empted by "Let us cultivate our garden."

Then the second act of *The Bourgeois Gentleman,* in which Monsieur Jourdain receives instruction from the professors of the sciences, arts, and graces, may be thought of as a small encyclopedia in the form of a farce and as the model for this history of the bourgeois savants. The *Dunciad* must not go without mention. And the ingenious reader may amuse himself by discovering all the analogies that may be drawn between *Bouvard and Pécuchet* and *Faust.*

II

"Bouvard et Pécuchet sont-ils des imbéciles?" The blunt question is the title of an essay, notable in the history of Flaubert criticism, which was published in 1914 by the eminent scholar René Dumesnil. It is the question which lies at the heart of the ambiguity of *Bouvard and Pécuchet*.

It will perhaps seem strange that ambiguity should be imputed to the novel. In England and America more people know about *Bouvard and Pécuchet* than have read it. The author's purpose as stated in his famous correspondence, and also the outline of the story, are part of our general literary information. Neither the purpose nor the story suggests the possibility of ambiguity. Flaubert's avowed intention, that of pillorying the culture of bourgeois democracy, does not seem likely to induce or even permit more than one meaning to appear. As for his plan of having two simple copying clerks undertake to master, seriatim, all the sciences and disciplines, and to come to grief or boredom with each one, it seems clear and schematic to a degree, even to a fault—it is hard to see why it should not be entirely within the control of the author's equally clear purpose. Yet it has been said by a French writer that of all the works of Flaubert it is *Bouvard and Pécuchet* that gives the critics the most trouble; that it is a book which is intricate, complex, and difficult to analyze; that its meaning is hard to come at.[2]

Indeed, so great is the ambiguity of *Bouvard and Pécuchet* that it is possible to conclude that the book quite fails to be what Flaubert intended it to be. Which need not, of course, prevent it from being something else of a very good sort.

The trouble starts with the fact that Bouvard and Pécuchet, as Dumesnil demonstrated, are *not* imbeciles. Perhaps it is too much to say, as Dumesnil does say, that they have the souls of apostles, but

---

[2] Claude Digeon, in his *Le Dernier Visage de Flaubert* (Paris: 1946), p. 94.

imbeciles they certainly are not, and we shall be able to go considerably further in their praise than this mere negation. There can be no doubt that Flaubert began with the intention of making them as foolish and ridiculous as possible. We are surely not free to suppose that he had any inclination to show them mercy because they were poor clerks and lived very limited lives. When the word bourgeoisie came to be used in this country in a social-political sense, it was likely to be restricted in its reference to people of pretty solid establishment. For the social group more or less analogous to that to which Bouvard and Pécuchet belonged we used other words, choosing them according to our political disposition—"white-collar workers," "office proletariat," "little people." But Flaubert made no such distinction. For him the bourgeoisie was the bourgeoisie from top to bottom. He saw the characteristics and the power of the class as continuous from the wealthy to the poor. If he had thought to call the small bourgeoisie the "little people," he would have done so contemptuously, having reference to the size of their ideas and ideals and impulses. And he feared them exactly for this littleness, which he believed they wanted to impose upon the world. It was by no means the straitened lives that Bouvard and Pécuchet lived for forty-seven years until the great moment when they met each other that induced Flaubert to let them off from being imbeciles. No doubt in reference to just this hole-and-corner existence he had at one time cruelly planned to call the book "The History of Two Cockroaches."

But two cockroaches cannot be friends with each other. And François Denys Bartholomée Bouvard and Juste Romain Cyrille Pécuchet —their Christian names once mentioned in their history are forever forgotten and may as well be memorialized here—are truly friends. This fact is of decisive importance in the novel—it defeats whatever intention Flaubert may have had to make his protagonists contemptible. To Flaubert friendship was not merely a relation: it was a virtue, as it was for Montaigne, as it was for Swift.

Bouvard and Pécuchet are able to be friends because they are sufficiently different in their natures, although at one in their minds.

Bouvard, as the sound of his name suggests, is the fleshier of the two, the more rotund, and the easier-going, the more sentimental, sensual, and worldly. Pécuchet, in accordance with his name, is lean and stringy; he is puritanical, passionate, pessimistic—a little more *sincere* than Bouvard. (Flaubert set great store by their names. When he overheard Zola say that he had found the perfect name for a character, Bouvard, he turned pale, and in the greatest agitation begged Zola not to use it. And he was much troubled when a banker named Pécuchet, a man he respected, played an important part in his financial life in 1875; the point of delicacy was settled by M. Pécuchet's death.)

Once in their life together, after many frustrations, at a moment when they are nervous and depressed, Bouvard and Pécuchet find that they can't stand the sight of each other; this is natural and transitory, and it but serves to emphasize the fullness and constancy of their devotion to each other. Their manner of life, we must recognize, has great charm. They are much harassed, much frustrated by practical as well as by intellectual matters, but their housekeeping, which is omnipresent in the story, is a pleasure to read about. Even when the economy falls quite to pieces and becomes sordid, it never quite belies the rich common poetry of their first meal, their first evening, their first morning in their own home. From their establishment we derive the pleasure which is afforded by the living arrangements of *Robinson Crusoe* or *The Swiss Family Robinson,* or Boffin's Bower, or Sherlock Holmes's rooms in Baker Street. Their enterprises are based on innocence and a pleasant sufficiency: they have a good deal in common with the respected author of "Speculations on the Source of the Hempstead Ponds, with some Observations of the Theory of Tittlebats," for Mr. Pickwick, another superannuated bourgeois bachelor, was devoted to the life of the mind, and his scientific adventures, although more primitive than those of Bouvard and Pécuchet, are alike in kind. They have affinity with Tom Sawyer—they are consciously boyish in their dreams of glory, in their dreams of love; for a moment, in their hydrotherapeutic phase, they have their Jackson's Island and are seen naked as Red Indians and gleefully splashing each other from their adjoining baths. Their life, despite its disappointments, is a kind of idyl, and it approaches the pastoral convention—there is no reason not to think of them as two shepherds tending their woolly flocks of ideas. Who would not want to read Bouvard's "Lament for Pécuchet," or, for the matter of that, Pécuchet's "Elegy for Bouvard," whichever came first; and whose heart would not be wrung by the event either poem recorded and the loneliness of the survivor at the double copying desk, the contriving of which had been the last ingenuity of the two friends?

Had they lived alone and pursued their studies and projects alone, it is possible that imbecility might have descended upon the mind of each. It is not until they meet each other that they really begin their intellectual life. Although they are always at one in their enthusiasm, they take sufficiently different views of questions to create between them a degree of dialectic; Flaubert, like Plato, conceived of friendship as one of the conditions of thought. Love and logic go together.

Not imbeciles, then, but certainly not without folly. Wherein does the folly of Bouvard and Pécuchet lie? In part their error is the same as that of their prototype, Monsieur Jourdain—they want to learn too quickly. They do not know the true mode of thought; they have no patience. They would not understand what many of the great researchers meant when they said that they stared at the facts until the facts spoke to them. They are committed to the life of the mind in general, but not, in the way of the true scholar, in particular. They are perhaps too thoroughly Whole Men; they lack the degree of benign limitation which permits an intense preoccupation, making a single subject seem the satisfaction of the demands of a whole temperament. And then we must remember their age; they are forty-seven when they begin, they have no time for patience— they are about the same age as Faust was when he expressed his sense of the inadequacy of all the disciplines. They are Faustian;

they must try everything, and to no intellectual moment are they able to say their *"Verweile doch!"*

But their measure of folly is not what makes Bouvard and Pécuchet comic characters. They are comic through the operation of the censorship which the race exercises over those who address themselves to the large enterprises of the spirit. This censorship undertakes to say who is to be allowed to engage upon what high adventures. It decides who, by reason of age or degree of pulchritude or social class, may fall in love, or have surpassing ambitions, or think great thoughts. Whether or not we are ourselves engaged in any of the great spiritual enterprises, we feel it our duty to protect their decorum and their *décor* by laughing at anyone who does not conform to the right image of the lover, the hero, or the thinker. This would be a more disagreeable human trait than in fact it is if we were not at the same time prepared to discover that some of the people whom we debar from their desires have their own special virtues. Leopold Bloom, although he has no ashplant and no irony and does not answer every question "quietly" as Stephen Dedalus does, but, on the contrary, is without dignity in love or thought, is yet seen to be a proper object of our respect and affection. Don Quixote is too old, too stringy, too poor, as well as too late in the day, for chivalry and courtly love, but he is not too much or too little of anything to be wise with a new kind of wisdom. The ancient inscription that Mr. Pickwick discovers is deciphered to read "Bill Stubbs, his mark," which he believes to be nothing but the operation of malice —he really has no mind at all except what makes him defy Dodson & Fogg and become the saint of the Fleet.

So with Bouvard and Pécuchet. They are funny because they are what they are: because they are middle-aged; because one is fat and one is thin; because they wear strange garments; because they are unmarried and awkward in love; because they are innocent; because they are clumsy and things blow up in their faces, or fall on them, or trip them up; because they are gullible and think they are shrewd; because they are full of enthusiasm. Being funny in themselves, being comically *not* the men for high enterprises, they are therefore funny when they undertake the intellectual life. Their comicality is *a priori,* it does not grow out of their lack of intelligence. When it comes to intelligence, many a man has less who can command a better laboratory technique than theirs. Granted that they begin each adventure in stupidity, as they progress through the intellectual disciplines these "simple, lucid, mediocre" minds (as Maupassant called them) are likely to see whatever absurdities are to be seen; they are the catalysts of the foolishness of others.

Then, whether or not they are properly to be called apostles, their degree of virtue and their generosity of spirit are unmistakable. Their hearts—and what is more, their minds—instinctively take the side of the insulted and injured. If they cannot stay long with one idea, they nevertheless live by the mind; the courage that this requires they abundantly have. It is not they who exemplify the vices of the bourgeoisie that Flaubert despised. For the bourgeoisie they have nothing but contempt. In their conflicts with the local priest, doctor, mayor, magnate, it is they who are in the right of things. They stand for intelligence: they are traitors to their class. And they suffer the consequences; they acquire the peculiar pathos of their dedication.

The evidence of their superiority gave umbrage. As they upheld immoral points of view, they were surely immoral themselves; slanders were invented about them.

Then a pitiable faculty developed in their spirit, that of perceiving stupidity and no longer tolerating it.

Insignificant things made them sad: adverisements in the newspapers, a smug profile, a foolish remark heard by chance.

Musing on what was said in the village, and on there existing as far as the Antipodes [other people like the members of the village bourgeoisie], they felt as though the heaviness of all the earth were weighing on them.

It is no wonder that more than one critic has considered whether Bouvard and Pécuchet must not be taken as standing for Flaubert himself, or for Flaubert and the good friend and neighbor of his

later years, Laporte, who found pleasure in helping accumulate the
material for *Bouvard and Pécuchet*.

III

Bouvard and Pécuchet, then, are not the objects of Flaubert's
satire. At most they are the butts of his humor, which is strongly
qualified by affection. They are never represented as doing anything
in the least ignoble or mean. They are "justified" characters. We
therefore naturally suppose that the savageness which the book was
intended to express is to be found in the exposition of the studies
which the two friends undertake—this surely will constitute the
fierce indictment of the bourgeois democracy.

But again our supposition is disappointed. The horrors of the culture of the bourgeois democracy play a considerably smaller part
than we anticipate. They are less horrible than we had expected.
And the animus with which they are exhibited turns out to be not
nearly so savage as we had been led to hope.

As I have said, a good many of the misadventures of Bouvard
and Pécuchet befall them simply because they are comic characters,
or because life is as it is. If their tenant farmer cheats them, if their
handyman diddles them, we cannot conclude that rural cupidity
and the unreliability of rural labor have been brought about by the
ascendancy of the bourgeoisie. If Bouvard, in two wonderful scenes,
witnesses the terrible power of sexuality, in human beings and in
peacocks, and cannot himself go much further in the direction of
passion than a warm flush of inclination, or if Pécuchet contracts
gonorrhea from his first sexual experience, we are not exactly being
given examples of the effect of the bourgeois swinishness. When the
hailstorm destroys the fruit which the two beginners have been almost successful in bringing to maturity, the phenomenon is not cultural but meteorological and, in its context, cosmological. That the
agricultural treatises differ from each other, that "as regards marl,
Puvis recommends it, Roret's handbook opposes it," this cannot

fairly be ascribed to the contemporary corruption of mind—it is of
the immemorial nature of farming: since the time of Cain, farmers
have exercised their moral faculties on just such differences of opinion. Pécuchet meditates on the inherent contradictions that seem to
exist between fruit and branch: "The authorities recommend stopping all the ducts. If not, the sap is injured, and the tree, of course,
suffers. For it to flourish, it would have to bear no fruit at all. Yet
those that are never pruned or manured yield fruit, smaller, indeed,
but better flavored"—this is not an indictment of the stupidity of
bourgeois-democratic pomology but a profound consideration of the
nature of life, cultural as well as arboricultural. In their true goodness of heart the two friends undertake to rear and educate a pair of
brutalized waifs; they fail not because their educational methods are
contemptible but because the human material has become intractable.

A considerable part of the intellectual criticism of the novel depends upon the inversion of the snobbish censorship to which I
have referred. This is the mode of comedy, which perceives that if
any abstruse discipline is confronted with an actual human being, no
matter how stupid—and, indeed, the stupider the better—it is the
person who is justified as against the discipline. A draper should not
be adept in arms nor study the arts of logic or language; still, when
put in company of the fencing master who can kill a man by demonstrative reason, or the rhetorician who shows him that *A* is sounded
with the mouth *so,* Monsieur Jourdain is not the greatest fool on the
stage, nor would he be if he had secured Aristotle as his teacher. In
any vaudeville dialectic the intellectual advantage always rests with
the obtuse or primitive person; the straight man, the patient teacher
who believes in the subject, is always discredited. No discipline
which is confronted with the simplicity, the intellectual *innocence,*
of Bouvard and Pécuchet can long maintain its pretense to value.

Then we must have in mind the large part that is played in the
book by intellectual and quasi-intellectual absurdities which are as
ridiculous as we want to call them, but about which it is impossible
for a sensible man to be seriously troubled. Two of the amusing

episodes of the novel concern themselves with Bouvard and Pécuchet training their memories by a compound of three mnemonic systems and hardening their bodies according to Amoros's manual of gymnastics. René Descharmes, in his wellknown work, *Autour de Bouvard et Pécuchet,* devotes a long chapter to one of the mnemonic systems, the most famous one of all, that of Feinagle, and he gives another chapter to the gymnastic manual. In Descharmes, as in Flaubert, the books are very funny. But we can scarcely believe that these books, and the treatises on hygiene and diet, were the kind of thing that was making Flaubert "rabid." As long as there have been printed books there have been mnemonic systems and they have been absurd; there have always been professors of physical training and they have always had a grandiose solemnity which may still be observed. Quackery is pretty constant in culture, and it is the detritus of culture, not its essence.

An American scholar and critic, Hugh Kenner, recently described *Bouvard and Pécuchet* as "the book into which Flaubert emptied his voluminous notes on human gullibility, groundless learning, *opinions chic,* contradictory authorities, ridiculous enthusiasms, the swill of the 19th century." But we must think with a certain tenderness of some of "the swill of the 19th century" because it has served as the intellectual aliment of certain of the best poets of our age, the men whom we most readily exempt from our general condemnation of our own culture and who have done most to make us aware of the awfulness of our culture and that of the nineteenth century. When Bouvard and Pécuchet involve themselves with the study of psychic and occult phenomena, their researches are no doubt less profound than those of William Butler Yeats, but not different in kind; and although they fall short of Yeats's degree of success in practice, still, on one occasion, they do startle themselves, their audience, and the reader by demonstrating an actual example of clairvoyance. Nothing that the delightful Robert Graves tells us about the Druids contradicts what Bouvard and Pécuchet discover in their study of the science of Celtic archaeology: "Some uttered prophecies, others chanted, others taught botany, medicine, history and literature: in short, all the arts of their epoch. Pythagoras and Plato were their pupils. They instructed the Greeks in metaphysics, the Persians in sorcery, the Etruscans in augury, and the Romans in plating copper and trading in ham." Then the passion of Bouvard and Pécuchet for antiquities, their lust for old documents and the cultural conclusions they base on their investigations and accumulations are no different from those of Ezra Pound, about whom Mr. Kenner has written so well; and they have Mr. Pound's responsiveness to comprehensive schemes of social and economic reform. Their knowledge of the emotions of the Waste Land is no less intense than that of T. S. Eliot, and based on a not dissimilar experience; with them as with him despair arises from culture and leads to religion.

Readers of literary bent, who have as an element of their pathos the belief that they are persecuted by science,[3] will set special store by those parts of the novel that have the effect of exposing the arrogance as well as the contradictions and absurdities of the physical science of the day. Everyone who has ever studied literature knows that physical science was the basis of the vulgar materialism of the nineteenth century. In this regard it is well to remember that Flaubert had no principled hostility to science as such—quite to the contrary, indeed. He takes note of the ridiculous statements that science can make, but much of the confusion that Bouvard and Pécuchet experience is the result of their own ineptitude or ignorance rather than of the inadequacy of science itself. It is not the fault of botany —although it may be the fault of a particular elementary textbook of botany—that they believe that all flowers have a pericarp, but look in vain for it when confronted by buttercups and wild strawberry.

Medicine, of course, is the natural prey of the comic—the treatment it receives in *Bouvard and Pécuchet* adds nothing in point of comic method to the classic one established by Molière. And this can

---

[3] It is not sufficiently understood that men of science have an analogous—homologous?—pathos to support them in their own troubles: they believe that they are systematically persecuted by the humanities.

serve to remind us of the extent to which the seventeenth and eighteenth centuries figure in the novel. These have become sacred eras, and persons of sensibility believe that either of them can show a virtue for every vice of the nineteenth century. Yet Flaubert represents them as the seedbed of literary stupidity.

> *Think of devices which can captivate,*

says Boileau.

> By what means think of these devices?

> *In all your speeches passion should be found,*
> *Go seek the heart, and warm it till it bound.*

How "warm the heart"?
The rules are not enough; genius is also necessary.
And genius is not enough. Corneille, according to the Académie Française, understands nothing of the theatre. Geoffroy depreciated Voltaire. Racine was jeered at by Subligny. Laharpe bellowed at the name of Shakespeare.

What we may call the primary or elemental religious experience of Bouvard and Pécuchet is treated by Flaubert with considerable seriousness and sympathy; it is the theological developments which follow upon that experience that he mocks. This theology cannot be said to be peculiar to the nineteenth century or to the bourgeois democracy.

Again, when it comes to philosophy, it is not merely the philosophy of the nineteenth century that brings Bouvard and Pécuchet to their despair. It is philosophy in general, what anyone except a logical positivist would say were the genuine problems of philosophy. These take, it is true, a specifically modern form, in part because Flaubert had had his say about ancient philosophy in *The Temptation of St. Anthony*. But they go back at least as far as the seventeenth century. "The famous *cogito* bores me," says Bouvard, just like any truthful person who has read Descartes. He and Pécuchet attempt Spinoza. They feel that "all this was like being in a balloon at night, in glacial coldness, carried on an endless voyage towards a bottomless abyss, and with nothing near but the unseizable, the motionless, the eternal. It was too much. They gave it up." As who does not? Their response to the *Ethics* is not foolish, not trivial; they have caught most accurately the emotion that Spinoza enforces upon us, and they know that it is impossible to live with. Yet Flaubert, at the time of writing the novel, had a devoted admiration for Spinoza, as we all have.

What is being mocked? For even literature, the great palladium of Flaubert's life, is not proof against the corrosive action of the simple, lucid, mediocre minds of Bouvard and Pécuchet. It is not merely bad literature that bores them after their first afflatus of enthusiasm; it is literature itself. The elements of each author that at first enchant them—the tone, the idiom, the system of distortion and extravagance—come to be the ground of their eventual boredom. It should perhaps be observed that their experience of literature does not include the very greatest writers, those to whom Flaubert gave his ultimate admiration, Shakespeare, Rabelais, Montaigne, etc. They do, however, read the modern authors for whom Flaubert had great admiration—Balzac, George Sand, Victor Hugo. And who would wish to be so pious as to say that boredom cannot attend our experience of even the very greatest writers?

The more we consider *Bouvard and Pécuchet,* the less the novel can be thought of as nothing but an attack on the culture of the nineteenth century. Bourgeois democracy merely affords the setting for a situation in which it becomes possible to reject culture itself. The novel does nothing less than that: it rejects culture. The human mind experiences the massed accumulation of its own works, those that are traditionally held to be its greatest glories as well as those that are obviously of a contemptible sort, and arrives at the understanding that none will serve its purpose, that all are weariness and vanity, that the whole vast structure of human thought and creation are alien from the human person. Descharmes concludes his study of *Bouvard and Pécuchet* with the statement that the import of the novel is comprehended in a verse from Ecclesiastes which Flaubert might well have used as an epigraph: "And I set my mind to search and investigate through wisdom everything that is done beneath the heavens. It is an evil task that God has given the sons of men with which to occupy themselves." The relevance of the pessimism of Ecclesiastes goes well beyond this single text.

The pessimism of *Bouvard and Pécuchet* is comparable with, although not the same as, that of *Gulliver's Travels*. Just as we may not lessen the depth of the pessimism of *Gulliver's Travels* by reading the book as if it were only Swift's response to the eighteenth century, so we may not lessen the depth of the pessimism of *Bouvard and Pécuchet* by reading it as if it were only Flaubert's response to the nineteenth century.

What does permit us to qualify the pessimism of *Bouvard and Pécuchet* is the comic mode in which it has its existence. The book is genuinely funny, and the comic nature of the two heroes invites us to stand at a certain distance from their woe. We are not dealing with, say, Musset's Octave, he who so advertised his self-pity by calling his history that of "a child of the century," by which he invites the reader to acknowledge a common paternity and thus approve his self-commiseration. Bouvard and Pécuchet permit us to laugh at ourselves in them and yet to remain detached from their plight. They are a *reductio ad absurdum* of our lives in culture, but we are not constrained to follow the reduction as far as it can take us.

They themselves qualify the pessimism of the book by their last act. Another famous copying clerk, an American, Melville's Bartleby the Scrivener, with the classic American pessimism which is more entire than any that the French have contrived, when he perceives the nothingness of society, simply curls up and wills to die, and dies. But when all is lost to Bouvard and Pécuchet, all is not lost: they procure the double copying desk, and the order of the day, which had come to them like a revelation, is *"Copier comme autrefois."* And so we last see them in the metamorphosis to which their lives entitle them, a sort of bachelor Baucis and Philemon, rustling their leaves at each other with a sweet papery sound. They have discovered the *"travailler sans raisonner,"* the virtue of work without philosophizing, which *Candide* inculcates. Yet the abrogation of abstruse research does not mean the abrogation of mind, for what they copy from the old papers which they indiscriminately buy are the absurdities they have learned to recognize. The results of their copying are to constitute, according to Flaubert's plan, the last part of the novel. Scholars have debated which of Flaubert's several collections of absurdities was to appear as the fruit of their efforts. The weight of the evidence seems to give that place to *The Dictionary of Accepted Ideas,* and most readers will be willing to accept this conclusion if only because of the pleasures of the *Dictionary* itself, which is the most elaborate of the collections.[4] But for the understanding of the novel itself it is almost enough to know that *something* was to follow, that, reduced as the two friends are, they have not lost their love of mind, to which they testify by recording the mind's failures.

IV

The pessimism of *Bouvard and Pécuchet* is qualified by certain other considerations. These are extraneous to the text, but our sense of the ambiguity of the novel justifies us in going beyond the text to see if we may gain further understanding from an awareness of the circumstances of its composition. Indeed, it is virtually impossible not to do something of this sort. In the time between his death and his centenary in 1921 the fame of Flaubert increased to the point where he was a classic of his language and the subject of an elaborate scholarship. His novels, which he had written according to his famous ideal of strict objectivity and stern impersonality, were read—and even when there was no excuse of ambiguity—more and more in the light of his personal legend, which seemed to grow ever greater in its power of appeal.

If there is such a thing as biographical success, Flaubert achieved

---

[4] The *Dictionary* may now be read in Jacques Barzun's translation, published by New Directions.

it in its fullest measure, for the last period of his life is as interesting, in both event and thought, as the early years in which his mind was formed and the middle years of his decisive productions; and its pathos is irresistible. This pathos, I venture to suppose, is similar in the effect it has upon the French reader to that which moves the English reader in the life of Swift. It is the pathos of the man whose savage pride induces him to have always before his mind the idea of mankind as a whole, and to regard the human actuality with an angry disgust so intense that it seems to him—and sometimes to others—like a madness. Those individuals whom he exempts from his general contempt for the human kind he grapples to himself with hoops of steel. If he is incapable of marriage and even of sexual love in any conventional sense, he can give to a few women an extreme devotion; and to many men he can give a friendship of surpassing respect and loyalty.

It was in his remarkably deep affections that Flaubert was struck again and again in his last years. "I am obsessed by the dead (my dead)," he wrote to Laure de Maupassant. "Is this a sign of old age? I think so." He was fifty-three. The year was 1873 and the necrology of the last four years had been long; many losses were still to come. His mother, his dearest friends, his literary colleagues and comrades-in-arms—their deaths accumulated and were augmented by the passing of people whom he did not love as he loved his mother, or George Sand, or Louis Bouilhet, or whom he did not respect as he did Jules de Goncourt, or Gautier, or even Sainte-Beuve, but who nevertheless embodied his past, such as Louise Colet, his former mistress, and Maurice Schlesinger, the husband of the woman Flaubert had loved with a virtually mystic passion since his adolescence and whom he had enshrined as the Mme. Arnoux of *A Sentimental Education*.

He could make of his life an altar of the dead, as witness the time, effort, and passion he gave to keep alive the memory of the cherished Louis Bouilhet. But he could also make it an altar of the living. Perhaps he would not have said with Henry James that life is nothing unless it is sacrificial, but he acted as if he believed this to be so when he offered up his independence for the happiness of his niece Caroline.

Caroline Commanville was the only child of Flaubert's only sister, who had died in 1846, and she had been reared by her grandmother and her uncle. To Caro, as she was called, Flaubert gave the full of the devotion of which he was capable. His love, characteristically enough, expressed itself in his solicitude for the grace of her mind. Something of his yearning tenderness for her, which appears so unabashedly in the letters which she published after his death, was lent to Bouvard and Pécuchet when, moved in part by belated parental impulses, they adopt the stray children to educate them for decorous and useful lives. Flaubert spent thirteen years on Caro's education, and the goal of his affectionate efforts was like that of Nature in Wordsworth's poem:

> This Child I to myself shall take;
> She shall be mine, and I shall make
> A Lady of my own

—a Lady who in her own person should be the answer to the vulgarity and stupidity of the time.

How far he did indeed succeed in his best hopes for the intellectual grace of Caro may be judged by American readers from the description of her which Willa Cather gives after meeting her at a hotel at Aix in 1930, when she was a woman of eighty-four. And nothing can suggest better the moral limitations of Miss Cather and her feminized universe than the fact that although she renders the most intense and delicate homage to the charm of Mme. Franklin-Grout (as she had become), speaking at length of her manners, her command of many languages, the purity of her passion for art, her friendship with her uncle's great friends, her closeness to her uncle himself, she gives no intimation that for the sake of Caro, and at her behest, Flaubert had put himself into financial jeopardy, surrendering the fortune upon which he depended for his literary life, and with very little thanks from the beneficiary.

Up to 1875 the business affairs of Caroline's husband Commanville seemed to justify an elaborate establishment in Paris and a fashionable and expensive way of life. Then it became clear that Commanville was on the verge of bankruptcy. To save the Commanvilles from disgrace Flaubert pledged his entire fortune—when it came to the bourgeois pieties he was to be outdone by no one. He gave up his pleasant flat in Paris and took cheaper rooms, and in general greatly curtailed his expenses. He sold the property at Deauville from which he derived his income. At one time it seemed probable that he would have to give up the house at Croisset, where he had lived virtually all his life. This horrified him and wrung from him an agonized cry—without it, he said, using the English word, he would have no *home*. George Sand offered to buy it if possible and let him live in it all his life, but the sale proved unnecessary. In all, Flaubert put at the disposal of the Commanvilles 1,200,000 francs, in return for which he was to receive a small allowance.

The full extent of the sacrifice can be properly understood only if we feel the force of Gautier's remark that Flaubert's bourgeois fortune was part of his creative endowment. The sacrifice being what it was, the Commanvilles' subsequent behavior gives the incident a Lear-like character. They did not pay the allowance promptly and Flaubert had to importune for it. They were angry when Flaubert, with much reluctance and humiliation, consented to allow his friends to procure a pension for him; they did not forgive the friends who had won his consent and campaigned for the pension. They felt he was a drain on their resources and called him "the consumer"; their own way of life continued to be expensive. They required him to enlist his friends in further help to them. When the devoted Laporte, who himself had lost his fortune, refused to commit himself further, they insisted that Flaubert break with him, which he did in great sadness.

These events, interesting in themselves, are significant for our purpose as constituting the circumstance in which Flaubert wrote the *Three Tales* and as having a bearing upon their common theme of the sacrifice of the self; and the *Three Tales* must inevitably be read as a gloss upon *Bouvard and Pécuchet*.

In September of 1875, with the Commanville affairs temporarily under control, Flaubert went to spend six weeks at Concarneau with his old friend, the naturalist Georges Pouchet. Flaubert's nerves were in a bad state; he was sadly distraught. He envied the calm with which his scientist friend went about his work. Unable to take up his own work on *Bouvard and Pécuchet,* he swam and walked to restore his equanimity and he began the story of *St. Julian*. He took it with him when he left Concarneau and finished it in January. In February he began *A Simple Heart,* which he completed in August. In August he began *Herodias,* which he finished the following February. The stories appeared as a newspaper serial and then in a volume; they were greeted with almost universal admiration—Flaubert's first popular success since *Madame Bovary*.

The part that these three stories play in Flaubert's artistic development cannot concern us here. Nor can we stop to consider all that they might be understood to say of Flaubert's inner life. What is of immediate consequence to us is the theme which they have in common and how that bears upon *Bouvard and Pécuchet*.

The stories are well known and need be recalled but briefly. All are associated with Flaubert's native Rouen. The legend of St. Julian is the subject of a window of the Cathedral; the Herodias story is told on the tympanum of the Cathedral's south portal. The Félicité of *A Simple Heart* was a servant girl whom Flaubert had known in his boyhood. The story of St. Julian, a Christianized version of the Oedipus legend, tells of a young nobleman brought up to arms and the chase; his passion for killing is exorbitant (the catalogue of the beasts he slays reminds us of nothing so much as the fifteen hundred volumes Flaubert read for *Bouvard and Pécuchet*), until one day it is prophesied to him by a gigantic and invulnerable stag that he will kill his own mother and father. The prophecy comes true despite Julian's best efforts to circumvent it. Julian, shunned by all mankind, lives as a hermit. One cold night there comes to his hut a

leper of extreme loathesomeness who asks for food, then for the
warmth of Julian's embrace, then for a kiss upon his ghastly mouth.
And as Julian's *caritas* extends to this last request, the leper appears
as Christ and carries Julian off in glory. *A Simple Heart* is a record
of a life of religious piety and of entire devotion to others. Virtually
the only events of Félicité's life are the deaths of those whom she
loves and serves. (It has been remarked that Félicité has a seizure on
the road very much like that which Flaubert suffered as the first
episode of his illness; other possible connections with Flaubert are
her cherishing of her nephew, her being exploited by her relatives,
her being left destitute by the death of her mistress, and her continuing to live by sufferance in the stripped and empty house.) *Herodias*
is the story of John the Baptist imprisoned by the Tetrarch Antipas,
of Salome's dance, and the severed head.

The religious elements of the three stories must not mislead us
about the condition of Flaubert's belief. The *Tales* are not to be
thought of as tentatives toward an avowal of faith. For this Flaubert's attitude toward religion was far too complex. Even in *Bouvard
and Pécuchet,* as I have noted, Flaubert treats simple, primary religious faith, or impulse to faith, with great gentleness; what dismayed him were the intellectual extrapolations from this simplicity.
Yet his response to religion is not comprised by the tenderness he
could show to simple faith and his contempt for systematic theology.
What his attitude to religion actually was in its considerable complexity has been well described by Philip Spencer in his *Flaubert:*
"He seems . . . to have regarded Christianity as a spent force. . . .
The only two elements in Catholicism to which Flaubert responded
were subordinate to the main tradition and divergent from it: the
hatred of life, the negation of life's goodness, which he thought he
discovered in Catholic philosophy, and, concomitant with it, the
rigorous self-abasement of asceticism. But his own religious feeling,
if such it can be called, was diffuse—a kind of creatureliness before
the mystery of creation. 'What draws me above all things,' he wrote
in 1857, 'is religion. I mean all religions, not one rather than another.

Each dogma on its own repels me, but I consider the feeling that created them as the most natural and poetical in humanity. I don't like philosophers who find there only fraud and foolishness.' " A man who can speak thus does not easily "turn to" religion, and the *Three Tales* must not be thought of even as the tribute to religion of an unbeliever who perceives the charms and advantages of faith and who regrets his inability to believe. Flaubert was a very serious man.

But we shall not be wrong if we think of the stories as a tribute to what Flaubert took to be a characteristic mode of Christianity, the "negation of life's goodness"—life's goodness in general and specifically the goodness of man's life in culture. In each of the stories the protagonist exists beyond the life in culture and stands divested of every garment that culture weaves. Julian passes beyond parental love, beyond social rank, beyond heroism and fame, beyond the domestic affections, beyond all the things, persons, and institutions that bind us to the earth, and he reaches that moment of charity which is the surrender of what Flaubert believed to be the richest luxury of culture, the self in the separateness of sensibility and pride that define it. Félicité, endowed by nature and culture with no other gift than that of the power to love and serve, is deprived of every person upon whom her love has fixed and is left with no other object to cherish than her poor stuffed parrot, the dumb effigy of the Speaking Bird, the Logos, the Holy Ghost. John the Baptist, naked and solitary, cries out from his prison-pit against the court of Antipas, and Flaubert is at his usual pains to specify not only the deeds but the artifacts—the garments and the food and the armament hidden beneath the palace—of which the Baptist's naked and solitary voice is the negation.

The *Tales,* that is, continue Flaubert's old despair of culture, which was, we may say, the prime condition of his art; it was a despair which was the more profound, we need scarcely say, because it was the issue of so great a hope. Emma Bovary had tried to live by the promises of selfhood which culture had seemed to make, and culture had destroyed her. Frédéric Moreau had ruined himself by never quite believing in the selfhood which culture cherishes as its dearest gift. Now Flaubert considers the condition of the spirit which puts itself as far as possible beyond the promises, the consolations, and the demands of culture; in each of the *Three Tales* he asks what remains when culture is rejected and transcended. The answer, given with a notable firmness and simplicity, is that something of highest value does remain—it is the self affirmed in self-denial: life is nothing unless sacrificial. And Bouvard and Pécuchet, sitting at their double copying desk, having a work and each other, but stripped of every idea, every theory, every shred of culture beyond what is necessary to keep men alive and still human, are, in their own mild negation of self, intended by Flaubert to be among the company of his saints.

Mansfield Park

SOONER or later, when we speak of Jane Austen, we speak of her irony, and it is better to speak of it sooner rather than later because nothing can so far mislead us about her work as a wrong understanding of this one aspect of it. Most people either value irony too much or fear it too much. This is true of their response to irony in its first simple meaning, that of a device of rhetoric by which we say one thing and intend its opposite, or intend more, or less, than we say. It is equally true of their response to irony in its derived meaning, the loose generalized sense in which we speak of irony as a quality of someone's mind, Montaigne's for example.[1] Both the excessive valuation and the excessive fear of irony lead us to misconceive the part it can play in the intellectual and moral life. To Jane Austen, irony does not mean, as it means to many, a moral detachment or the tone of superiority that goes with moral detachment. Upon irony so conceived she has made her own judgment in the figure of Mr. Bennet of *Pride and Prejudice,* whose irony of moral detachment is shown to be the cause of his becoming a moral nonentity.

Jane Austen's irony is only secondarily a matter of tone. Primarily it is a method of comprehension. It perceives the world through an awareness of its contradictions, paradoxes, and anomalies. It is by no means detached. It is partisan with generosity of spirit—it is on the side of "life," of "affirmation." But it is preoccupied not only with the charm of the expansive virtues but also with the cost at

[1] See Irony in Fowler's *Modern English Usage.*

which they are to be gained and exercised. This cost is regarded as being at once ridiculously high and perfectly fair. What we may call Jane Austen's first or basic irony is the recognition of the fact that spirit is not free, that it is conditioned, that it is limited by circumstance. This, as everyone knows from childhood on, is indeed an anomaly. Her next and consequent irony has reference to the fact that only by reason of this anomaly does spirit have virtue and meaning.

In irony, even in the large derived sense of the word, there is a kind of malice. The ironist has the intention of practicing upon the misplaced confidence of the literal mind, of disappointing comfortable expectation. Jane Austen's malice of irony is directed not only upon certain of the characters of her novels but also upon the reader himself. We are quick, too quick, to understand that *Northanger Abbey* invites us into a snug conspiracy to disabuse the little heroine of the errors of her corrupted fancy—Catherine Morland, having become addicted to novels of terror, has accepted their inadmissible premise, she believes that life is violent and unpredictable. And that is exactly what life is shown to be by the events of the story: it is we who must be disabused of our belief that life is sane and orderly. The shock of our surprise at the disappointment of our settled views is of course the more startling because we believe that we have settled our views in conformity with the author's own. Just when we have concluded in *Sense and Sensibility* that we ought to prefer Elinor Dashwood's sense to Marianne Dashwood's sensibility, Elinor herself yearns toward the anarchic passionateness of sensibility. In *Emma* the heroine is made to stand at bay to our adverse judgment through virtually the whole novel, but we are never permitted to close in for the kill—some unnamed quality in the girl, some trait of vivacity or will, erects itself into a moral principle, or at least a vital principle, and frustrates our moral blood-lust.

This interference with our moral and intellectual comfort constitutes, as I say, a malice on the part of the author. And when we respond to Jane Austen with pleasure, we are likely to do so in part because we recognize in her work an analogue with the malice of the experienced universe, with the irony of circumstance, which is always disclosing more than we bargained for.

But there is one novel of Jane Austen's, *Mansfield Park,* in which the characteristic irony seems not to be at work. Indeed, one might say of this novel that it undertakes to discredit irony and to affirm literalness, that it demonstrates that there are no two ways about anything. And *Mansfield Park* is for this reason held by many to be the novel that is least representative of Jane Austen's peculiar attractiveness. For those who admire her it is likely to make an occasion for embarrassment. By the same token, it is the novel which the depreciators of Jane Austen may cite most tellingly in justification of their antagonism.

About this antagonism a word must be said. Few writers have been the object of an admiration so fervent as that which is given to Jane Austen. At the same time, she has been the object of great dislike. Lord David Cecil has said that the people who do not like Jane Austen are the kind of people "who do not like sunshine and unselfishness," and Dr. Chapman, the distinguished editor of Jane Austen's novels and letters, although dissenting from Lord David's opinion, has speculated that perhaps "a certain lack of charity" plays a part in the dislike. But Mark Twain, to take but one example, manifestly did not lack charity or dislike sunshine and unselfishness, and Mark Twain said of Jane Austen that she inspired in him an "animal repugnance." The personal intensity of both parties to the dispute will serve to suggest how momentous, how elemental, is the issue that Jane Austen presents.

The *animality* of Mark Twain's repugnance is probably to be taken as the male's revulsion from a society in which women seem to be at the center of interest and power, as a man's panic fear at a fictional world in which the masculine principle, although represented as admirable and necessary, is prescribed and controlled by a female mind. Professor Garrod, whose essay, "Jane Austen, A Depreciation," is a *summa* of all the reasons for disliking Jane Austen, expresses a repugnance which is very nearly as feral as Mark Twain's; he implies that a direct sexual insult is being offered to men by a woman author who "describes everything in the youth of women which does not matter" in such a way as to appeal to "that age in men when they have begun to ask themselves whether anything matters." The sexual protest is not only masculine—Charlotte Brontë despised Jane Austen for representing men and women as nothing but ladies and gentlemen.

The sexual objection to Jane Austen is a very common one, even when it is not made explicit. It is not valid, yet it ought to be taken seriously into account. But then there is Emerson with his characteristic sexual indifference, his striking lack of animality, and Emerson's objection to Jane Austen is quick and entire, is instinctual. He says that she is "sterile" and goes on to call her "vulgar." Emerson held this opinion out of his passion of concern for the liberty of the self and the autonomy of spirit, and his holding it must make us see that the sexual reason for disliking Jane Austen must be subsumed under another reason which is larger, and, actually, even more elemental: the fear of imposed constraint. Dr. Chapman says something of this sort when he speaks of "political prejudice" and "impatient idealism" as perhaps having something to do with the dislike of Jane Austen. But these phrases, apart from the fact that they prejudge the case, do not suggest the biological force of the resistance which certain temperaments offer to the idea of society as a limiting condition of the individual spirit.

Such temperaments are not likely to take Jane Austen's irony as a melioration of her particular idea of society. On the contrary, they are likely to suppose that irony is but the engaging manner by which she masks society's crude coercive power. And they can point to *Mansfield Park* to show what the social coercion is in all its literal truth, before irony has beglamoured us about it and induced us to be comfortable with it—here it is in all its negation, in all the force of its repressiveness. Perhaps no other work of genius has ever spoken, or seemed to speak, so insistently for cautiousness and constraint, even for dullness. No other great novel has so anxiously asserted the need to find security, to establish, in fixity and enclosure, a refuge from the dangers of openness and chance.

There is scarcely one of our modern pieties that it does not offend. Despite our natural tendency to permit costume and manners to separate her world from ours, most readers have no great difficulty in realizing that all the other novels of Jane Austen are, in essential ways, of our modern time. This is the opinion of the many students with whom I have read the novels; not only do the young men controvert by their enthusiasm the judgment of Professor Garrod that Jane Austen appeals only to men of middle age, but they easily and naturally assume her to have a great deal to say to them about the modern personality. But *Mansfield Park* is the exception, and it is bitterly resented. It scandalizes the modern assumptions about social relations, about virtue, about religion, sex, and art. Most troubling of all is its preference for rest over motion. To deal with the world by condemning it, by withdrawing from it and shutting it out, by making oneself and one's mode and principles of life the very center of existence and to live the round of one's days in the stasis and peace thus contrived—this, in an earlier age, was one of the recognized strategies of life, but to us it seems not merely impracticable but almost wicked.

Yet *Mansfield Park* is a great novel, its greatness being commensurate with its power to offend.

Mansfield Park was published in 1814, only one year after the publication of *Pride and Prejudice,* and no small part of its interest derives from the fact that it seems to controvert everything that its predecessor tells us about life. One of the striking things about *Pride and Prejudice* is that it achieves a quality of transcendence through comedy. The comic mode typically insists upon the fact of human limitation, even of human littleness, but *Pride and Prejudice* makes comedy reverse itself and yield the implication of a divine enlargement. The novel celebrates the traits of spiritedness, vivacity, celerity, and lightness, and associates them with happiness and vir-

tue. Its social doctrine is a generous one, asserting the right of at
least the *good* individual to define himself according to his own
essence. It is animated by an impulse to forgiveness. One understands very easily why many readers are moved to explain their
pleasure in the book by reference to Mozart, especially *The Marriage of Figaro*.

Almost the opposite can be said of *Mansfield Park*. Its impulse is
not to forgive but to condemn. Its praise is not for social freedom
but for social stasis. It takes full notice of spiritedness, vivacity,
celerity, and lightness, but only to reject them as having nothing to
do with virtue and happiness, as being, indeed, deterrents to the
good life.

Nobody, I believe, has ever found it possible to like the heroine
of *Mansfield Park*. Fanny Price is overtly virtuous and consciously
virtuous. Our modern literary feeling is very strong against people
who, when they mean to be virtuous, believe they know how to
reach their goal and do reach it. We think that virtue is not interesting, even that it is not really virtue, unless it manifests itself as
a product of "grace" operating through a strong inclination to sin.
Our favorite saint is likely to be Augustine; he is sweetened for us
by his early transgressions. We cannot understand how any age
could have been interested in Patient Griselda. We admire Milton
only if we believe with Blake that he was of the Devil's party, of
which we are fellow travelers; the paradox of the *felix culpa* and the
"fortunate fall" appeals to us for other than theological reasons and
serves to validate all sins and all falls, which we take to be the signs
of life.

It does not reconcile us to the virtue of Fanny Price that it is re-
warded by more than itself. The shade of Pamela hovers over her
career. We take failure to be the mark of true virtue and we do not
like it that, by reason of her virtue, the terrified little stranger in
Mansfield Park grows up to be virtually its mistress.

Even more alienating is the state of the heroine's health. Fanny
is in a debilitated condition through the greater part of the novel.

At a certain point the author retrieves this situation and sees to it that Fanny becomes taller, prettier, and more energetic. But the first impression remains of a heroine who cannot cut a basket of roses without fatigue and headache.

Fanny's debility becomes the more striking when we consider that no quality of the heroine of *Pride and Prejudice* is more appealing than her physical energy. We think of Elizabeth Bennet as in physical movement; her love of dancing confirms our belief that she moves gracefully. It is characteristic of her to smile; she likes to tease; she loves to talk. She is remarkably responsive to all attractive men. And to outward seeming, Mary Crawford of *Mansfield Park* is another version of Elizabeth Bennet, and Mary Crawford is the antithesis of Fanny Price. The boldness with which the antithesis is contrived is typical of the uncompromising honesty of *Mansfield Park*. Mary Crawford is conceived—is calculated—to win the charmed admiration of almost any reader. She is all pungency and wit. Her mind is as lively and competent as her body; she can bring not only a horse but a conversation to the gallop. She is downright, open, intelligent, impatient. Irony is her natural mode, and we are drawn to think of her voice as being as nearly the author's own as Elizabeth Bennet's is. Yet in the end we are asked to believe that she is not to be admired, that her lively mind compounds, by very reason of its liveliness, with the world, the flesh, and the devil.

This strange, this almost perverse, rejection of Mary Crawford's vitality in favor of Fanny's debility lies at the very heart of the novel's intention. "The divine," said T. E. Hulme in *Speculations*, "is not life at its intensest. It contains in a way an almost anti-vital element." Perhaps it cannot quite be said that "the divine" is the object of Fanny's soul, yet she is a Christian heroine. Hulme expresses with an air of discovery what was once taken for granted in Christian feeling. Fanny is one of the poor in spirit. It is not a condition of the soul to which we are nowadays sympathetic. We are likely to suppose that it masks hostility—many modern readers respond to Fanny by suspecting her. This is perhaps not unjustified, but as we try to understand what Jane Austen meant by the creation of such a heroine, we must have in mind the tradition which affirmed the peculiar sanctity of the sick, the weak, and the dying. The tradition perhaps came to an end for literature with the death of Milly Theale, the heroine of Henry James's *The Wings of the Dove,* but Dickens exemplifies its continuing appeal in the nineteenth century, and it was especially strong in the eighteenth century. Clarissa's sickness and death confirm her Christian virtue, and in Fielding's *Amelia,* the novel which may be said to bear the same relation to *Tom Jones* that *Mansfield Park* bears to *Pride and Prejudice,* the sign of the heroine's Christian authority is her loss of health and beauty.

Fanny is a Christian heroine: it is therefore not inappropriate that the issue between her and Mary Crawford should be concentrated in the debate over whether or not Edmund Bertram shall become a clergyman. We are not, however, from our reading of the novel, inclined to say more than that the debate is "not inappropriate"—it startles us to discover that ordination was what Jane Austen said her novel was to be "about." In the letter in which she tells of having received the first copies of *Pride and Prejudice,* and while she is still in high spirits over her achievement, she says, "Now I will try and write something else, and it shall be a complete change of subject— ordination." A novelist, of course, presents a new subject to himself, or to his friends, in all sorts of ways that are inadequate to his real intention as it eventually will disclose itself—the most unsympathetic reader of *Mansfield Park* would scarcely describe it as being about ordination. Yet the question of ordination is of essential importance to the novel.

It is not really a religious question, but, rather, a cultural question, having to do with the meaning and effect of a *profession.* Two senses of that word are in point here, the open avowal of principles and beliefs as well as a man's commitment to a particular kind of life work. It is the latter sense that engages us first. The argument between Fanny and Mary is over what will happen to Edmund as a person, as a *man,* if he chooses to become a clergyman. To Mary, every clergyman is the Mr. Collins of *Pride and Prejudice;* she thinks of ordination as a surrender of manhood. But Fanny sees the Church as a career that claims a man's best manly energies; her expressed view of the churchman's function is that which was to develop through the century, exemplified in, say, Thomas Arnold, who found the Church to be an adequate field for what he called his talents for command.

The matter of a man's profession was of peculiar importance to Jane Austen. It weighs heavily against Mr. Bennet that, his estate being entailed, he has made no effort to secure his family against his death, and by reason of his otiosity he is impotent to protect his family's good name from the consequences of Lydia's sexual escapade. He is represented as being not only less a man but also less a gentleman than his brother-in-law Gardiner, who is in trade in London. Jane Austen's feelings about men in relation to their profession reach their highest intensity in *Persuasion,* in the great comic scene in which Sir Walter Elliot is flattered by Mrs. Clay's telling him that every profession puts its mark upon a man's face, and that a true gentleman will avoid this vulgar injury to his complexion. And in the same novel much is made of the professional pride of the Navy and the good effect it has upon the personal character.

In nineteenth-century England the ideal of professional commitment inherits a large part of the moral prestige of the ideal of the gentleman. Such figures as the engineer Daniel Doyce of *Little Dorrit* or Dr. Lydgate of *Middlemarch* represent the developing belief that a man's moral life is bound up with his loyalty to the discipline of his calling. The concern with the profession was an aspect of the ethical concept which was prepotent in the spiritual life of England in the nineteenth century, the concept of duty. The Church, in its dominant form and characteristic virtue, was here quite at one with the tendency of secular feeling; its preoccupation may be said to have been less with the achievement of salvation than with the performance of duty.

The word grates upon our moral ear. We do what we should do,

but we shrink from giving it the name of duty. "Cooperation,"
"social-mindedness," the "sense of the group," "class solidarity"—
these locutions do not mean what duty means. They have been invented precisely for the purpose of describing right conduct in such
a way as *not* to imply what duty implies—a self whose impulses and
desires are very strong, and a willingness to subordinate these impulses and desires to the claim of some external nonpersonal good.
The new locutions are meant to suggest that right action is typically
to be performed without any pain to the self.

The men of the nineteenth century did not imagine this possibility. They thought that morality was terribly hard to achieve, at the
cost of renunciation and sacrifice. We of our time often wonder
what could have made the difficulty. We wonder, for example, why
a man like Matthew Arnold felt it necessary to remind himself almost every day of duty, why he believed that the impulses must be
"bridled" and "chained down," why he insisted on the "strain and
labour and suffering" of the moral life. We are as much puzzled as
touched by the tone in which F. W. H. Myers tells of walking with
George Eliot in the Fellows' Garden at Trinity "on an evening of
rainy May," and she, speaking of God, Immortality, and Duty, said
how inconceivable was the first, how unbelievable the second, "yet
how peremptory and absolute the third." "Never, perhaps, have
sterner accents affirmed the sovereignty of impersonal and unrecom-
pensing Law. I listened, and night fell; her grave majestic counte-
nance turned towards me like a sybil's in the gloom; it was as
though she withdrew from my grasp, one by one, the two scrolls of
promise, and left me the third scroll only, awful with inevitable
fate."[2]

[2] But if we are puzzled by the tone of this, we cannot say that it is a tone inappropriate to its subject. The idea of duty was central in the English culture of the
nineteenth century, and in general when Englishmen of the period speak about duty
in propria persona they speak movingly. This makes it all the stranger that when they
express the idea through a literary form they scarcely ever do so in an elevated manner. They seem to have thought of duty as an ideal to be associated in literature
chiefly with domestic life or with dullness. As a consequence, everyone was delighted
with the jig in *Ruddigore:* "For duty, duty must be done,/ The rule applies to every-

The diminution of faith in the promise of religion accounts for much but not for all the concern with duty in nineteenth-century England. It was not a crisis of religion that made Wordsworth the laureate of duty. What Wordsworth asks in his great poem "Resolution and Independence" is how the self, in its highest manifestation, in the Poet, can preserve itself from its own nature, from the very sensibility and volatility that define it, from its own potentiality of what Wordsworth calls with superb explicitness "despondency and madness." Something has attenuated the faith in the self of four years before, of "Tintern Abbey," the certitude that "Nature never did betray/The heart that loved her": a new Paraclete is needed and he comes in the shape of the Old Leech Gatherer, a man rocklike in endurance, rocklike in insensibility, annealed by a simple, rigorous religion, preserved in life and in virtue by the "anti-vital element" and transfigured by that element.

That the self may destroy the self by the very energies that define its being, that the self may be preserved by the negation of its own energies—this, whether or not we agree, makes a paradox, makes an irony, that catches our imagination. Much of the nineteenth-century preoccupation with duty was not a love of law for its own sake, but rather a concern with the hygiene of the self. If we are aware of this, we are prepared to take seriously an incident in *Mansfield Park* that on its face is perfectly absurd.

The great fuss that is made over the amateur theatricals can seem to us a mere travesty on virtue. And the more so because it is never made clear why it is so very wrong for young people in a dull coun-

---

one./ Unpleasant though that duty be,/ To shirk the task were fiddledeedee." It was left to foreigners to deal with the idea as if it were of *tragic* import. Melville in *Billy Budd* and Vigny in his military stories exploited the moral possibilities of the British naval tradition of Nelson and Collingwood which even Wordsworth had been able to represent only abstractly and moralistically in his "character" of the Happy Warrior; and Conrad is the first English novelist to make the idea of duty large and interesting. It is hard to believe that the moral idea which Emily Dickinson celebrates in her brilliant poem on Thermopylae and associates with high intelligence is the same idea that Tennyson celebrates in "The Charge of the Light Brigade" and associates with stupidity.

try house to put on a play. The mystery deepens, as does our sense that *Mansfield Park* represents an unusual state of the author's mind, when we know that amateur theatricals were a favorite amusement in Jane Austen's home. The play is Kotzebue's *Lovers' Vows* and it deals with illicit love and a bastard, but Jane Austen, as her letters and novels clearly show, was not a prude. Some of the scenes of the play permit Maria Bertram and Henry Crawford to make love in public, but this is not said to be decisively objectionable. What is decisive is a traditional, almost primitive, feeling about dramatic impersonation. We know of this, of course, from Plato, and it is one of the points on which almost everyone feels superior to Plato, but it may have more basis in actuality than we commonly allow. It is the fear that the impersonation of a bad or inferior character will have a harmful effect upon the impersonator, that, indeed, the impersonation of any other self will diminish the integrity of the real self.

A right understanding of the seemingly absurd episode of the play must dispel any doubt of the largeness of the cultural significance of *Mansfield Park*. The American philosopher George Mead has observed that the "assumption of roles" was one of the most important elements of Romanticism. Mead conceived of impersonation as a new mode of thought appropriate to that new sense of the self which was Romanticism's characteristic achievement. It was, he said further, the self's method of defining itself. Involved as we all are in this mode of thought and in this method of self-definition, we are not likely to respond sympathetically to Jane Austen when she puts it under attack as being dangerous to the integrity of the self as a moral agent. Yet the testimony of John Keats stands in her support—in one of his most notable letters Keats says of the poet that, as poet, he cannot be a moral agent; he has no "character," no "self," no "identity"; he is concerned not with moral judgment but with "gusto," subordinating his own being to that of the objects of his creative regard. Wordsworth implies something of a related sort when he contrasts the poet's volatility of mood with the bulking permanence of identity of the Old Leech Gatherer. And of course not only the poet but the reader may be said to be involved in the problems of identity and of (in the literal sense) integrity. Literature offers the experience of the diversification of the self, and Jane Austen puts the question of literature at the moral center of her novel.

The massive ado that is organized about the amateur theatricals and the dangers of impersonation thus has a direct bearing upon the matter of Edmund Bertram's profession. The election of a profession is of course in a way the assumption of a role, but it is a permanent impersonation which makes virtually impossible the choice of another. It is a commitment which fixes the nature of the self.

The ado about the play extends its significance still further. It points, as it were, to a great and curious triumph of Jane Austen's art. The triumph consists in this—that although on a first reading of *Mansfield Park* Mary Crawford's speeches are all delightful, they diminish in charm as we read the novel a second time. We begin to hear something disagreeable in their intonation: it is the peculiarly modern bad quality which Jane Austen was the first to represent—insincerity. This is a trait very different from the *hypocrisy* of the earlier novelists. Mary Crawford's intention is not to deceive the world but to comfort herself; she impersonates the woman she thinks she ought to be. And as we become inured to the charm of her performance we see through the moral impersonation and are troubled that it should have been thought necessary. In Mary Crawford we have the first brilliant example of a distinctively modern type, the person who cultivates the *style* of sensitivity, virtue, and intelligence.

Henry Crawford has more sincerity than his sister, and the adverse judgment which the novel makes on him is therefore arrived at with greater difficulty. He is conscious of his charm, of the winningness of his personal style, which has in it—as he knows—a large element of *natural* goodness and generosity. He is no less conscious of his lack of weight and solidity; his intense courtship of Fanny is, we may say, his effort to add the gravity of principle to his merely natural goodness. He becomes, however, the prey to his own charm, and in his cold flirtation with Maria Bertram he is trapped by his impersonation of passion—his role requires that he carry Maria off from a dull marriage to a life of boring concupiscence. It is his sister's refusal to attach any moral importance to this event that is the final proof of her deficiency in seriousness. Our modern impulse to resist the condemnation of sexuality and of sexual liberty cannot properly come into play here, as at first we think it should. For it is not sexuality that is being condemned, but precisely that form of asexuality that incurred D. H. Lawrence's greatest scorn—that is, sexuality as a game, or as a drama, sexuality as an expression of mere will or mere personality, as a sign of power, or prestige, or autonomy: as, in short, an impersonation and an insincerity.

A passage in one of her letters of 1814, written while *Mansfield Park* was in composition, enforces upon us how personally Jane Austen was involved in the question of principle as against personality, of character as against style. A young man has been paying court to her niece Fanny Knight, and the girl is troubled by, exactly, the effect of his principledness on his style. Her aunt's comment is especially interesting because it contains an avowal of sympathy with Evangelicism, an opinion which is the reverse of that which she had expressed in a letter of 1809 and had represented in *Pride and Prejudice,* yet the religious opinion is but incidental to the affirmation that is being made of the moral advantage of the profession of principle, whatever may be its effect on the personal style.

Mr. J. P. —— has advantages which do not often meet in one person. His only fault indeed seems Modesty. If he were less modest, he would be more agreeable, speak louder & look Impudenter;—and is it not a fine Character of which Modesty is the only defect?—I have no doubt that he will get more lively & more like yourselves as he is more with you;—he will catch your ways if he belongs to you. And as to there being any objection from his *Goodness,* from the danger of his becoming even Evangelical, I cannot admit *that.* I am by no means convinced that we ought not all to be Evangelicals, & am at least persuaded that they who are so from Reason and Feeling, must be happiest & safest. Do not be frightened from the connection by your Brothers having most wit. Wisdom is better than Wit, & in the long run will certainly have the laugh on her side; & don't be frightened by the idea of his acting more strictly up to the precepts of the New Testament than others.

The great charm, the charming greatness, of *Pride and Prejudice* is that it permits us to conceive of morality as style. The relation of Elizabeth Bennet to Darcy is real, is intense, but it expresses itself as a conflict and reconciliation of styles: a formal rhetoric, traditional and rigorous, must find a way to accommodate a female vivacity, which in turn must recognize the principled demands of the strict male syntax. The high moral import of the novel lies in the fact that the union of styles is accomplished without injury to either lover.

Jane Austen knew that *Pride and Prejudice* was a unique success and she triumphed in it. Yet as she listens to her mother reading aloud from the printed book, she becomes conscious of her dissatisfaction with one element of the work. It is the element that is likely to delight us most, the purity and absoluteness of its particular style.

The work [she writes in a letter to her sister Cassandra] is rather too light, and bright, and sparkling; it wants to be stretched out here and there with a long chapter of sense, if it could be had; if not, of solemn specious nonsense, about something unconnected with the story; an essay on writing, a critique on Walter Scott, or the history of Buonaparté, or anything that would form a contrast, and bring the reader with increased delight to the playfulness and epigrammatism of the general style.

Her overt concern, of course, is for the increase of the effect of the "general style" itself, which she believes would have been heightened by contrast. But she has in mind something beyond this technical improvement—her sense that the novel is a genre that must not try for the shining outward perfection of style; that it must maintain a degree of roughness of texture, a certain hard literalness; that, for the sake of its moral life, it must violate its own beauty by incorporating some of the irreducible prosy actuality of the world. It is as if she were saying of *Pride and Prejudice* what Henry James says of one of the characters of his story "Crapy Cornelia": "Her grace of ease was perfect, but it was all grace of ease, not a single shred of it grace of uncertainty or of difficulty."[3]

Mansfield Park, we may conceive, was the effort to encompass the grace of uncertainty and difficulty. The idea of morality as achieved style, as grace of ease, is not likely ever to be relinquished, not merely because some writers will always assert it anew, but also because morality itself will always insist on it—at a certain point in its development, morality seeks to express its independence of the grinding necessity by which it is engendered, and to claim for itself the autonomy and gratuitousness of art. Yet the idea is one that may easily deteriorate or be perverted. Style, which expresses the innermost truth of any creation or action, can also hide the truth; it is in this sense of the word that we speak of "mere style." *Mansfield Park* proposes to us the possibility of this deception. If we perceive this, we cannot say that the novel is without irony—we must say, indeed, that its irony is more profound than that of any of Jane Austen's other novels. It is an irony directed against irony itself.

In the investigation of the question of character as against personality, of principle as against style and grace of ease as against

---

3 This may be the place to remark that although the direct line of descent from Jane Austen to Henry James has often been noted, and although there can be no doubt of the lineage, James had a strange misconception of the nature of the art of his ancestress. "Jane Austen, with her light felicity," he says in *The Lesson of Balzac,* "leaves us hardly more curious of her process, or of the experience that fed it, than the brown thrush who tells his story from the garden bough." He says of her reputation that it is higher than her intrinsic interest and attributes it to "the body of publishers, editors, illustrators, producers of the present twaddle of magazines, who have found their 'dear,' our dear, everybody's dear, Jane so infinitely to their material purpose." An acid response to the "dear Jane" myth is always commendable, but it seems to have led James into a strange obtuseness: "The key to Jane Austen's fortune with posterity has been in part the extraordinary grace of her facility, in part of her unconsciousness . . ." This failure of perception (and syntax) is followed by a long, ambiguous, and unfortunate metaphor of Jane Austen musing over her "work-basket, her tapestry flowers, in the spare, cool drawing room of other days." Jane Austen was, it need scarcely be said at this date, as little unconscious as James himself either in her intentions or (as the remarks about the style of *Pride and Prejudice* show) in her "process."

grace of difficulty, it is an important consideration that the Craw-
fords are of London. Their manner is the London manner, their
style is the *chic* of the metropolis. The city bears the brunt of our
modern uneasiness about our life. We think of it as being the scene
and the cause of the loss of the simple integrity of the spirit—in our
dreams of our right true selves we live in the country. This common
mode of criticism of our culture is likely to express not merely our
dissatisfaction with our particular cultural situation but our dislike
of culture itself, or of any culture that is not a folk culture, that is
marked by the conflict of interests and the proliferation and conflict
of ideas. Yet the revulsion from the metropolis cannot be regarded
merely with skepticism; it plays too large and serious a part in our
literature to be thought of as nothing but a sentimentality.

To the style of London Sir Thomas Bertram is the principled an-
tagonist. The real reason for not giving the play, as everyone knows,
is that Sir Thomas would not permit it were he at home; everyone
knows that a sin is being committed against the absent father. And
Sir Thomas, when he returns before his expected time, confirms
their consciousness of sin. It is he who identifies the objection to the
theatricals as being specifically that of impersonation. His own self
is an integer and he instinctively resists the diversification of the self
that is implied by the assumption of roles. It is he, in his entire
identification with his status and tradition, who makes of Mansfield
Park the citadel it is—it exists to front life and to repel life's mu-
tabilities, like the Peele Castle of Wordsworth's "Elegiac Verses," of
which it is said that it is "cased in the unfeeling armor of old time."
In this phrase Wordsworth figures in a very precise way the Stoic
doctrine of *apatheia,* the principled refusal to experience more emotion than is forced upon one, the rejection of sensibility as a danger
to the integrity of the self.

Mansfield stands not only against London but also against what
is implied by Portsmouth on Fanny's visit to her family there.
Fanny's mother, Lady Bertram's sister, had made an unprosperous
marriage, and the Bertrams' minimal effort to assist her with the

burdens of a large family had been the occasion of Fanny's coming to live at Mansfield nine years before. Her return to take her place in a home not of actual poverty but of respectable sordidness makes one of the most engaging episodes of the novel, despite our impulse to feel that it ought to seem the most objectionable. We think we ought not be sympathetic with Fanny as, to her slow dismay, she understands that she cannot be happy with her own, her natural, family. She is made miserable by the lack of cleanliness and quiet, of civility and order. We jib at this, we remind ourselves that for the seemliness that does indeed sustain the soul, men too often sell their souls, that warmth and simplicity of feeling may go with indifference to disorder. But if we have the most elementary honesty, we feel with Fanny the genuine pain not merely of the half-clean and the scarcely tidy, of confusion and intrusion, but also of the vulgarity that thrives in these surroundings. It is beyond human ingenuity to define what we mean by vulgarity, but in Jane Austen's novels vulgarity has these elements: smallness of mind, insufficiency of awareness, assertive self-esteem, the wish to devalue, especially to devalue the human worth of other people. That Fanny's family should have forgotten her during her long absence was perhaps inevitable; it is a vulgarity that they have no curiosity about her and no desire to revive the connection, and this indifference is represented as being of a piece with the general indecorum of their lives. We do not blame Fanny when she remembers that in her foster father's house there are many rooms, that hers, although it was small and for years it had been cold, had always been clean and private, that now, although she had once been snubbed and slighted at Mansfield, she is the daughter of Sir Thomas's stern heart.

Of all the fathers of Jane Austen's novels, Sir Thomas is the only one to whom admiration is given. Fanny's real father, Lieutenant Price of the Marines, is shallow and vulgar. The fathers of the heroines of *Pride and Prejudice, Emma,* and *Persuasion,* all lack principle and fortitude; they are corrupted by their belief in their delicate vulnerability—they lack *apatheia*. Yet Sir Thomas is a father, and a father is as little safe from Jane Austen's judgment as he is from Shelley's. Jane Austen's masculine ideal is exemplified by husbands, by Darcy, Knightley, and Wentworth, in whom principle and duty consort with a ready and tender understanding. Sir Thomas's faults are dealt with explicitly—if he learns to cherish Fanny as the daughter of his heart, he betrays the daughters of his blood. Maria's sin and her sister Julia's bad disposition are blamed directly upon his lack of intelligence and sensibility. His principled submission to convention had issued in mere worldliness—he had not seen to it that "principle, active principle" should have its place in the rearing of his daughters, had not given them that "sense of duty which alone can suffice" to govern inclination and temper. He knew of no other way to counteract the low worldly flattery of their Aunt Norris than by the show of that sternness which had alienated them from him. He has allowed Mrs. Norris, the corrupter of his daughters and the persecutor of Fanny, to establish herself in the governance of his home; "she seemed part of himself."

So that Mansfield is governed by an authority all too fallible. Yet Fanny thinks of all that comes "within the view and patronage of Mansfield Park" as "dear to her heart and thoroughly perfect in her eyes." The judgment is not ironical. For the author as well as for the heroine, Mansfield Park is the good place—it is The Great Good Place. It is the house "where all's accustomed, ceremonious," of Yeats's "Prayer for His Daughter"—

> How but in custom and ceremony
> Are innocence and beauty born?

Yet Fanny's loving praise of Mansfield, which makes the novel's last word, does glance at ironies and encompasses ironies. Of these ironies the chief is that Lady Bertram is part of the perfection. All of Mansfield's life makes reference and obeisance to Sir Thomas's wife, who is gentle and without spite, but mindless and moveless, concerned with nothing but the indulgence of her mild, inexorable wants. Middle-aged, stupid, maternal persons are favorite butts for

Jane Austen, but although Lady Bertram is teased, she is loved. Sir Thomas's authority must be qualified and tutored by the principled intelligence, the religious intelligence—Fanny's, in effect—but Lady Bertram is permitted to live unregenerate her life of cushioned ease.

I am never quite able to resist the notion that in her attitude to Lady Bertram Jane Austen is teasing herself, that she is turning her irony upon her own fantasy of ideal existence as it presented itself to her at this time. It is scarcely possible to observe how *Mansfield Park* differs from her work that had gone before and from her work that was to come after without supposing that the difference points to a crisis in the author's spiritual life. In that crisis fatigue plays a great part—we are drawn to believe that for the moment she wants to withdraw from the exigent energies of her actual self, that she claims in fancy the right to be rich and fat and smooth and dull like Lady Bertram, to sit on a cushion, to be a creature of habit and an object of ritual deference, not to be conscious, especially not to be conscious of herself. Lady Bertram is, we may imagine, her mocking representation of her wish to escape from the requirements of personality.

It was Jane Austen who first represented the specifically modern personality and the culture in which it had its being. Never before had the moral life been shown as she shows it to be, never before had it been conceived to be so complex and difficult and exhausting. Hegel speaks of the "secularization of spirituality" as a prime characteristic of the modern epoch, and Jane Austen is the first to tell us what this involves. She is the first novelist to represent society, the general culture, as playing a part in the moral life, generating the concepts of "sincerity" and "vulgarity" which no earlier time would have understood the meaning of, and which for us are so subtle that they defy definition, and so powerful that none can escape their sovereignty. She is the first to be aware of the Terror which rules our moral situation, the ubiquitous anonymous judgment to which we respond, the necessity we feel to demonstrate the purity of our secular spirituality, whose dark and dubious places are more numerous and obscure than those of religious spirituality, to put our lives and styles to the question, making sure that not only in deeds but in *décor* they exhibit the signs of our belonging to the number of the secular-spiritual elect.

She herself is an agent of the Terror—we learn from her what our lives should be and by what subtle and fierce criteria they will be judged, and how to pass upon the lives of our friends and fellows. Once we have comprehended her mode of judgment, the moral and spiritual lessons of contemporary literature are easy—the metaphysics of "sincerity" and "vulgarity" once mastered, the modern teachers, Lawrence and Joyce, Yeats and Eliot, Proust and Gide, have but little to add save in the way of contemporary and abstruse examples.

To what extremes the Terror can go she herself has made all too clear in the notorious passage in *Persuasion* in which she comments on Mrs. Musgrove's "large, fat sighings" over her dead scapegrace son. "Personal size and mental sorrow have certainly no necessary proportions," she says. "A large bulky figure has as good a right to be in deep affliction as the most graceful set of limbs in the world. But fair or not fair, there are unbecoming conjunctions, which reason will patronize in vain—which taste cannot tolerate, which ridicule will seize." We feel this to be unconscionable, and Henry James and E. M. Forster will find occasion to warn us that it is one of the signs of the death of the heart to regard a human being as an object of greater or less *vertu;* in fairness to Jane Austen we must remember that the passage occurs in the very novel which deals mercilessly with Sir Walter Elliot for making just this illegitimate application of taste to life. But although this aesthetic-spiritual snobbery is for Jane Austen a unique lapse, it is an extension, an extravagance of her characteristic mode of judgment, and it leads us to see what is implied by the "secularization of spirituality," which requires of us that we judge not merely the moral act itself but also, and even more searchingly, the quality of the agent. This is what Hegel has in mind when he is at such pains to make his distinction between character and personality and to show how the development of the idea of personality is one of the elements of the secularization of spirituality. Dewey followed Hegel in this when, in his *Ethics*, he said that moral choice is not really dictated by the principle or the maxim that is applicable to the situation but rather by the "kind of selfhood" one wishes to "assume." And Nietzsche's conception of the Third Morality, which takes cognizance of the *real*—that is, the unconscious—intention of the agent, is the terrible instrument of criticism of this new development of the moral life. We are likely to feel that this placing of the personality, of the quality of being, at the center of the moral life is a chief glory of spirit in its modern manifestation, and when we take pleasure in Jane Austen we are responding to her primacy and brilliance in the exercise of this new mode of judgment. Yet we at times become aware of the terrible strain it imposes upon us, of the exhausting effort which the concept of personality requires us to make and of the pain of exacerbated sensitivity to others, leading to the *disgust* which is endemic in our culture.

Jane Austen's primacy in representing this mutation in the life of the spirit constitutes a large part of her claim to greatness. But in her representation of the modern situation *Mansfield Park* has a special place. It imagines the self safe from the Terror of secularized spirituality. In the person of Lady Bertram it affirms, with all due irony, the bliss of being able to remain unconscious of the demands of personality (it is a bliss which is a kind of virtue, for one way of being solid, simple, and sincere is to be a vegetable). It shuts out the world and the judgment of the world. The sanctions upon which it relies are not those of culture, of quality of being, of personality, but precisely those which the new conception of the moral life minimizes, the sanctions of principle, and it discovers in principle the path to the wholeness of the self which is peace. When we have exhausted our anger at the offense which *Mansfield Park* offers to our conscious pieties, we find it possible to perceive how intimately it speaks to our secret inexpressible hopes.

Author's Note

"The Poet as Hero" was written as the introduction to *The Selected Letters of John Keats* (The Great Letters Series, edited by Louis Kronenberger; New York: Farrar, Straus and Young, 1951).

The essay on *Little Dorrit* was written as the introduction to the edition of the novel in the New Oxford Illustrated Dickens (London: Geoffrey Cumberlege, Oxford University Press, 1953). It was published in *Kenyon Review*, Autumn, 1953.

The essay on *Anna Karenina* was written as the introduction to the Limited Editions Club edition of the novel (Cambridge, England: 1951).

The essay on *The Bostonians* was written as the introduction to the Chiltern Library edition of the novel (London: John Lehmann, 1953).

"Wordsworth and the Rabbis" was read at the celebration of the centenary of Wordsworth's death which was held at Princeton University on April 21 and 22, 1950. It was published, with a different title ("Wordsworth and the Iron Time"), in *Wordsworth: Centenary Studies Presented at Cornell and Princeton Universities,* edited by Gilbert T. Dunklin (Princeton, N.J.: Princeton University Press, 1951). By permission of the Princeton University Press it was also published in *Kenyon Review,* Summer, 1950.

"George Orwell and the Politics of Truth" was written as the introduction to George Orwell's *Homage to Catalonia* (New York: Harcourt, Brace and Company, 1952). It was first published in *Commentary,* March, 1952.

"William Dean Howells and the Roots of Modern Taste" was written as a lecture given at Harvard University in 1951. It was first published in *Partisan Review,* September–October, 1951.

"Flaubert's Last Testament" was written as the introduction to *Bou-*

vard and Pécuchet, translated by E. W. Stonier and T. W. Earp (Norfolk, Conn.: New Directions, 1954). It was first published in *Partisan Review,* November–December, 1953.

The essay on *Mansfield Park* was written as the chapter on Jane Austen for the fifth volume of the *Pelican Guide to English Literature,* edited by Boris Ford. It was first published in *Partisan Review,* September–October, 1954.

From Tradition to Political Reality

STUDIES IN BRITISH HISTORY AND CULTURE

VOLUME VII

From Tradition to Political Reality

*A Study of the Ideas Set Forth in
Support of the Commonwealth
Government in England,
1649-1653*

by
MARGARET A. JUDSON

Published for
The Conference on British Studies and Wittenberg University
by ARCHON BOOKS

Library of Congress Cataloging in Publication Data

Judson, Margaret Atwood, 1899-
   From tradition to political reality.

   (Studies in British history and culture ; 7)
   Bibliography: p.
   Includes index.
   1. Great Britain—Politics and government—
1649-1660. 2. England—Intellectual life—17th
century. I. Title. II. Series.
DA425.J84   320.9′41′063   79-20978
ISBN 0-208-01836-0

First published 1980 as an Archon Book,
an imprint of The Shoe String Press, Inc.,
Hamden, Connecticut
for
The Conference on British Studies
and
Wittenberg University
Springfield, Ohio

Printed in the United States of America

CONTENTS

FOREWORD

Studies in British History and Culture was founded in January, 1965, as a joint publishing venture of the Conference on British Studies and the University of Bridgeport; Stephen Graubard and Leland Miles were the Senior Editors, and the New York University Press was printer. Three volumes were published in the series under this arrangement, the last being in 1970. A five year hiatus then occurred when the University of Bridgeport decided that it could no longer fund the series. Fortunately, Wittenberg University volunteered to become copublisher with the conference and with Archon Books. Since that time the series has published three books.

The intention of the conference and the editors in establishing the monograph series was to publish works of vigorous research, original interpretation, and literary grace which fell between the regular article and the full length book. The editors were especially seeking works which would challenge traditional viewpoints or advance new theses and works which would integrate particular events with larger themes.

In this seventh volume of the series, Margaret Judson discusses many of the arguments put forward in defense of the Commonwealth between 1649 and 1653. She passes by some of the men best known in our own day such as Hobbes, Harrington, Milton, Winstanley, Vane, and Martin in order to concentrate on another group, less well known to us but famous in their own time. Such men included Marchamont Nedham, Henry Parker, Anthony Ascham, John Dury, John Owen, and Ephraim Elcock. Some of these writers began by relying on the Bible. It was not difficult for them to find texts in the Old Testament to prove that God the Father disliked monarchy, or texts in the New to prove that St. Paul believed in obedience to the higher powers. Such arguments were fleshed out with references to English Puritan divines and also to a few Dutch thinkers, notably Grotius. Quite soon, however, more secular arguments were resorted to. There was of course a general desire for peace and survival. Might not the present government be in power as the result of God's providence? From this it was not very far to the position of defending the government in possession, without any theological flourishes. Appeals could also be made to an age-old English commonwealth, which had survived many different regimens without any essential change. And from such arguments it was not very much further to a defense of the present government on grounds of personal security and private advantage. These were the seventeenth-century equivalents of "the best Prime Minister we have" and "you never had it so good" positions of recent years. Between 1649 and 1653, therefore, political thought took giant strides towards the purely secular approach that is characteristic of modern times. Professor Judson's interesting thesis will encourage many students to read for themselves the Thomason Tracts, now available on microfilm.

Stephen Baxter
Leland Miles
Senior Editors

PREFACE

The research for this study began in the summer of 1952 when I read a number of the Thomason Tracts in the British Library, which were published after the execution of Charles I in 1649. I was surprised to discover, in addition to royalist and radical authors, a number of writers who set forth both traditional and more modern pragmatic ideas to justify the Rump government. Since historians and political scientists had at that time paid little attention to these ideas, I decided to explore them further.

I wish to express my appreciation to the Guggenheim Foundation for the fellowship which enabled me in 1954 to carry on a substantial part of the research for this book. I am also indebted to the Rutgers Research Council which, since my retirement in 1967, has supported the work necessary to complete this study and has provided generous financial assistance toward its publication. I wish to thank the Alexander Library of Rutgers University, which has provided me with a study in which to work.

The staff of that library, and also the staffs of the British Library, the Folger and Union Theological libraries, as well as the Harvard, Yale, and Princeton libraries, have graciously assisted me in my work.

In the text spelling, punctuation, use of capitals, and dating of these seventeenth-century tracts have been modernized. In the footnotes and bibliography I have kept the dating given on the tract itself.

Highland Park, New Jersey   M. A. J.
Oct. 1979

INTRODUCTION

The trial and execution of Charles I stunned most Englishmen and sent shock waves through European capitals. Yet these revolutionary actions did not bring in an entirely new government nor one which rested upon a revolutionary ideology. The Levellers with their democratic ideas never came to power, and the republican members of the Rump government, few in number, particularly in the first year of the Commonwealth, were primarily concerned with demonstrating that government could actually function without a monarch at its head.

Although the government lacked any one firm ideological base, there were a number of men who used pen or pulpit to explain and justify it to the people. For many years scholars interested in the political ideas set forth between 1649 and 1653 concentrated their attention upon Hobbes, the English giant among political theorists, whose *Leviathan* appeared in 1651; or upon the continuing Leveller and emerging Digger thought; or upon Milton's prose tracts justifying and exalting Charles's execution and denouncing monarchy. Because of his fame and official position,[1] Milton was once regarded, particularly by literary scholars, as the government's main defender. However, any careful reader of the Thomason

Collection in the British Library could discover in those numerous contemporary tracts that the Rump government was justified and defended by a broad spectrum of ideas set forth by known and unknown preachers and pamphleteers. For a long time these ideas remained largely unnoticed by scholars.

In recent years, however, some of these ideas have been brought to light and their significance pointed out, first by Perez Zagorin[2] and more recently by John Wallace[3] and Quentin Skinner.[4] As a historian long concerned with constitutional and political ideas in seventeenth-century England, I hope to contribute another chapter to complement those which these historians have written.[5]

The ideas set forth in defense of the Rump government between February 1649 and its expulsion in April 1653 constitute an illuminating chapter in intellectual history in a transitional period. In these few years defenders of the regime set forth both old and new approaches to human society and its government. The Scriptures were not forgotten. In the forties they had provided ammunition for Puritan preachers urging revolutionary action against Charles's government. In 1649 and succeeding years, the tables were turned as many preachers and pamphleteers quoted scriptural endorsement for the "powers that be." More importantly, writers called attention to the many recent manifestations of God's providence. Did providence not proclaim clearly that God Himself was founder and protector of this government? And should not man respond by cooperating with God and thus playing his part here and now "in his own generation"?

If religious arguments played their part in the defense of the government, so did those which were secular. It was the secular questions writers asked and answered in this period of the Puritan Revolution which, looking to the future, were the most significant. With the abolition of the monarchy, so indispensable in earlier constitutional and political thinking in England, some writers now asked if England still remained a viable community to which Englishmen of different creeds and ideologies now owed allegiance. To answer this critical question, writers insisted that the age-old commonwealth of England lived on, although without the monarch, its traditional head. The way in which some writers pointed out and developed this concept of England as a cohesive community now existing on its own, discussed in chapter 3, is a major thesis of this study.

Writers also asked searching questions concerning the actual government which existed and functioned before their eyes. Could men ignore this reality? Did they owe their allegiance to the government in possession, or must they remain faithful to solemn oaths which earlier had been given the king? And if they did owe allegiance to this government, how could it be justified? The more philosophically minded writers went further, asking what were the essential values to man and his earthly interests of government per se.

Such searching questions had been asked earlier by greater thinkers than these preachers and pamphleteers, but what is significant is that so many writers were raising them during those critical years between 1649 and 1653. The objective of chapters 4 and 5 is to examine these more modern, essentially pragmatic ideas concerning government set forth at this particular time when a struggle for the minds of men was going on. In that battle of words a new climate of political thinking emerged which in the future increasingly would enter into the way political thinkers analyzed government as such. A consideration of this new climate of thought is therefore the other main thesis of this study.

In addition to these major theses, the long-standing conventional religious ideas, considered in chapter 2, afford the intellectual historian an opportunity to see in sharp relief over a short period of time the range of ideas which were set forth in support of this particular government.

It is essential then to examine this government, its composition, its policies, and its achievements. For too long this government, in particular its domestic policies and its internal politics, has been given insufficient attention, even by Gardiner. Now, however, owing to the work of Ivan Roots, David Underdown, Blair Worden, and Gerald Aylmer,[6] the Commonwealth government has been portrayed and analyzed so carefully that it cannot be ignored or passed over quickly as a mere prelude to Cromwell's Protectorate. These contemporary historians have given us a detailed and convincing treatment of a period which long baffled historians because of their preconceptions and also because of the scarcity of primary sources available for its study.

Now much more is known about the members of the Commons and council who shaped governmental policy. Many, perhaps most, of these men were not radically different in their social background, their education at university and inn of court, even in their earlier experience in county or town government, from other members of the Long Parliament elected in the forties. Those who remained in the Commons after Pride's Purge (some of whom signed Charles's death warrant) were not the "scum of the earth" as their enemies liked to portray them.[7] Moreover, between February and August 1649, many members who had voluntarily stayed away returned to their seats, thus strengthening the moderate composition of the Commons. As Worden aptly says, "Most Rumpers, like most members of the Long Parliament of the 1640's, belonged to the ship money generation." They too wished above all "order, peace, plenty, protection of property rights, exclusion of central government from local affairs."[8] Although they had carried out a political revolution, the majority of them certainly did not desire extensive and disruptive social changes in England.

The Rumpers can no longer be classified simply as Independents who had won out over the Presbyterians. According to Worden, "there were at least as many rumpers whom we can confidently describe as religious presbyterians as there were rumpers who were clearly religious independents or sectaries."[9] It was the republican Henry Martin himself who, commenting upon Walker's charges against the Independents and Cromwell, wrote:

> It is clear to me that a whole Parliament can have no plot at all: they are so numerous and mingled in temper and education, age and interests, that so great a party as he [i.e., Walker] calls Independents could not drive on any project of that bulk, so long a brewing, with secrecy sufficient for such an enterprise.[10]

In short, the Rump government was made up of men with widely different views. If republicans like Martin, Ludlow, and the Chaloner brothers were there, so also were lawyers like St. John and Whitelocke who believed fundamentally in mixed monarchy.

The policies pursued by this government can best be characterized as pragmatic. Above all, the Rump was determined that despite Charles's execution a functioning government carry on without interruption. The many Englishmen fervently desiring peace needed to be convinced that without a monarch or House of Lords, the Commons and its appointed council could actually rule the country. As different problems arose the government reacted to them and handled them one by one. In reading today the *Journals of the House of Commons*, the *Calendar of State Papers Domestic*, or the *Acts and Ordiances* for this period, one is struck by the attention given to whatever needed to be done at the moment, rather than by any long-range planning—revolutionary or otherwise. At times the reader of these sources could easily believe that he was following records for an earlier period.

For this government to remain in control of England it needed to meet the threats to its security, and until after Worcester in September 1651, there were many. At home, numerous royalist plots needed to be discovered and prevented. The Levellers needed once and for all to be crushed. Presbyterian preachers, who used the pulpit to defy the government, had to be silenced. If Ireland lent itself to royalist plots, Cromwell and his army needed to end this dangerous threat to the Commonwealth as quickly as possible. When Scotland rallied around Prince Charles, it too needed to be invaded to provide the necessary security for the Commonwealth. The Commons themselves declared in September 1649:

> The great work we have first to do, is to establish the being and safety of the Commonwealth upon sure foundations, which are undermined by more enemies than are visible to all. This provided for, we shall not be wanting daily to remove or add what shall be for the well-being of it, either in conveniency or ornament . . .[11]

In carrying on a functioning government within England and in meeting the threats to its security, the leaders of the government were more concerned to increase its support at home than to satisfy the more radical members pushing for far-reaching and immediate reforms.[12] According to Worden, Cromwell himself for quite a time recognized that it was necessary to pursue moderate policies in order to secure a broad base of support.[13] As early as 8 February 1649, the House declared that they were "fully resolved to maintain the fundamental laws of this nation for the good of the people."[14] In their declaration of 17 March 1649, they explained again in greater detail that they had appointed judges and were determined to keep both the central courts at Westminster and those on circuit functioning.[15] Although the new government had killed the king, abolished monarchy, and done away with the House of Lords, the Commons, whose members survived the Purge, had been legally elected in the forties. They still remained, and so did the laws and the sytem of courts. The government and some of its supporters liked to point out the legality or quasi-legality of their position.[16]

This government, however, was wise enough not to dash completely the radical and utopian hopes of some of its own members and supporters. In a number of official declarations and public thanksgivings they spoke of carrying on the work of the Lord for his chosen people, and proclaimed that they would turn England into a land where justice and happiness would prevail and tyranny and oppression would be abolished forever.[17]

In addition to broadening its base of support, this Commonwealth government used many other means to ensure that it remain in power. In the first place, the Rump passed three acts declaring unequivocally that the Commons were supreme. The fact that members had been purged and no new elections held did not deter the Rump from asserting its own supremacy. On 4 January, after the Purge but before the king's trial, the resolution was passed "that the Commons of England, in Parliament assembled, do declare that the people are under God the original of all just power." The same act also stated "that the Commons of England, in Parliament assembled, being chosen by, and representing the people, have the supreme power in this nation."[18] In the act of 19 May 1649 declaring England a Commonwealth, "the supreme authority of this nation" was again stated to be "the representatives of the people in Parliament."[19] The Treason Act of 14 May 1649 spelled out specifically:

> that if any person shall maliciously or advisedly publish by writing, printing, or openly declaring that the said government is tyrannical, usurped or unlawful; or that the Commons in Parliament assembled are not the supreme authority of this nation; or shall plot, contrive, or endeavor to stir up or raise force against the present government, or for the subversion or alteration of the same, and shall declare the same by any open deed, that then every such offence shall be taken, deemed and adjudged, by the authority of this Parliament, to be high treason.[20]

Even before the first act of treason was passed five royalists,

Hamilton, Holland, Norwich, Capel, and Owen, were tried and three of them executed. The government was determined to show that royalist resistance would not be allowed. In the first months of the new government, the Levellers presented the most dangerous threat to it. New Leveller pamphlets appeared, local unrest encouraged by the Levellers broke out, and in late April the army Levellers mutinied. Their revolt was crushed in May at Burford by the army under Cromwell. Although the Levellers continued to cause trouble for the new government, they no longer constituted a major threat to its existence. The Presbyterians always presented a problem to the government and their ministers were sought out and punished. In May 1651 three important Presbyterian ministers, Love, Jenkins, and Case, were accused of plotting against the government and were arrested and tried. On 22 August Love was executed. According to Worden, this broke the back of clerical opposition to the Rump.[21]

Joseph Frank has shown how the government increased its control over the press. Although "the story of censorship was inconsistent," Frank states that "by mid-October [1649] every licensed London newspaper had been silenced, many of them forever. Thereafter, except for a few fitful months, a relatively free weekly press was, if not dead, moribund."[22] The most important journalist the government secured to champion its own cause was Marchamont Nedham, one of the editors of the royalist *Mercurius Pragmaticus*. For a handsome consideration, Nedham changed his spots and in May 1650 came forth with his *Case of the Commonwealth of England Stated*.[23] Within a few weeks the first issue of *Mercurius Politicus* appeared. In this influential newsletter Nedham cleverly inserted, along with the news, many of the ideas he had set forth in the *Case of the Commonwealth*.

The most controversial and hotly debated means employed by the Rump to secure loyal officials, preachers, scholars, and citizens was the famous engagement. It was eventually decided that a promise to be faithful to the Rump government had to be cast in purely secular terms without reference to God, king, or the legitimacy of the Rump. In the latter days of February 1649, members of the council were required to promise that they would be faithful to the existing government. In October other important officials—members of Parliament, judges, lawyers, university officials and fellows, many ministers, and other prominent officers or citizens—were required to "subscribe" the engagement. Finally, on 2 January 1650 the Rump passed an act requiring that every male aged eighteen or over "do declare and promise that I will be faithful to the Commonwealth of England, as it is now established, without a King or House of Lords."[24]

The word "oath," obviously with a religious connotation, is not used in the relevant material concerning the engagement in the *Journals of the House of Commons* nor in the act of January 1650. Men are asked to declare or promise to be faithful to or to "subscribe" the engagement.[25] The engagement was cast in purely secular terms and asked loyalty only to a de facto government. Needing wide-based support, the government was obviously endeavoring to make a declaration of loyalty as easy as possible for people of different persuasions, conservatives and moderates as well as radicals. The government must have hoped that men who had formerly sworn an oath of loyalty to the king could "subscribe" the secular engagement without having a troubled conscience.[26] It should be noted that a number of the arguments writers advanced in support of the engagement were primarily secular in nature.

Although royalists, Levellers, some Presbyterians, and many others were distressed about the different means used by the Rump to maintain itself in power, the solid accomplishments of the government, especially in its first two years, deserve more attention than some earlier historians gave them.[27] Too often these historians viewed this government through their own democratic or republican eyes or were looking for social change. Because the Commonwealth government did not measure up to their expectations they pointed out (rightly, to be sure) that the government was an oligarchy desirous only of perpetuating itself in power, stubbornly refusing to allow new, more democratic elections, and failing to achieve important reforms in religion, the laws, or in society in general. These historians dwelt upon the cruel treatment of Ireland without always explaining Ireland's threat to the Rump's very existence.

However, the government clearly performed reasonably well those basic functions which any government, whatever its nature or ideology, should provide. After years of civil war with the resulting breakdown of established institutions and patterns of life in town and country, this Rump government was bringing a measure of peace to a war torn land, thus preserving an England which could still claim men's loyalties. Interesting as Leveller and Digger demands and ideas are to us in the twentieth century, those revolutionary ideas and demands threatened to undo that peace which Englishmen of differing social strata so fervently desired.

Under the Rump government the courts soon began to function as judges again went on circuit. Whitelocke stated "that the Judges of Assizes had much settled the people's minds as to the present government in their charges to the grand juries."[28] Men felt more secure about their property holdings. Not only did this government for the most part keep the peace at home and bring about a partial return to prewar conditions, but it met even more successfully the threats to its security from Ireland and Scotland. It demonstrated that a government without a monarch could act effectively and decisively. Consequently it was this government, and not that of Prince Charles in exile, which beginning in December 1650 won the official recognition of foreign governments, Catholic as well as Protestant. By 1652 the navy, refurbished and strengthened under Vane's administration, was winning victories reminiscent of those of Elizabeth's reign.

There is no doubt that too little was done to bring about even moderate reforms—to say nothing of establishing a heaven upon earth—as promised at times in the declarations of the parliaments. Nevertheless an important step toward religious toleration was taken when the Elizabethan recusancy laws were abolished. Also, a commission was appointed to bring about reforms in the laws, which later resulted in a few needed changes. Although the means used by the government to keep itself in power may be deplored, there was, except for Ireland, no widespread reign of terror. Particularly before Worcester, as Worden says, "the Rump had served its purpose."[29]

The practical and solid achievements of this government constitute the background for many of the ideas preachers and pamphleteers set forth in its defense, for there was no one ideology upon which they could or did rely. Had the Levellers come to power, they had at hand their own democratic ideology which had been set forth over the past few years, but this ideology now was directed against the Rump government.

And what of republican ideology? In their declaration of 17 March 1649 the Commons extolled the virtues of a republic.[30] Republican members of the Rump, Martin above all, played a leading role in the strategy and actions which the Rump used to eliminate the need for the monarchy in the actual functioning of the government.[31] Martin, however, was no theorist. Although Henry Vane the Younger later became an important theorist, between 1649 and the expulsion of the Rump in April 1653 he concentrated his attention on problems of administration. His theoretical writings do not begin until 1654 when he went into retirement.[32]

In the years between 1649 and 1653 John Milton used his pen in the service of the Commonwealth. In the *Tenure of Kings and Magistrates* (February 1649) Milton lashed out against the Presbyterians who had denounced the king's execution and continued to attack the Rump. In *Eikonoklastes* (October or November 1649) Milton strove mightily to destroy the sacred image of the royal martyr eulogized in *Eikon Basilike*. When the great European scholar Salmasius wrote to arouse European princes to support Prince Charles, it was Milton, the great English scholar, who answered him argument by argument in *A Defense of the People of England* (February 1651).

Valuable as the contribution of these tracts was to the Rump, Milton seemed more concerned to attack his enemies than to set forth a clear or consistent republican ideology.[33] Moreover, he appears to have been largely unaware of or unconcerned with the political realities of the situation. How men of moderate views were torn between loyalty to the old monarchical regime and allegiance to the new government in possession does not seem to have played a significant part in his thinking.[34] The ideas Milton set forth in these tracts seem to stand alone and appropriately should be treated by a Milton scholar.[35]

Marchamont Nedham, who came to the support of the Rump, did set forth a clear case for republicanism. Nevertheless, his major work in this period, *The Case of the Commonwealth of England Stated* (May 1650), devoted at the end of the tract only 18 pages out of 122 to the "excellency of a free state above a kingly government." In his weekly journal, *Mercurius Politicus*, Nedham at times did wax eloquent on the "advantages of a free state." Nevertheless, his main ideological contributions to the support of the Rump took other forms which will be apparent in succeeding chapters.[36]

It must not be inferred that republican ideas played no part in the justification of the Rump government. Writers employed a great range of ideas, often in the same tract or sermon. They reminded readers of the virtues of republican Venice and the successes in trade and on the seas of the Dutch. Nedham proclaimed that a free state prevents "corruption and faction" among the rulers and fosters "a more magnanimous, active, and noble temper of the spirit" in the people.[37] Nevertheless, after reading a multitude of tracts, mainly those in the Thomason Collection from between 1649 and April 1653, my distinct impression is that republican ideology played only a minor role in the ideological support of the government, particularly in the critical period between February 1649 and September 1651. For a number of reasons, then, republican ideas as such have not been included in this study.[38]

The sources for the ideas set forth in defense of the Rump government which will be considered in this study can be found in the formal declarations or acts of the Commons, as well as in the casual phrases of letters of the council or of individuals. Charges given by a judge at assize or by a justice of the peace at quarter sessions are revealing, as are questions raised and answers given by men genuinely perplexed as to whether they owed loyalty to the existing government or to the king to whom they had earlier sworn allegiance. By far the most important sources are the numerous pamphlets and sermons preserved in the Thomason Tracts for these years. Many but not all of these tracts supporting the government have to do with the engagement controversy. Although the names of a number of the writers and preachers are known, the authors of some of the most significant tracts are anonymous.

No clear pattern emerges concerning either the type and motivation or the ideology and approach of the different men who wrote in support of the government. In the forties Henry Parker had been the most important theorist undergirding the claims of Parliament.[39] Between 1649 and 1651 Parker continued to use his pen in support of the Commons. Another theorist, Anthony Ascham, had argued in 1648 before the king's execution in favor of a government actually in possession.[40] After Charles's execution this important and influential theorist developed more fully his ideas concerning society and government. The pragmatically minded chameleon, Marchamont Nedham, became one of the government's most vigorous supporters. Another was the dull, repetitious, and unimaginative John Dury, so different from Nedham in his approach. Although Dury had opposed Charles's execution, as early as March 1649 he

11

produced his first pamphlet in support of the government.[41] In July 1649 he was made deputy keeper under Whitelocke of the library at St. James.[42] In the continuing battle of words over the engagement controversy, Dury seemed to rise to each occasion and produce another pamphlet. In rewarding men as dissimilar as Nedham, Parker, and Dury, it is apparent that the government was anxious to secure all the support it could from writers on its behalf, however different they might be in their arguments or ideology.

It is well known that John Owen, friend of Cromwell and a favorite preacher before the Commons, received material benefits and emoluments, an important one being the deanery of Christ Church, Oxford.[43] An interesting case is that of John Rocket, a minister from Nottinghamshire, whose estate had been sequestered because of his "practices against the state."[44] The council later reported that they had "received good assurance of the man's penitence and willing recognition of his deviations in some late transactions laid to his charge."[45] Apparently Rocket was freed from prison and thanked the council by writing *The Christian subject,* a tract supporting the government, which was published in November 1651.

Undoubtedly further research would reveal benefits which other writers and preachers received. To speak up on behalf of the government between 1649 and 1653 could mean, then as now, that a government job might be continued or a more favorable one obtained. It might mean that you or your relatives would be unmolested or taxed lightly, a church living could be kept, or a more lucrative one secured. One wonders if Sergeant Francis Thorpe, who used the occasion of the York assizes to explain and justify the new government, received a special reward. Did William Sclater, John Shaw, and Richard Saunders who, in their sermons at the assizes, strongly endorsed the government? When the council became alarmed by the hellfire sermons Presbyterian ministers delivered against the regime and the engagement, other preachers such as John Price used their pulpits to denounce "the cloudy clergy."[46]

Illuminating as it would be to discover answers to these questions, it would be a mistake to overemphasize the rewards men received for championing the government's cause. Some of its strong supporters had other objectives in mind. Years before the Rump came into power, Dury had worked at home and abroad to bring about peace and understanding and ultimately religious unity among the warring Protestant churches.[47] To achieve these ends, however, Dury believed that a peaceful society under an effective government was essential. And was not the Rump the answer of the moment to the anarchy or revolution which Dury feared might well have followed Charles's execution? John Owen believed that God would best be served and religious toleration achieved in an orderly way if a firm government held the reins.

There were some convinced radicals, too, who wrote on the government's behalf. John Goodwin, one of Parliament's ardent champions in the forties and a staunch advocate of Pride's Purge and Charles's execution, must have believed that the Rump would fulfill its promise and provide for new elections. The preacher Thomas Brooks was another supporter who must have hoped for a more democratic regime.[48]

The type or nature of the arguments writers and preachers used differed widely. Francis Rous, the old parliamentarian, and the prolific Dury were two who looked to the Scriptures and to providence to justify their contentions, but each also injected secular arguments into their writings. Nedham and the anonymous author of the important pamphlet commonly called the *Northern subscriber's plea* (1651) presented their case in secular terms, but each included religious arguments as well. Perhaps more than anyone Dury seized upon almost every argument that can be found in these years. It is the range and variety of the arguments the supporters of the government employed which will be one of the objectives this essay endeavors to show.

In an age when many writers still piled authority upon authority to convince their readers, what were the favorite sources to which these authors turned? They did not look primarily to legal precedents, since the king's trial and execution were completely illegal, as lawyers well knew. Scripture, however, was at hand, and passages in both the Old and New Testaments provided ammunition upon which writers loved to rely. Perhaps even more popular was the concept of providence, for had not God clearly demonstrated his approval of the Rump? How some men interpreted God's role in the English political scene at this time is a fascinating story. Earlier Puritan divines, particularly William Perkins and William Ames,[49] were favorite authorities. Among secularly minded writers, Grotius was often relied upon and quoted. In his first work *A Discourse*

(1648), Ascham literally appropriated many of Grotius's basic ideas. Ascham himself soon became a favorite authority. Dury must have been widely read, for references to him in the tracts were frequent. Professor Skinner has demonstrated that Hobbes not only influenced others, but that he himself deliberately played a part in the engagement controversy.[50]

It should not be forgotten, however, that many of those writers supporting the government must have been keenly aware of the actual situation between 1649 and 1653. They saw that England's social fabric, despite the stresses and strains it had undergone, remained intact. A functioning government was keeping the peace (at home at least), handling its numerous daily problems with considerable success, and winning recognition in Europe. Here was visible proof before their very eyes not only of what mighty acts God was performing for England, but also of what man himself "in his own generation" could achieve.

I

THE TRADITION OF MONARCHY VS. THE DESIRE FOR PEACE

The greatest obstacle writers faced when they spoke out on behalf of the Commonwealth government was the deeply held conviction that monarchy was not only indispensable in the English polity but indeed "the perfectest state of government," as John Pym, the great parliamentarian, had pronounced in 1621.[1] Even before Charles's head fell on the block, the Commons knew full well that for centuries monarchy had been essential for the normal functioning of the English government. They clearly understood, as Henry Robinson, a defender of the new government, wrote later concerning the courts, that "we had little but what was our king's. We had nothing of our own."[2] Recognizing this dilemma, the Commons quickly passed a number of acts to make it as legal as possible for a government to carry on without a king. On 29 January 1649, the day before Charles's execution, an act was passed "for the alteration of several names and forms used in courts, writs, etc. . . . and setting of proceedings in courts of law . . ."[3] The day of his execution, an act was passed "prohibiting the proclaiming of any person to be King of England, Ireland, or the Dominion thereof."[4] On 9 February there followed "an act for repeal of several clauses in the statutes of 1 Elizabeth and 3 Jacobi touching the oaths of allegiance, obe-

15

dience, and supremacy."[5] The next day the freemen of the city of London were required by act of Parliament to swear "to be true and faithful to the Commonwealth of England." On 17 February an act authorized "justices of peace, sheriffs, and other ministers of justice therein named, to act and proceed in the execution of their offices and duties until their several commissions shall come unto them."[6] The same day, again by act of Parliament, it was ordered that in all presentments and indictments in courts of law, "the name of the keepers of the liberty of England by authority of Parliament" shall be substituted for the name of the king.[7] Not until a month later, on 17 March, did Parliament pass the act for "the abolishing the kingly office in England and Ireland and the Dominions thereunto belonging."[8] As late as 19 May the act was passed formally declaring England a Commonwealth.[9] It was obviously more important that the government function without interruption and as "legally" as possible without a king than that precious time be taken to label or theorize upon the form and nature of this government.

Acts and actions as definite as those just listed made it possible for the government to carry on without interruption, but no act, least of all Charles's execution, could wipe out the belief in monarchy as the natural, best, and only form of government for England. In its long history the English government had always had a monarch as its head. England had become a nation under the leadership of those kings who were strong and the institutions of which the king was most often the creator and legally the head. Since before the Norman Conquest it was the king's peace which had prevailed; it was due to the king, his writs, and his judges, that the common law courts had developed. It was monarchy more than any other institution which had built the English state.

Over the centuries monarchy and law had developed together. Whitelocke explained in the famous conference Cromwell held with lawyers in 1651 that "the laws of England are so interwoven with the power and practice of monarchy that to settle a government without something of monarchy in it would make so great an alteration in the proceedings of our law that . . . we can [not] well forsee the inconveniences that will arise thereby."[10] The same interweaving of monarch and law was argued later by Whitelocke and other members of a committee appointed by the Commons in April 1657 to try to convince Cromwell that he should accept the title of king. Whitelocke explained that the ancient title of king and not the new one of protector had been "known by the law of England for many ages, many hundreds of years to-gether received, and the laws fitted to it."[11]

According to William Lenthal, Master of the Rolls, the title of king "carries more in it of weight than a meer title; . . . the whole body of the law is carried upon this wheel, it is not a thing that stands upon the top meerly, but runs through the whole 'life and veins of the law.' "[12] Another speaker, either the Lord Chief Justice Glynn or the Lord Chief Justice St. John, pointed out that a "king has run through so many ages in this nation, and has governed the nation by that title and style, that it is known to the law."[13]

It was Glynn who, stressing the interweaving of king and law in England's long history, made the additional significant point that "the king's duty [was] known in reference to the people, and the people's duty known in reference to him." "The assumption of the title of any king is without need of any other authority to protect the people, and bind the people to obey you."[14]

Monarchy had also played key nonlegal roles in English history and society. It had long been regarded as a vital part of the social order—a concept which had not been challenged, except by the Levellers, during the years of civil war. "A gentleman's honor, his most precious possession, whether he was royalist or parliamentarian, descended to him ultimately from the king and immediately from his family."[15] Again, it was the king who appointed to those numerous governmental offices so sought by thousands of Englishmen desiring to rise in the social and economic scale. The leading royalist theorist, Robert Filmer, who looked upon the king as the father of his country, would have been viewed sympathetically by many Englishmen accustomed through family and church discipline to accept the father's authority in the family unit.[16]

Monarchy was also regarded as necessary to provide the social stability that so many Englishmen continued to desire in their war torn land. "To shake the throne would be to shake the whole structure of society,"[17] and even to shake the universe itself to those who still believed in the "great chain of being" in which a king occupied a key position in the hierarchy reaching from God to man. Perhaps most important, there was "a mystique of kingship" which the trial and execution of Charles as a crowned king had endeavored to eradicate.[18] This drastic action, however, failed to obliterate Englishmen's belief in monarchy. As Don Wolfe wrote,

Each Englishman had a precious possession in his image of the king, an image that made him kin to all other subjects in time of crisis or despair. Never had this vision of kingship been more persuasive than that of Charles at prayer before the block of execution.[19]

According to W. C. Abbott,

> Englishmen believed that national unity and order were embodied in a sovereign who was more than an individual, more even than the highest official in the state, whose person was sacred and whose office, whoever held it, was in some mystical fashion bound up with the life of the whole people.[20]

Whether the monarchy was regarded from a traditional or legal point of view, because of its social and economic advantages in English society of the period, or because it represented a mystical and yet personal and national image for Englishmen, this belief in monarchy lived on after Charles's execution. It acted as a formidable ideological obstacle for those writers endeavoring to change the thinking and behavior of Englishmen.

It is hardly necessary to point out that royalists of differing shades of opinion, both believers in absolute or in limited mixed monarchy, held fast to their belief in monarchy and worked actively or waited passively for the return of Prince Charles. But it should never be forgotten that this belief in monarchy had lived on through the civil wars in the minds of men who had sided with Parliament's cause and had fought Charles I on the battlefield. Between the outbreak of war in 1642 and Pride's Purge in December 1648, parliamentarians differed sharply on the terms of a treaty with the king to end the war. How much power the king should have in different areas—military, appointing, foreign affairs, religion—led to many bitter disputes in and out of Parliament. It seems fair to surmise that many, if not most, parliamentarians believed in some form of limited mixed government, but one in which the king remained a partner with the Lords and the Commons. To abolish kingship or make the king a mere figurehead was not in the thinking of many members of Parliament, at least until late in 1648. They had waged war against Charles, but not against the institution of monarchy. Very few parliamentarians, if any, would agree with the republican Henry Martin that the king was a mere man with private family interests. To most Englishmen, parliamentarians as well as royalists, Charles was a king around whose person and office there had gathered for centuries both general and specific powers, and whose position was regarded as indispensable in the English polity.

It was not necessary to believe in the divine right of kings to hold Charles's position sacred, for many important Englishmen were bound to him by oaths regarded as promises solemnly made before God to be loyal to their king. The determination of the Commons to "defend the king's majesty's person and authority" had been most solemnly set forth in article three of the Solemn League and Covenant and had never been revoked.[21] Among the numerous writers and speakers supporting Charles between November 1648 and January 1649 was William Prynne, who pointed out that Parliament had stated numerous times during the civil war that "it never intended the least hurt, injury, or violence to the king's person, crown, dignity or posterity."[22]

The supporters of the new government were well aware of the strength of the monarchical tradition and of the numerous statements and oaths in which the Commons had professed their loyalty to the king and to the monarchy. They also knew that to most men such oaths were regarded as particularly binding, so they devoted page upon page in their numerous pamphlets to reinterpreting by casuistical arguments the underlying meaning or "end" of the oaths or to explaining them away. They understood full well how essential to the acceptance of the new government it was that the consciences of Englishmen who had taken these oaths be quieted. Recognizing this deep-seated, long-established belief in monarchy is necessary for understanding the nature of the ideas put forth in support of the new government.

A most illuminating pamphlet in which this belief in monarchy is revealed was written by Nathaniel Ward, the cobbler of Agawam. His *Discolliminium or A most obedient reply to a late book called Bounds and Bonds*[23] attacked the views of Ascham and others who had argued that men should take the engagement. It is significant that Ward must at some time have disapproved of Charles's policies for he had emigrated to New England in 1634. Ward did not believe in absolute monarchy but, in common with many on both sides of the controversy, in the mixed government of kings, Lords, and

19

Commons.[24] Moreover, he admitted that at times submission might have to be made to those who through force were in plenary possession.[25] Such submission, however, was not to a true authority. Throughout his pamphlet, Ward expressed the sentiments which many moderates must have held. He argued against the prevailing views of the supporters of the government and concluded that monarchy was best. His own "political creed" concerning England was that the "mind of God is, and the condition of this land requires, that we should be ruled by the highest form of government the realm can afford. Authority divested of majesty is very despicable."[26] It is dangerous, even blasphemous to break "oaths, vows and covenants," which are "the high prerogative of God and godly nations, the violating of them a kind of climbing his couch, and pulling down Reuben's curse on the violaters heads." Moreover, since monarchy has prevailed for so long a time in England, "men will find the transmutation of an ancient and suitable form of state a far harder task than a first constitution, yea give me leave to say, it will be found the next work to a creation."[27]

Ward reluctantly admitted that a government other than monarchy could rightfully exist in England, but insisted that "it is in the mind of God that every nation should be governed by a national ordinance."[28] No government, such as that of the existing Commons, should be accepted or obeyed "till it hath obtained a national confirmation in one kind or other, and this confirmation has not been sought or given."[29] If the king had to forfeit his power even in a mixed monarchy it could not be relinquished to the other partners in government, as Grotius claimed, but only to "the whole state, or their complete representatives."[30]

Even writers who urged that men support the Commonwealth government knew well how deeply rooted in the minds of men monarchy was. In reading the numerous tracts of John Dury, one is aware of how hard he is trying to dispel the notion of monarchy, and particularly of the oaths associated with it. Albertus Warren, an advocate of the new government on utilitarian grounds, tells us frankly that men "think too much of the indispensable necessity of monarchy."[31] According to the author of a tract entitled *The Engagement vindicated*, monarchy did most resemble God's government but, the author insisted, "this doth not prove it the most accommodate to human affairs."[32]

If it was difficult and unnatural to try and execute a king, it was equally, if not more, difficult and unnatural to justify a government which had abolished monarchy. How this task was attempted, how older ideas were employed and adapted to the changed situation, and how essentially new ideas concerning society and government emerged, will be shown in succeeding chapters.

If a continuing belief in monarchy made it difficult for Englishmen to support the new government, a strong factor which worked on its behalf was the profound desire for peace. Few if any men had really wanted a civil war. At each stage in the war's progression a group emerged in Parliament which, ardently desiring peace, wanted to come to terms with the king. In the countryside, club men proclaimed their intention of remaining neutral in the contest. "The fear of plunder and fire, the peril of losing all one's possessions at the hands of mutinous soldiers or a marauding army, the dread of pillage, arson and violence by a brutal soldiery, all run like a nightmare refrain in diaries of the time."[33] The desire for peace in their war torn society became even stronger when fighting broke out again in the second civil war in 1648. For important Englishmen possessing landed property, peace was essential if they were to retain, regain, or increase their landed holdings. For men engaged in commerce and industry, peace was also a necessary prerequisite. To carry on normal business activities within their town led the important townsmen of Newcastle to support any ruler in London who brought peace.[34] Shocked as Englishmen were by Charles's execution, there must have been some who quietly hoped, as Cromwell, Ireton, and other regicides believed, that peace might be possible now that Charles by his maneuvers could no longer endanger it.

After the execution of the king the new Commonwealth government knew well that it must bring peace to England if it hoped to win the support of large numbers of Englishmen. The Rumpers were keenly aware of the threats to their authority from the royalists, the Levellers, the Irish, and the Scotch. The government and its supporters claimed credit for saving Englishmen from continued confusion and violence in their war weary society. The first objective of the government, according to the Commons's declaration of March 1649, was "to prevent a new war . . . and to establish a firm and safe peace."[35] In Parliament's September 1649 *Vindication of their Proceedings*, reference is made to Parliament's discovery of "the dangerous practices of several interests against the present government and peace of the commonwealth." In particular the Levellers, whose views would result in anarchy, were denounced.[36]

The government was ever on the alert to discover possible sources of unrest and dissent, to nip them in the bud, and to remind Englishmen of the blessings of peace which this government had achieved. In its letters to various officials, the council asked them to be on the lookout for those breaking the peace in their localities. Presbyterian ministers were particularly dangerous for they were using the pulpit in and out of London to stir up the people against the government. Letter after letter urged local officials to curb these preachers. The justices of assize in Lancashire were instructed to let the people know that their "seditious preachers, in their praying and preachings against the present government," could make that county "a seat of war."[37] The consul at Smyrna was advised from London of the "evidences" of God's providence "to settle the Commonwealth in good and peaceable condition."[38] After the battle of Worcester in 1651, the *Weekly Intelligencer* reminded people criticizing the government that they should be more aware of "the things that belong unto their peace."[39]

Some members of the royalist opposition clearly saw that their hopes of a return to monarchy were reduced if the Commonwealth government should be able to maintain the peace. Ormond wrote to Sir Edward Nicholas that "nothing [was] more dangerous to the English monarchy . . . than that the rebels [i.e., the government] should have means, by easing the people, to gain their affections, and by a perfect tranquillity to have power, leisure, and reputation to establish their tyranny at home and their alliances abroad."[40]

To men searching their souls whether or not to accept the new Commonwealth government, the peace it provided was a powerful argument in its favor. William Lowe thanked Colonel Harley for a book sent him, apparently dealing with the question of loyalty. Lowe replied that he could find nothing in the book "that forbids us to endeavour the common good of the people of England, or to live quietly in our callings under the present government."[41] The diary of Adam Martindale provides insight into one man's tortuous problem. Turning to Scripture for help as to whether or not he should take the engagement, Martindale wrote, "if the people of God in Babylon were to seek the peace of that city and pray unto the Lord for it, which was more than to be merely true and faithful, though the King of Babylon was a usurper over the Jews, then we may engage to be true and faithful to the usurpers over us."[42]

Writers supporting the government recognized the propaganda value of stressing peace. Whether editors of newspapers, lay pamphleteers, ministers or theorists, all sounded the same note—that civil dissension must stop, that peace was essential, and that this government had achieved it or was bringing it about. At a session in Truro the magistrate Robert Bennet reminded the people that "by the good providence of God we are once more met upon the employment of justice, the conservation of our civil peace."[43] In March and April 1649 when Leveller activities threatened to undo the peace, John Dillingham, editor of the *Moderate Intelligencer*, urged his readers to support the government despite its high taxes for it was giving England peace, whereas, he reminded his readers, thirty years of war had devastated Germany.[44]

After the army's victory over the Levellers at Burford, John Owen pointed out in his sermon to the Commons 7 June 1649 that had the Levellers succeeded, they would have "wrapped us in confusion." The present "rulers of the nation," however, Owen said, are "in the ways of peace, protection and safety."[45] Both Presbyterians and Independents were urged by the author of *Vox Pacifica* to accept this government because "the ship of this commonwealth is now near her harbor, fraught with peace and the blessed means of plenty and freedom."[46] Ministers were admonished by Richard Saunders not to be seditious. "Let it not be said, truly professors of religion are now the greatest state incendiaries. Oh! do not your hearts tremble to think of blood again?"[47]

What was the purpose of the oath of loyalty to the king you once took, Saunders asked the ministers who hesitated or refused to take the engagement. Those oaths and covenants had actually been taken, he explained, with the "public peace, welfare, and good as the chief end. And will not the keeping of them [i.e., the oaths]... in maintaining the pretended right of the late king's son be the only way to war, disorder, confusion, blood?"[48] Enoch Grey, a Puritan minister, argued in a similar way concerning oaths. "Such," he wrote, "as cannot be kept with the peace and stability of nations (all casuists acknowledge) leave no obligation upon the conscience because reason and rule is the bond of justice."[49]

For Christians, above all, peace was absolutely essential, as a number of preachers pointed out. Enoch Grey asked that prayers for peace be made "because of the house of the lord our God, let us seek the good of England in the peace whereof is our peace, the peace of our precious wives and of our dear children."[50] In the numerous tracts of John Dury supporting the government and urging that men take the engagement, the importance of peace was interwoven with many of his other arguments. To Dury peace was essential if religious unity, so close to his heart, was to be achieved.[51] Dury frequently reminded his readers that peace was the government's objective and that it was actually being brought about. In *A disengaged survey*,[52] he chose for his text Rom. 12:18, "If it be possible as much as lyeth in you, live peaceably with all men." Like Saunders and Grey, Dury maintained that oaths formerly taken to the king did not bind because they were but "circumstantials" at the present time when a government existed which provided "righteousness and peace." To abide by former oaths in such a situation might again "throw them into blood and confusion."[53]

Throughout his treatise on *The Christian subject,* John Rocket waxed eloquent on the importance of peace. Taking as his text 1 Tim. 2:1-2, he explained that Paul, when he asked for prayers for those in authority, put peace first "because it is the common ingredient that makes sweet all things . . . is the groundwork of all other happiness."[54] The present magistrates had brought peace, Rocket explained. They had worked for the preservation and peace of the whole body politic.[55] "War is no friend to truth in itself, nor to the powerful and constant practice of godliness." God is "God of Peace" and Christ "King of Peace."[56]

Writers whose approach to the questions at issue was primarily secular also put great emphasis on peace. Anthony Ascham, the political theorist whose writings influenced so many preachers and pamphleteers supporting the government, premised much of his theory upon the necessity for peace in human society. Ascham believed that peace was essential for the little or common man—far more important to him and to society than the form of government. Writing in 1648 after the civil war but before the execution of the king, he said concerning one of his important concepts, reason of state, "[it] is not busied so much about inward piety and virtue, as it is about public quiet and repose."[57] In each of his tracts produced in 1649, *A combat between two seconds* (July), *The bounds & bonds of public obedience* (August), and *Of the confusions and revolutions of governments* (November), Ascham pointed out the dangers of

24

confusion if individuals did not accept and support the Rump government. In *Combat*, he argued against giving "up all to a popular confusion."[58] In his *Bounds & bonds* he declared that peace was perhaps the main objective of government. "States cannot," he wrote, "look so strictly after virtue, as after public quiet."[59] Again in *Confusions and revolutions* he sounded the same note. Here he denounced the Leveller concept of a state of nature which would be one of confusion.[60] He even said that confusion was in some ways worse than war in which some public order prevailed, whereas confusion "levels all, both public and private."[61]

The pragmatic realist Francis Osborne pointed out to the gentry and nobility that it would be most indiscreet "for people so long beaten by the cruel storms of a civil war to refuse for the present any harbour, though never so incommodius, and to venture again the wreck of so sacred a vessel as the commonwealth."[62] In his *Case of the Commonwealth of England Stated* Nedham, like Osborne basing his arguments largely on practical grounds, demonstrated how both the royalists and Levellers in their desire to overthrow the government were endangering the peace which had been achieved.[63]

Peace was a recurring theme of lay pamphleteers, of preachers, and of the government itself, each of whom was well aware of men's deep longing for peace. This government providing peace, as its champions proclaimed, was a government deserving of men's allegiance whatever their former oaths had been. Whether the approach of a writer was essentially religious or secular the value of peace played an important part in his arguments. Because of the limited evidence it is impossible to prove that the government was supported because men valued the internal peace it brought. Nevertheless there is little doubt that peace and all its blessings influenced many men as they considered the question of loyalty—active or passive—to the government.

II

Scriptures, Providence, and the Government

The arguments set forth by preachers and pamphleteers in defense of the Rump government took many forms. Some were primarily religious in nature, others secular, and many intertwined both approaches in the same pamphlet or sermon. In this chapter the arguments which looked primarily to the Scriptures or to God's providence will be presented.

Writers relied upon numerous passages from both the Old and New Testaments to convince their readers to accept the new government. As John Blackleach wrote, "If you keep close to God's rule, you shall not err."[1] The deep-seated belief in monarchy as the best (even divinely ordained) form of government for England was countered by reminders of the many wicked kings of Israel whom God had chastised. These writers also knew that God had spoken in Scripture against a monarchical form of government. In *Endeavours aiming at the Glory of God,* Blackleach turned to the Old Testament to show that "government by succession . . . was none of God's institution," whereas "government by judges is plainly proved to be the best form of government, being God's immediate direction, most blessed and approved for God's glory, and for a peoples greatest good, comfort and safety."[2] Blackleach urged "the people of England to cleave close to the most pure, most immediate and first institution of government recorded in the holy scriptures," namely government by judges. "The scripture is evident," he wrote, that such a government was "Gods own immediate institution."[3] According to the Scriptures, God ordained judges for Israel and made clear His dislike of kings. Since England was "not now a separated people from the true Israel of God, [nor are we] strangers to those laws which God then in those times gave to them,"[4] we should pay heed to God's advice to his chosen people.

John Cook agreed that "monarchy [is] no creature of God's making." Both Scripture and reason prove "that monarchical government is against the mind of God."[5] "The scripture is very clear that God's people were governed by Parliament."[6] The first kings came from the people, not from God. "God has protested against monarchy in . . . [many] places of Scripture, and therefore to contend for it, is flat rebellion against the majesty of heaven, to make ourselves wiser than God."[7] It was "a free state" which came closest to the "word of God," according to the *Moderate Mercury*.[8] Writers were obviously trying to convince their readers that there was no divine link from God to monarch as so many believed, but that on the contrary, God in his Scriptures had clearly spoken against monarchy.

If numerous passages from the Old Testament could be cited as demonstrating God's disapproval of monarchy, the New Testament spoke out in favor of submission to the powers that actually existed. The famous passage of Scripture quoted time and time again by writers supporting the Commonwealth government was, "Let every soul be subject unto the higher powers. For there is no power but of God; the powers that be are ordained of God. Whosoever therefore resisteth the power, resisteth the ordinance of God, and they that resist shall receive to themselves damnation" (Rom. 13:1-2).

This scriptural pronouncement provided the foundation for the important pamphlet written by the old parliamentarian, Francis Rous, which appeared in April 1649.[9] Rous explained in some detail that the Roman government to which Rom. 13:1-2 and other passages in the New Testament commanded obedience, had come to power illegally by the use of force. Likewise many kings of England had come to the throne illegally by the use of force, and yet had received the obedience of their people.[10] As Rous explained, that obedience was lawful.

> ... when a question is made whom we should obey, it must not be looked at what he is that exercises the power, or by what right or wrong he has invaded the power, or in what manner he does dispense it, but only if he have power. For if any man do excel in power, it is now out of doubt, that he received that power of God; wherefore without all exception thou must yield thyself up to him, and heartily obey him. . . .

> And indeed how can it be otherwise? for when a person or persons have gotten supreme power, and by the same excluded all other from authority, either that authority which is thus taken by power must be obeyed, or else all authority and government must fall to the ground; and so confusion (which is worse than tituler tyranny) be admitted into a commonwealth.[11]

Rous contended that "confusion and destruction" must be prevented and peace and order must prevail. When the Scriptures speak of obeying the powers, they "speak not of the future, but of the present time."[12] Only by obeying the powers that be can peace be maintained and the Commonwealth preserved. By his use of Rom. 13:1-2 and other New Testament passages, Rous made in the first months of the new regime a persuasive appeal to Englishmen desiring peace above all else.

The effectiveness of this argument was weakened, as Skinner has shown,[13] by the assertion of several writers and preachers, mainly Presbyterian, that this passage of Scripture really meant that subjects must obey the lawful authority and not mere power as such. Nevertheless, Rom. 13:1-2 and other New Testament passages enjoining obedience continued to be quoted by writers in support of the government. As one anonymous author wrote, "the place of Scripture, Romans 13:1 (amongst other things) is very full and pregnant to prove the being of our present powers from God."[14] Even the secularly minded Francis Osborne, who based much of his argument on force and possession, reminded his readers that "the apostle Paul commands Christians to submit to the present power for conscience sake, and justifies this precept so far by his own example as to appear before a court of justice" even though the judges in the court were corrupt.[15] The cautious John Dury admitted that the former government was legal, but cited 1 Cor. 6:12 and 10:23 that things may be lawful and yet not "most expedient for the public state."[16]

The sermon preached before the judges in Exeter 23 March 1651 by Richard Saunders is an example of the way in which a preacher, undoubtedly influenced by Ascham's views, could interpret the meaning of Rom. 13:1-2 to justify, even legalize, the allegiance demanded by the Rump.[17] As indicated by the title to his sermon, *Plenary possession makes a lawful power*, legality no longer depended upon long-established laws but upon a government in possession which was able to maintain order and peace. In interpreting the word *subject* in Rom. 13:1-2, Saunders explained that the translation of the Greek word *subjection* means "let every soul be set in order under the higher powers."[18] The word *subject* includes "whatever is necessary to prevent the dissolving of the frame of government, and what may perfect and secure the same."[19] Through this interpretation of the scriptural word *subject* in Rom. 13:1-2, Saunders was reminding his readers that the present government which had achieved order should be able to do whatever proved to be necessary to maintain itself in power.

The word of God as revealed in Scripture, both in the Old and New Testaments, served well many writers who labored to persuade Englishmen that God disapproved of monarchy but had also proclaimed that men owed allegiance to the new government.

Another argument, essentially religious in nature, employed by writers to justify obedience to the new government focused on the vital role played by God's providence in establishing and maintaining the new government. If a quantitative approach were used to count the different arguments supporting and justifying the government, the argument based on God's providence could turn out to be the winner. There is hardly a pamphlet or sermon among the large number which were read in which some reference to or longer discourse on God's providence does not occur. Some writers such as Nedham or Osborne seem to be paying only lip service to this concept, hoping, presumably, that their reference to it would help to convince some religiously minded doubters. For other writers such as Thomas Brooks, John Owen, and the anonymous author of

29

England's apology, God's providence appears to be a living and burning reality. Impossible as it is to ascertain the sincerity of many writers employing this argument, there is no doubt that God's providence loomed large in the thinking of seventeenth-century Englishmen, as their diaries and letters amply attest.

The concept of providence and its role in human affairs was obviously not an idea newly discovered in 1648 or 1649. On the contrary, it was a profound belief deeply embedded in Protestant, particularly Calvinist, thought in England.[20] In the sixteenth, and in the first half of the seventeenth, century the concept of providence had taken many shapes and forms. Puritans had relied upon it to guide, motivate, and activate them in their determination to remedy wrongs they deplored in church and state. When, for example, in 1641 and 1642 the Long Parliament seemed to falter in its work, it was Puritans like Stephen Marshall or Jeremiah Buroughs who goaded them on.[21] When finally the civil wars had been won, the king tried and executed, and the Commonwealth government established, who could deny that God's providence had led and brought them through the turmoil to victory? Attractive and appealing to modern scholars as Leveller and Digger ideas are today, these ideas were, I suggest, dismissed as dangerous or impossible by large numbers of Englishmen of differing shades of opinion who trusted in God's works and believed His hand had guided them through the turmoil in England between 1640 and 1653.

Certainly, the feeling of guilt about the execution of Charles and the disturbing questions about the authority of the Rump could be answered for many by reminding them of God's providence and His support of their cause. On 10 January 1649, even before the king's execution, the Commons announced, "We therefore despairing of any good return of justice from the king, did appeal unto the great God of heaven and earth for the same, who after four years of war, did give a clear and apparent sentence on our side."[22] The author of the tract *England's apology* called Charles's execution "the first clear and thorough act of justice that was executed in the western world."[23] It was God's providence—his intervention in human affairs—which prevented anyone from rescuing the king at that time, "all men being under a divine restraint, and awed by the dreadfulness of God's justice in such an act."[24] After the execution England, by God's providence, "had been blessedly led into a commonwealth."[25] The Commons declared in September 1649 that amidst the troubles in the country and divisions within the government, "through the good providence of God, we have been kept together, as weak instruments in the hand of our great God, serving our generations."[26]

Above all, as the Commons, pamphleteers, and preachers proclaimed again and again, "the great God of battle"[27] had blessed their cause by a steady succession of military victories. "At Naseby God set up his standard," and no battles had been lost since that time.[28] "Witness the great advantage the enemy had of us at Naseby; the miraculous rally at Dublin . . . the deliverance beyond all reason . . . at Dunbar . . ."[29] "We cannot but see the hand of God reached out unto us, for the upholding of this government." There has been nothing like it since "the drying up of the Red Sea."[30] After the siege of Dublin was raised in 1649, William Cooper, preaching to the Commons, declared, "there was very much of God in it and little of man."[31]

The success of the English armies under Cromwell in Scotland was often spoken of as especially miraculous. It was God who chose to give the victory at Dunbar to the English, rather than to the Scotch, even though they had "the covenant on the palms of their hands."[32] In his sermon after the success, Thomas Brooks thanked God who gave them the victory, reminding his listeners that "the manifestations of God in his providence are the most precious things in the world."[33] "Despair not; God is with us," George Wither cried in *Carmen Eucharisticon*.

> We have seen God marching, so
> With our Friends, against our Foe,
> As he did, long time ago.
> When his Israel was oppress't
> And, securing us from fear;
> When our hopes, at lowest were,
> When dispis'd, we did appear,
> And our perill most increst.[34]

Another ditty labelled *A Word of councel to the disaffected* runs as follows:

31

Will ye not fear? hath not the Almighty shown
His works of wonder? Will ye not them own?
. . . .
Think when ye thought come was the critic hour
That none could help, how God still showed his power
Think thus, and let your stubborn wills submit
To him that chang'd the world, still orders it.[35]

Because God had acted decisively on their behalf, how could men question his providence? Thus Puritan ideas of resistance to authority, so important in the civil war, were superseded, for a time at least, by Puritan support of the new government brought about by God's providence. To resist it was to sin against the Almighty himself. If God's word, as revealed in Scripture, commanded men to obey the powers that be, His works, as revealed through His providence, spoke even more persuasively.

Even writers who advanced secular arguments appealed to Providence to persuade men to accept God's decree. Henry Robinson, for example, who believed in only the relative good of the existing regime, nevertheless wrote that "we may discern a bright star of providence leading us directly to it [i.e., the government]." Those men opposed to the government "may well be said to fight against the very arm of the almighty."[36] The author of *A discourse concerning the Engagement*, more commonly known as the *Northern subscriber's plea*, set forth a modern point of view concerning the nature and function of government per se, regardless of its kind.[37] Nevertheless, this author stated that God's providence was "the main foundation upon which we build an obedience, being of most and direct influence upon our consciences. . . . The policies of nations are some of God's works upon the wheels, which He orders and frames as seemeth good to Himself."[38] John Drew, who supported the author of the *Northern subscriber's plea*, put it this way: "If the falling of a sparrow to the ground hath something of providence in it, much more those wonderful appearings of God antecedent, concomitant, and subsequent to our change of government. . . . We never looked at providence as an ordinance of God for the determining a right, but seeing the hand of the almighty in important events, we think ourselves bound to acknowledge it."[39]

England now, perhaps more than ever, was regarded by many writers as a promised land or second Israel, especially chosen by

God for his purposes. As the author of *England's apology* explained, in the civil wars the Parliament was only against the king's person but ultimately God "had a further higher design. . . . God hath given us an opportunity against our wills to make ourselves the freest and happiest nation on this earth, and we are the first of so large a continent that God hath advantaged with such a blessing."[40] God is "so in love with England's liberties that our unworthiness and unsuitableness cannot stop him in this course of grace and mercy," and He "has been acting and doing us good, without our observance."[41] "How can a model of the workings of God for his people be drawn in fairer and clearer colors?"[42]

In *The Potent Potter*, a sermon preached before the Commons 19 April 1649, John Warren called England in the period before the execution of the king, "a goodly vessel . . . in comparison with other nations." Now, however, under God's hand, it would become a much finer nation.[43] "As the clay is in the hand of the potter, so is England in the hand of God," who is shaping it to his purposes. "Shall God begin to build and never finish what he has begun?"[44] William Cooper preached a sermon on God's saving Jerusalem. In this act, Cooper explained, "the Lord comes forth armed with His almighty creating power stretching out the heavens, laying the foundation of the earth, and forming the spirit of man within him."[45] The implication was clear. God had used and would continue to use "His almighty creating power" for his beloved England.

If God's providence had brought about the king's execution, established the government, given it great victories, and would lead them to the promised land, why should anyone question the validity of the government and the engagement men were asked to sign? Yet many were sorely perplexed. Had Parliament not sworn in the Solemn League and Covenant to be faithful to the king? In all the tedious, long, often casuistical arguments spun out in answer to this dilemma, it would appear to be God's providence which weighed most persuasively in the minds of men. Who could fail to see that in 1649, 1650, and 1651, God Himself had not only created but favored the government? Could man, despite former oaths to the king, ask for a higher authority than God to whom to yield his fealty? As Dury wrote, no oath can prevent God from giving government "to whomsoever he pleases."[46] Many can't tell of the "titles of government but none [are] too ignorant to tell of God's

33

choice. . . . To neglect a present duty by an over-ruling providence fostered upon us, upon pretence of former obligations to the contrary, when not withstanding God hath razed the foundations of those obligations, what can it be but to rebel against the ordinance, not only of men, but of God himself, against the universal good . . . of a nation, against our obligation, to that public authority, under whose shadow we sit down in peace."[47] According to the author of *Certain Particulars*, "at such a time as this, wherein God has chalked out His own way, we are rather to stand adoring His work, than to make headway against it."[48] Because conditions had changed since the oath to the king was taken, a man was no longer bound by it. "And certainly God that changes time and governments, would rather have us soberly to follow His providence, than to think we, by our opposition, can cross Him in His way."[49]

In one of the numerous ditties of the times, both God's works (providence) and his word (Scriptures) are invoked as the highest sanction for man's obedience.

> But ye are ty'd to fathers, and their heirs
> What say ye then if God new powers prepares.
> To present rule his word commands ye bow
> Shall God's command be crossed by your vow.[50]

Although man should obey and not defy God's providence, man himself should actively respond to its call. Walzer has aptly phrased covenant theology as "a way of activating men and not of controlling God."[51] "What the covenant did was to suggest a disciplined and methodical response to grace, a new, active and willing obedience to command."[52] Although God is omnipotent, man must respond to Him and cooperate with His plan. Not only must man—individually and collectively—thank God for the blessings bestowed upon him and his nation, not only should he passively accept God's providence, but he must actively assist Him in the task at hand.

In the earlier decades of the seventeenth century Puritan preachers, writers, and speakers had often reminded their audience that men should be doers. As Richard Sibbes said, "first consider what is our part; and as far as God prevents [i.e., goes before] us with light, and affords us help and means, we must not be failing in our duty."[53] In 1628 Alexander Leighton had called upon Parliament to act.

> As God has set you forth (right honourable) for this great work of reformation; so your choice and place require you to be men of activity . . . Joshua did well to pray, but he must up and do.[54]

In 1640 Stephen Marshall, preaching before the Commons, exhorted them to be "up and doing, and the Lord be with you in his cause."[55] In 1641 Sir Henry Vane the Younger reminded Parliament that they should act (against episcopal government in the church) for they had "been called, continued, preserved, and secured by the immediate finger of God, as it were for this work."[56]

Sermons preached before the Commons in 1649 and succeeding years reminded members of the Commons of their continuing responsibilities. Although God had achieved such tremendous victories, man needed to continue to be a doer, helping God in the great work still to be carried on. John Cardell preached to the Commons the day after Charles's execution on Matt. 11:19, "Wisdom is justified of her children." He reminded his audience that God cannot be "unmindful of His covenant with, or of his several promises and engagements unto his own people."[57] "The God of Heaven by his providence . . . hath called you to a very great work in a very difficult and dangerous time."[58] God desired that great things be done and expected the Commons to cooperate with Him. They were to be concerned with liberty and justice, and to be wise to see who should be punished and who spared. "Consider that the work itself is God's work, and that He hath engaged himself by way of promise, to be with you in it."[59]

After the victory at Dunbar in 1650, Thomas Brooks exhorted Parliament not to "let slip any opportunity wherein you may honor a good God, and be serviceable to your generation."[60] God had owned them and they should now "cleave" to God. "Oh, let not God have cause to say, lo here is a Parliament, here is a Common-Wealth that I have owned in the face of all their sins . . . and they have disowned me, when troubles and trials have been upon them."[61] God expected them to work "for common justice, and righteousness towards all men."[62] The Scots had sinned but they, so greatly favored by God, needed to "endeavor with all your might to make a conquest of all those enemies that be within you."[63]

On 9 August 1649 John Shaw "of Christ's College Cambridge and now preacher of God's word at Kingdom upon Hull," delivered a sermon at York Cathedral before the judges, justices of the peace, and gentry gathered there for the assizes. "My lords," Shaw proclaimed, "God hath hitherto carried you on courageously and undauntedly in the cause of God and the commonwealth, [now] you ride on in God's way and prosper."[64] William Cooper was most explicit in what he admonished Parliament to do, which was to thank God for his victories and "reciprocate" by listening to the cries of "poor prisoners and those many files of petitions that lie dormant in your hands, and were never read over."[65] The fiery author of *England's apology* was also concerned with man's response to Providence. Believing that God was "in love"[66] with England and "would have the glory of making this nation a commonwealth,"[67] this writer asserted that after such favors we should be humiliated "that we have not answered God in our duties, suitable to these manifestations. . . . God has given us our choice whether royal bondage, or English liberty."[68] Man's duty was to take the engagement to the Commonwealth. "No former covenant can bind me from obedience to a present duty, and serving my generation according to specific opportunities; obedience to civil powers is a duty at present. . . . Disobedience to them [the civil powers] is sinful, it being a resistance of an ordinance of God."[69]

John Owen, friend of Cromwell and a believer in religious toleration, concludes this section on Providence and man's response to it. This important and influential minister in the period of the Commonwealth[70] and at least some of the Protectorate preached before Parliament 7 June 1649, after the defeat of the Levellers at Burford. The title of the sermon, *Human Power Defeated*,[71] suggests God Himself was responsible for the defeat of the Levellers who, had they succeeded, "would have destroyed the Parliament and their own commander (Cromwell)," would have caused confusion and chaos, and whose "common workmen" would have "enjoyed their lust" for a season.[72] Speaking to those "that are rulers of this nation in the ways of peace, protection and safety," Owen exhorted them to continue to "be in the ways of God and do the things of God. . . . The ways of the Lord are your locks; step but out of them, they will be cut and you will become like other men."[73] Owen was a staunch supporter of the government, but he frequently reminded it to continue to work for the Lord in His spiritual endeavors for England.

In a sermon preached before Parliament 28 February 1650[74] on "a day set apart for solemn humiliation throughout the nation,"[75]Owen talked of Ireland. God had given the victory there to England, but now He expected the government to do its part by spreading the Protestant gospel in Ireland. "Your work," Owen proclaimed, "whereunto (while you are in his ways) God is engaged, is your safety and protection. God's work whereunto you are engaged, is the propagating of the kingdom of Christ, and the setting up of the standard of the gospel. So far as you find God going on with your work, go you on with His. . . . Do your utmost for the preaching of the gospel in Ireland."[76] Parliament must thank God for His victory in Ireland by doing their part in that land.

After the victory at Worcester, Owen preached a thanksgiving sermon[77] exhorting Parliament not only to thank God but to "meet" the Lord in three ways: "(1) in the way of his providence, (2) in the way of his worship, (3) in the way of his holiness."[78] Never had there been a time, Owen pointed out, when there had been such evidence of the "presence, power, and providence" of the "Holy One of Israel . . . in disposing of all affairs here below according to the counsel of his own will."[79] God was using England for His purposes. "In the carrying on of the interest of Christ and the gospel, God will work wonderful providential alterations among nations, states, and men on earth."[80] Nations "are to be civilly moved, that they may be spiritually established. . . . God hath gone with you, I hope, now to the end of your work, leave him not until he comes to the end of His."[81] This was the responsibility of Parliament.

Owen's views on providence and man's relation to it in his own "generation" are set forth most explicitly in the sermon he preached at Ireton's funeral on 6 February 1652.[82] Here Ireton is likened to Daniel, for both were keenly aware of God's "providential alterations"[83] or changed conditions in their own society. Knowing well that governments might change, Ireton was "wise to discern the seasons."[84] He always sought to discover God's will, but also the particular role which he himself should play at the right moment. He also possessed "a civil wisdom, or a sound ability of mind for the management of the affairs of men, in subordination to the providence and righteousness of God. . . . He ever counted it his wisdom to look after the name of God, and the testification of his will, in every dispensation of providence, wherein he was called to serve."[85] What Daniel "had in speculation was this man's [i.e., Ireton's] part to follow in action. He was an eminent instrument in the hand of God in as tremendous providential alterations, as such a spot of the world has at any time received, since Daniel foresaw in general them all."[86] He "closed with the mind of God, with full purpose of heart to serve the will of the Lord in his generation."[87]

This eulogy set forth in awesome tones the concept of God's providence and man's relation to it. According to Owen, Ireton, convinced of God's providence, played superbly his own part in his generation, cooperating fully with God but always using his own awareness of what must be done in a particular situation at a particular time, and always "laboring" with "undefatigable industry in the pursuit of the work committed to him."[88] Ireton was an example, visible to all, of God and man working together to bring about a better England in the years from 1647 to 1653.

Few men have played their part on earth as well as Owen claimed Ireton did, but beyond a doubt, those who listened to or read the numerous sermons and tracts would not forget that man—individually and collectively—had his own part, his "generation's work," to perform in cooperation with God. In any full study of the growing emphasis in seventeenth-century English thought upon man, his rights and responsibilities, his interests and powers, one chapter should be on the response of man to the long-established idea of providence. This concept proved to be a living, dynamic one which played a vital part in the thinking of English writers and preachers who faced the great changes within their nation and its government.

III

The Continuing English Commonwealth

It was natural, in the climate of thinking in mid-seventeenth-century England, for the government and its champions to turn to the Scriptures and the great manifestations of God's providence in support of their position. Not content, however, to rely only upon religious arguments, these supporters of the government looked also to more political and social concepts to justify their case. They proclaimed that although the monarchy, so fundamental in the past, had been abolished, nevertheless England as a viable entity still existed. Whether this entity was called nation or community or more precisely state or commonwealth, it was a fundamental reality to which all Englishmen owed a loyalty more basic than they owed to a king. In discussions of ideas of the period, this significant entity has not received the recognition it warrants. This chapter, therefore, sets forth the background of this concept and the shape it took in the writings of many pamphleteers at this critical period.[1] Moreover, there is considerable evidence, which will be brought out at the end of this chapter, that the concept of England as a cohesive entity influenced even some doubtful royalist souls to take the engagement.

This belief in an organic whole was an old one whose full history has yet to be written. In past centuries, however, the king had been regarded as an indispensable part of it—in fact the head entrusted with the welfare of the whole body. From the estate of the king, the term *state* had evolved. S. B. Chrimes pointed out that as early as the fifteenth century,

> Political thought was becoming less exclusively a theory of monarchy, and rather more a theory of the state . . . even though theory was still shot through and through with notions of kingship. . . . there are indications, from the century as a whole, of the currency of a conception of the *respublica*, commonweal, or State, which transcends theory of a purely monarchical derivation. Talk of the body politic, elaborate anthropomorphic conceits, concern for the *respublica Angliae* and the 'whole weal publique' . . . are all significant commonplaces of everyday political thought.[2]

These terms continued to be used in the sixteenth and early seventeenth centuries.[3] The statute 3 Jac. l.c.2 asserted, Maitland pointed out, that Guy Fawkes "had attempted the destruction of his Majesty and 'the overthrow of the whole state and commonwealth.' "[4]

From the point of view of the law, however, it has generally been held that when in 1641 Pym and St. John charged Strafford with committing treason against the state by undermining its unity, they were introducing a new concept of treason—an offense which had always been regarded as legally possible only when committed against the king. In 1965, however, Conrad Russell stated[5] that in addition to treason against the king, there had existed a parallel theory of "treason against the state, or against the stability of the kingdom," and that "the essence of this doctrine of treason is the idea of making a division between the king and the people."[6] If Russell is correct (and his thesis is a convincing one), then the concept of the entity called the state had been accorded legal meaning long before Pym and St. John employed it against Strafford.

Whatever the term *state* meant legally, there is ample evidence that it, *commonwealth*, and *kingdom* were frequently employed by leaders of Parliament in their disputes with the king in the 1620s and again between 1640 and the outbreak of the war in 1642. These

40

parliamentary leaders claimed the right to discuss matters, such as religion, appointments to high office, and foreign affairs, which for the most part had earlier been considered within the king's governing power. To support their claims parliamentary speakers in the twenties turned, not to arguments based on law and precedent, but to the general contention that they, being representatives of the realm, had a right and responsibility to consider all matters related to the state or commonwealth. "I have read nothing in the negative," a Mr. Wentworth said in the 1621 Parliament, "what business for the commonwealth we may not treat of or meddle with."[7]

It is significant that as early as 1621 Pym used the argument he employed twenty years later against Strafford. In the debates in the 1621 Parliament, Pym asserted that a certain speech attacking the Puritans constituted an offense to the state because the speaker sought to menace the great unity between king and people by bringing the Puritans "into the ill opinion of the king."[8] In that same Parliament George Moore said in his attack on Bacon, "were the Lord Chancellor never so great . . . yet the commonwealth (the mother of us all) is to be preferred before all."[9] In the 1624 Parliament a book by Richard Montagu was denounced because it was "so offensive to the state."[10] In 1628 Pym attacked Manwaring, the Arminian theologian, on the ground that if his views prevailed this would alter the form of the English government which can not be changed "without apparent danger of ruin to the state."[11]

Such statements[12] in which members of Parliament insisted that they, as well as the king, had a responsibility to discuss any and all matters of concern to the nation, whose representatives they were, certainly must have made some Parliament men more aware of the existence and importance of England as a cohesive entity. When the king won the ship money case against Hampden, it was Clarendon who later wrote that men "no longer looked upon it as the case of one man, but the case of the kingdom."[13] When the Long Parliament convened in November 1640, its leaders were determined not only to talk about their responsibility towards the state and commonwealth, but to exercise it. They impeached or attainted the king's ministers and judges and passed statutes drastically curtailing the authority of the king. Until the summer recess in 1641, the king signed these statutes demanded by the Houses, thereby still carrying out in a legal sense his responsibility as king for the welfare of the whole. The time came, however, as the rift widened between king and Parliament, when the Lords and Commons claimed sole responsibility for the kingdom's welfare and safety. In their proclamations concerning the militia bill, they insisted that they were "intrusted with the safety of the kingdom and peace of the people."[14] This same claim was asserted bluntly in their declaration of 14 May 1642. Admitting that normally king and Parliament were trusted and acted together for the safety and welfare of all in the commonwealth,

> yet since the prince being but one person is more subject to accidents of nature and chance, whereby the commonwealth may be deprived of the fruits of that trust which was in part reposed in him, in cases of such necessity, that the kingdom may not be enforced presently to return to its first principles, and every man left to do what is right in his own eyes, without either guide or rule, the wisdom of this state hath intrusted the houses of Parliament with a power to supply what shall be wanting on the part of the prince.[15]

In the latter part of this declaration it should be noted that the words "wisdom of this *state*" are used.

"Wanting" as this particular prince was, and far reaching as the claims of the two Houses often were, Parliament stated sincerely in declaration after declaration during the course of the war that they were fighting for king and Parliament.[16] Likewise, the royalists under Clarendon's wise leadership often asserted that they were fighting not only for the king and his traditional powers and rights, but also for Parliament, its legal privileges, and for Magna Carta. In the midst of the civil war, the contestants were frequently not far apart in their official statements and propaganda appeals. One may conjecture that this similarity of stated aims helped to keep alive during years of fighting the belief that an English commonwealth more fundamental than either king or Parliament still remained. Up until Pride's Purge the hope persisted that some agreement with the king might be worked out.[17] It seems reasonable to assume that practically all the members of the Lords and Commons still regarded a monarch, even one with greatly reduced powers, as essential in their polity. I know of no consideration by parliamentary leaders or of any parliamentary declaration where an entity, called state or commonwealth, is discussed without implying that the king was in some way a part of it.

The most important writer on Parliament's behalf during the civil war was Henry Parker, who in a series of pamphlets set forth a theory of parliamentary sovereignty. As early as July 1642 Parker declared that Parliament was "indeed the state itself,"[18] and also that the whole "kingdom is not so properly the author as the essence itself of Parliament."[19] His identification of Parliament as a state or kingdom is understandable in view of the long-prevailing concept that Parliament, the representative of the people, was for all practical purposes the people itself. Although Parker does not seem in 1642 to have removed the king completely out of Parliament or the state, his theories would leave the king little, if any, real power. It was natural, then, that after the abolition of monarchy this important theorist would use his pen in staunch support of a state or kingdom without a king.[20]

In examining the charges and speeches made against Charles in his trial, it is apparent that the arguments used against him do not follow a consistent pattern, some endeavoring to be as legal and constitutional as possible under the circumstances, others following more general and theoretical lines. Of course all actions against Charles, beginning with Pride's Purge, were illegal and revolutionary—the Purge itself, the Commons declaring themselves the supreme power, the act setting up the court to try the king, the charge and final sentence against the king.

If actions of the Commons were illegal, so also were any arguments based on the law and constitution. In their more general theoretical arguments, however, it should be noted that the king's accusers had considerable insight into the beliefs which had long been held concerning the function of the king and his place in their polity. These men trying the king demonstrated, in the first place, that they were keenly aware of England as a community or body to whom a true king was ultimately responsible. They often identified this whole with the Commons or with the people of England. Occasionally they employed, as in the actual charge against the king,[21] the word *commonwealth*. To them that term did not imply a new entity or form of government but the English people as a body politic.

In the second place, the men trying the king seemed to have a clear perception of the long-standing beliefs concerning the role and function of the king as head of the commonwealth. They asserted that the king had betrayed his trust as head of the body politic. Instead of keeping the peace, the kings's peace, he had waged war upon his people, as many witnesses were called to attest. Instead of protector of his people he had become their destroyer. Instead of defender of the laws he, their king, had broken them. Perhaps most important, instead of acting as a true king should for the public interest or general welfare, he had acted on the basis of his private interests. Because he had failed to act as a true king, he must be termed a tyrant and no longer be permitted to continue as the leader of his people.[22] Cutting off his head might be regarded symbolically as an act freeing the body politic to stand alone.

After the execution of the king the concept of an entity, called England, nation, state, or commonwealth, lived on and played an important part in the thinking of the years between 1649 and 1653. Although several modern historians investigating local areas have shown that local circumstances played an important part in determining men's loyalties in this period,[23] the fact that the term commonwealth was an old one, denoting an organic whole, was also a factor when men weighed their obligations and interests.

Soon after the Rump government came into power Sergeant Thorpe was faced with the task of pointing out to the grand jury at the York assizes "that statutes belonging to this nation [which the king had signed] . . . being duly observed, do really [still] promote the peace and plenty of this commonwealth."[24] In discussing treason he carefully explained that, when earlier statutes referred to treason against the king, the "name and word king . . . is frequently used to set forth the public interest of the people." What was once called "the king's peace, the king's coin, etc., really means the public concernment of the people being for their public use and benefit." When ancient statutes condemned levying war against the king, they really meant that treason was levying "war against the kingdom and the government of it."[25] It seems clear that Thorpe had a concept of an all-embracing entity, as well as its government, and was endeavoring to explain that earlier statutes couched in the king's name actually referred to the kingdom. In one sense such statements can be regarded as the necessary rationalization which had to be made when the government, desiring to maintain the law and order required for a peaceful society, depended upon statutes made when England possessed a king as head of the common-

44

wealth. From the point of view, however, of the ideas set forth in support of the Rump government, it is significant that Thorpe turned from king to kingdom and from the king's peace and coin to the "public interest of the people."

In the area of foreign affairs one of the pertinent questions which arose concerned the titles, forms, and ceremonies which the new government should use in its dealings with foreigners. Sir Oliver Fleming proposed to the council of state that foreigners should pay as much deference to it as had been given to kings, for the "high and great titles" of kings had not been "given them as particular men, but in relation to the greatness and potency of the commonwealth from whence all their titles were derived."[26] Consequently, this commonwealth continued to merit the same respect, and its government should be approached by foreigners in their dealings with it with all the form and ceremony previously accorded the king. In his advice to the council of state Fleming, like Thorpe, seems to have a concept of the commonwealth as a whole, stemming from the past when the king was a part, and continuing on its own without the king under a different form of government.

In the official statements and records of Parliament,[27] there is evidence that both before and after the act on 19 May 1649 declaring England a commonwealth, there is frequent use of the term commonwealth in a general sense as well as a form of government. In the act itself the term commonwealth is, in my view, used in two ways. In the first part of that act it is stated that "the people of England *are* and shall be, and, are hereby constituted, made, established, and *confirmed* to be a *commonwealth* and free state."[28] The words I have italicized—namely, *are, confirmed,* and *commonwealth*—imply that England had long been a commonwealth, that that fact is now confirmed, and that it is the English people, though without a king, who now constitute that commonwealth. The second part of the act declares that in the future this commonwealth shall "be governed as a commonwealth and free state [should be] by the supreme authority of this nation, the representatives of the people in Parliament."[29] The use of the word *commonwealth* in two ways—one for the larger whole and the other for the form of its government—could be and actually was confusing at times to contemporaries, as will be shown later.[30]

If the government and its officials at times thought of the commonwealth as a society of Englishmen, so did a number of pamphleteers. Even before the death of the king, the fiery Puritan John Goodwin justified the army's use of force in Pride's Purge, because the actions of those members excluded from Parliament were breaking "a poor nation in pieces."[31] For Goodwin the law of nature, necessity, and also the love of country and nation were the "law of God himself written in the fleshy tables of men's hearts."[32] According to Professor Mosse, Goodwin believed that God "legitimized" such an action as Pride's Purge if done "for the common good." It was the "godly state" and not the "ruler" that essentially concerned Goodwin. When that was in danger extraordinary actions were justifiable.[33] Another pamphleteer, the author of *Rectifying Principles,* announced before the execution of the king that the "state at large, or kingdom is king, head chief, etc."[34]

This concept of the "state at large" was a basic consideration in the thinking of many preachers and pamphleteers. To Enoch Grey, "treason against a state was more criminal than against a king, the whole being greater than a part."[35] "He was a wise statesman," Grey also wrote, "who said England is a strong body which can never die, unless it kills itself: to divide among ourselves will produce infallible ruin: in folly and fury we may wound the nation, but it is beyond our art, or the skill of angels and men to heal it, such may the confusion be."[36] John Rocket was another writer pleading the government's cause who also had a concept of the greater whole which must not be allowed to dissolve. "Let every man take his oar and with all the might and strength he has row in some part of the ship of this nation to preserve it from sinking and splitting against those many rocks that appear in every passage of this commonwealth."[37] The Puritan minister, John Shaw, wished to impress the importance of the commonwealth upon the public officials, the mayor, justices of the peace, and judges gathered together at York Minster, on 9 August 1649. "The love of this commonwealth," Shaw reminded them, "is deeply rooted in your heart (deeper than the loss of Calais in Queen Mary's time) . . . which public frame of spirit is a thing most highly commendable."[38] Each of these writers, Grey, Rocket, and Shaw, either said or implied that this entity they were concerned to preserve was of long standing, and more important than the form of its government.

Several of the most important writers supporting the government, namely Ascham, Parker, Dury, and Elcock, made much of the point that this larger whole—call it England, nation, commonwealth, community, society, or state—had long existed and continued to live on after the execution of the king and the abolition of monarchy. Before the death of the king, the theorist Anthony Ascham had seemed to be aware of the deep divisions in England and to sense the troubles ahead. Nevertheless, he believed that despite these divisions there still was an English society which would continue to exist. Ascham wrote in 1648:

> That it is ill supposed that the legislature acts of former ages are not ours. For we are still the same society or body politique, which dies not, no fundamental change intervening. Though the particular persons of past ages be no more, yet the society is the same; just as the Rhine is the same river as it was at the beginning although its waters still run away and at every moment buried in the sea. . . . A community [cannot] be properly said to change because it still holds to the same end viz, the preservation of the whole.[39]

The question posed in *Anglia Liberata* was whether this body lived on after the execution of the king.[40] Specifically, did the treaties made earlier with the Netherlands hold? William Macdonnell, a Scotsman, insisted that they no longer prevailed,[41] whereas a Dutchman and an anonymous Englishman contended that they did. According to the Dutchman, "the English people and nation is and abides the same it was, the individuals decay, the species remains."[42] The English people were the same as when the treaty with Holland was made. "The people that is now," according to the Englishman, "is the same in specie, that it was a hundred or perhaps a thousand years since . . . This noble nation of England seems now to renew her age again like the eagle, under the sweet influence of liberty."[43] Since she was the same nation as earlier, the treaties still held.

It is not surprising that Henry Parker, the most important theorist supporting Parliament in the civil war, now proclaimed clearly that England's existence as a state or community was not affected by the execution of the king and the abolition of monarchy. "The change of rule in a nation," Parker wrote, "does not change the nation; forasmuch as the manner of rule is changeable and accidental, and so does not give being, or support the essence of a state."[44] It was to the state and not to a king, that a man's allegiance was primarily due. "Our allegiance has been formerly engaged to the state of England governed in such a form: that form is now changed and now our allegiance to the state cannot be continued in the old form, without danger to the substance, without ruin to the end, for which allegiance so engaged."[45]

Although the form of government had changed, Parker insisted that the commonwealth "is the same now under this form of regiment as it was before under monarchy."[46] God insisted on obedience "to the state."[47] Englishmen could not be "neuters . . . because they are natives, and members of this state, and owe allegiance to government, howsoever they may except against this or that form of government." The engagement asked "fidelity from Englishmen to their common mother."[48] Although Parker seemed at times to use the terms *state* and *government* interchangeably, he clearly recognized that an entity more comprehensive than government, whatever its form, had long existed in England, that it still prevailed, and that men's loyalties were primarily owed to it.

John Dury, the most prolific pamphleteer supporting the government, at times also wrote of this larger entity. In his most important pamphlet, the *Considerations*,[49] he stated that this entity or commonwealth had existed earlier when there was a king "for in a kingdom there is a commonwealth as the intrinsical substance of the being thereof; for which all things are to be done by the king and lords as the public servants thereof and ministers, not masters of state."[50] In a later pamphlet Dury wrote, "For the having of a king and house of lords were never by the rulers of Christianity and natural equities understood to be useful but in order to the common-wealth."[51] The man doubting whether or not he should take the engagement should consider, Dury explained in the *Considerations*, "whether the national tie and association by which we were a commonwealth while we were yet called a kingdom hath ever been dissolved." That tie still existed, Dury contended, and Parliament had worked to keep it intact.[52] "The intent of the engagement is to this effect, that seeing there is still [i.e., without a king] a national tie and association remaining amongst the people of this land, whereof the common good ought to be procured truly,"[53] men should be loyal to the greater whole and also to the government— i.e., Parliament—which God had placed over it. If men demurred to take the engagement because of former loyalty and oaths to the king they should remember that "the ground of all these obligations is nothing else, but the welfare of the commonwealth, which was intrinsical to that which was called the kingdom." In those former oaths to the king, Dury explained, "you were bound for the commonwealth's sake, which in the bosom of the kingdom was then, and is now without it extant, and in being by itself."[54] If a man refused to take the engagement, Dury insisted in a later pamphlet, he had to admit "that it is unlawful for a subject to promise that he will be true and faithful to the commonwealth wherein he lives, because the form of government is not the same which it was before."[55]

In this pamphlet, the *Objections,* Dury suggested (without fully explaining himself) that taking the engagment to the government or powers that be was actually "more than what the engagement in express terms doth require of you."[56] Essentially he must have meant that in taking the engagement one was asked to be loyal to the commonwealth as an entity and not as a form of government. However, in another pamphlet, *Two Treatises,* he implied that the engagement asked one to be loyal to both the larger entity and to its government. "It [i.e., the engagement] does clearly oblige us to do our duty to the commonwealth collectively and representatively without a king."[57]

John Dury was not a consistent or a logical thinker. At times in urging that men take the engagment to the commonwealth, he spoke of it as the larger entity, at other times as its existing government. Nevertheless, there seems little doubt that beginning with the *Considerations,* Dury set forth a concept of a comprehensive entity, society, nation, or commonwealth which had existed when England was a kingdom, which lived on after the king's execution, and to which, next to God, an Englishman's highest loyalty was owed.[58] It is impossible to ascertain whether or not he took this concept from Ascham, whom he had probably read by November 1649. In the *Considerations,* first published in December 1649, there is no marginal reference to any authority, although this omission is no proof that he had not read Ascham. Dury was one writer, like several others treated so far in this chapter, who did not necessarily have to rely upon a particular authority such as Ascham to believe that England had long been a commonwealth under kingly government, and that this entity continued to exist even without a king as its head.

Ephraim Elcock was another important writer who had much to

say on the commonwealth as a long-standing entity. His tract, *Animadversions on a book, called, A plea for non-scribers*, was assisted through the press by his "loving friend and servant in Christ" J. D., who must be John Dury.[59] According to Dury, who wanted the tract made public, there is "something more sharp in it than my genius did affect."[60] Non-subscribers to the engagement erred, Elcock asserted, when they thought of the commonwealth as "a particular form of government." On the contrary the commonwealth was "the people or community of England, in the form of a commonwealth, as the kingdom of England was the people of England under that form of monarchy."[61] This commonwealth was "not a thing of yesterday's erection, but the commonwealth, which has heretofore been, does now more clearly appear," though the king and Lords have been cast out.[62] Clearly Elcock, like Dury and several others discussed in this chapter, believed that a commonwealth had long existed in England and possessed sufficient power to preserve itself. Turning to Aristotle's *Politics* for support, Elcock wrote, "A politick body is a society of men, according to nature having in itself . . . sufficiency for preservation of itself, constituted for being or well being or . . . commodious life." Such a society by its very nature needs a "sufficiency for all things conducible to its own civil happiness," even the change of the magistrate.[63]

Englishmen had earlier taken oaths of allegiance not to the king but to this society "or polity or commonwealth, the universality of the people, being represented by their chosen delegates, in whom all majesty and supreme power of the commonwealth resided, the king being an honorary servant of the commonwealth"[64] In taking the engagement now to the same continuing society, non-subscribers would not be breaking former oaths to the king who had been only a subordinate officer to the supreme commonwealth. Changing magistrates does "not make a new kind of government, as long as the supreme primary power and the soul (as I may call it) which moves and quickens the whole politick body, remains one and the same."[65] The commonwealth remained though king and Lords had been cast out.

In some parts of his argument Elcock identified this society not only with the people of England, but with the Commons.[66] This point of view can be seen clearly when he discussed coordinate government. A popular argument with non-subscribers to the engagement ran as follows:[67] the English government had been one of equal coordinates, king, Lords, and Commons, no one of which could legally take away another's power. According to Elcock, however, the Commons were not coordinate, but possessed a "nomothetic [i.e., law-giving] faculty and so is not properly under a law."[68] Their coordination is "originaliter and fontaliter,"[69] whereas the king's is derivative. In another part of the tract, Elcock wrote, "The whole community or universality of the nation is a commonwealth, having a nomothetic power in itself paramount to all magistrates, and this universality is represented by the house of commons."[70]

To Elcock it was "natural and properly fundamental . . . that a people inhabiting together in one land, be a commonwealth having all power to themselves, for self preservation, and are to be governed by whom themselves shall choose."[71] Elcock also viewed the Commons as possessing not only nomothetic power but legislative sovereignty—a concept which had been developed in the pamphlet warfare of the 1640s.[72] Elcock's statement is crystal clear on this point.

> Whole legislative power being in the representatives of the people who (as an house) are above all our common law and positive statutes, and may change, alter, and abrogate them, as they see most rationally convenient for the public utility of the people.[73]

Elcock's acceptance of the legislative sovereignty of the Commons, coupled with his concept of a commonwealth or community of the people of England, existing before and continuing after the execution of a "subordinate magistrate," the king, were indeed set forth and explained "sharply," as Dury had written. Elcock was a pamphleteer who set forth some of the most important concepts used in support of the commonwealth between 1649 and 1653.[74]

One of the most illuminating tracts on the commonwealth and its binding ties was written by an author who may have been Thomas Paget.[75] He explained that the commonwealth was not a new creation but one which had existed for centuries. "Englishmen for many generations have as a nation lived nationally in England, and had been combined in a politic body or commonwealth according to the rights and customs of this nation, chosen and consented unto by the people hereof. Thus is the commonwealth of England to be estimated."[76] In England, the traditional ties binding the people together were of long standing and "more natural and fundamental" than those binding Joseph to Egypt or Christ to Caesar.[77] Despite the change of government there was still the same English language and same territorial boundaries, the same Magna Carta, the same courts at Westminster and in the counties, the same Christian religion. "And principally it [i.e., the government] enacteth laws by Parliamentary power."[78] The commonwealth of England with these traditional binding ties still lived on.

As in earlier centuries the commonwealth had survived great changes, so, the author explained, it continued to do. In its long history the country had been governed by "Britains, Saxons, Danes, and Normans—refining and reforming laws and government as need has required, yet none of these variations may be said to abrogate or disanul the identity of the commonwealth of England."[79] In later centuries this commonwealth continued to exist despite many changes and reforms—even the severance of all ties with Rome—and remained "the same commonwealth still, yea, and English blood and spirits are yet remaining amongst us. . . . English patriots, in their love and zeal of their native country, should show themselves to be true and faithful to the commonwealth of England, in whose hands soever the government is established."[80] Reading this author's account of the English commonwealth as an entity bound together in the past and in the present by ties more fundamental than any one form of government could provide contributes significantly to our understanding of the term *commonwealth*.

The anonymous author of *Certain Particulars* also set forth a valuable interpretation of this entity. "By the commonwealth may be understood the public affairs and welfare of the place wherein his lot is cast to inhabit, and so much the word *res publica* doth hold forth." In the margin next to this definition he cited from Augustine's *De Civitate* and Cicero's *Rhetoric*, "Respublica est res populi."[81] To promise to be faithful in the engagement meant to be faithful to a commonwealth as the author defined it or, in other words, "to seek the welfare of the common affairs of this nation, and of those grand privileges which have cost our ancestors and ourselves such large expense both of bullion and blood," privileges such as Magna Carta, frequent parliaments, and the right to have our own governors "so far as they derive their power from the people."[82] In this last phrase, the unknown author included among his "grand privileges" not only their past heritage but their present form of government, "wherein the original of government lies in the people, both to depose magistrates abusing their trust, and to elect and choose others in their places."[83]

This concept of a commonwealth of long standing, which was more all-embracing than the existing Commonwealth government, played a part in the arguments over whether or not men should take the engagement. Late in the winter of 1649-50, when this dilemma continued to trouble many men, conferences were held in London in the hope of reaching some understanding and possibly reconciliation through discussion among men with differing views. According to the *Memorandums of the conferences,*[84] there was much talk about the government of the commonwealth and the protection and peace it was bringing to Englishmen. In addition, "something also was declared concerning the word commonwealth, that if the meaning thereof were explained to be that which I. D. has in his *Considerations,* that then it was conceived few or none would scruple at the subscribing of the engagment."[85] In other words, the anonymous author of the *Memorandums* believed John Dury's [i.e., I. D.'s] interpretation of the commonwealth as given in his *Considerations,* which has been set forth earlier in this chapter, would have satisfied some perplexed men.

Another revealing pamphlet is entitled *Conscience puzzled, about subscribing the new Engagement.*[86] Could a person who had earlier taken the oath of allegiance and subscribed to the covenant take the engagement with a good conscience? The answer, the author explained, depended upon the meaning of the term commonwealth—whether it was truly an all-embracing entity or the name of the existing government without king or Lords. "If by commonwealth be meant the whole company of men and women, both of higher and lower rank, contained within the bounds and territories of these dominions. So we were wont to call the commonwealth in the time of monarchy . . . For unto the commonwealth in this sense we must be faithful, whatsoever government it be under."[87] If men were not true to it without king or Lords, they had not been true to it before.[88]

The same distinction between the commonwealth as an entity and its present government was made by Robert Filmer, the best-known contemporary political theorist on behalf of patriarchal absolute monarchical government.[89] Because Filmer made this clear distinction he explained that men could with good conscience take the engagement to the commonwealth at large. As he explained the situation, the engagement contained two parts, "1. a promisary part: to be true and faithful to the commonwealth of England. 2. a declaratory part: as it is now established without king and house of lords."[90] Filmer contended that "the commonwealth was not created by the present government."[91] On the contrary, it had existed under kingly rule. "Though there be not a kingdom in every commonwealth, there is a commonwealth in every kingdom; in that the weale of the commons ought to be the chief and first care of the kings."[92] In taking the engagement, Filmer argued, men were essentially affirming their loyalty to the long-established commonwealth. With the death of the king the "outward manifestation of justice" had changed but the commonwealth "remaines what it was, and hath a just title to every man's fidelity that is a member of it, who as well by natural right as municipal known laws are obliged to endeaver its preservation, and not only its being, but well being."[93]

The well-being of the commonwealth obviously meant to Filmer the return of king and Lords.[94] Therefore in taking the engagement men really "engage to endeavour the restoring it to the most glorious and happy being it is capable of, according to those ancient bases and fundamental lawes upon which it was first raised."[95] Without preserving the commonwealth (or England as a viable entity), as the promissory part of the oath asked, it might be more difficult for the king and Lords to return.

Filmer explained that even the second or declaratory part of the engagement oath could be taken. Although the new Commonwealth government had not been legally established, to accept this new exercise of usurped de facto power might be a matter of "self preservation" of necessity "for your estate,"[96] and also a matter of "prudence."[97] Moreover the long-established commonwealth might not endure without some government, which helped to preserve its being, though not its well-being.

In the conclusion of his tract Filmer summed up his views as follows:

> Now I conceive without any just exception an engager may thus declare himself for the sense he subscribes in it. That he

promises to be true and faithful to the commonwealth of England, as it was originally, and by our ancient and known lawes, formed and constituted (there being no new establishment of a commonwealth,) but of a present government without king and lords, for the exercise and administration of justice in the same commonwealth it was before which I must and doe submit to though not approving of the change.

For though there be a cutting off something that should remain, the body politique or commonwealth is the same it was; and though panting and gasping and longing for recovery of its natural head, and the exercise of those vital influences that should animate and preserve it in a healthful condition, and though for the present it be sine rege, it is not sine regime, it wants its well-being but it retains (an esse) a being though sickly and imperfect under the present government. And would fail if there were not at all in which respect you ought passively to submit to it till it shall please God to restore you to the blessing of the former.[98]

Strong advocate of monarchy and even absolute monarchy as Filmer was, he nevertheless held with a number of other writers of widely differing views that there had been and still was, despite the eclipse of king and monarchy and resulting change in the form of government, a commonwealth to which men owed allegiance.

If Filmer, an ardent royalist, saw the distinction between commonwealth at large and the prevailing Commonwealth government, so in a quite different sense did those radical democrats, Lilburne and Winstanley. Unlike Filmer they did not desire the return of the king but a future, more perfect commonwealth than the present one. In a pamphlet explaining the grounds and reservations upon which he took the engagement, Lilburne based his consent upon the fact that the government had declared "the people to be the sovereign or true fountain of all just power amongst men, and to them by God's assistance I will be true and faithful. . . . By the commonwealth I understand all the good and legal people of England to be meant."[99] Concerning the present so-called Commonwealth government, he did not mean the present Parliament or council of state or army, because the "engagement makers own a higher power than themselves."[100] In their declaration of 17 March 1649 they had stated that they were elected as trustees by the people, over whom they were not supreme. Consequently Lilburne explained that he took the engagement conditionally, "to be true to them as far as they are true to their trust."[101] The present rulers were not the commonwealth named in the words of the engagement. The commonwealth, he insisted, was the people of England possessing the right to have annual and successive parliaments, trial by jury, due process of law, etc. To that more perfect commonwealth, but one which would include some past laws and procedures, as well as future aspirations, Lilburne could be true.[102]

Even the Digger philosopher Gerrard Winstanley, as a pamphlet recently discovered and printed by Professor Aylmer makes clear[103] argued in favor of taking the engagement because he thought the present government was a step towards a true commonwealth. Winstanley maintained that no commonwealth had or could exist under kingly or tyrannical government, but pointed out that the existing government in "two acts of state" have freed "the people from obedience to the king, and from all that hold claiming under him" and have declared, "England a free commonwealth." The aim of this state government, Winstanley explained, was "that all Englishmen may have their freedom in and to the land, and be freed from the slavery of the Norman conquest. . . . As it [the government] doth establish successive Parliaments, by taking away king and house of lords, so it gives a full liberty to all sort of people that are English men (and who are called upon by the state to subscribe the taking of it) to have their freedom in the choosing of their representatives."[104] "A commonwealth government implies a government by our equals, chosen out freely for a time." If the representatives forgot this truth and ruled by their wills, thus bringing in "kingly power," they would corrupt the true meaning of commonwealth government.[105] Because Winstanley believed that the present rulers had at least the concept of a true commonwealth and were moving in that direction, he argued in favor of taking the engagement.

In contrast to Winstanley and Lilburne, who looked ahead to a future more ideal commonwealth, almost all of the other writers discussed in this chapter looked back. They pointed out that Englishmen themselves had long been members of a society or commonwealth bound together by common ties. Despite the strains and divisions of the civil war and even the execution of the king and abolition of monarchy, these writers insisted that this larger entity lived on. Vital as the monarchy had been in the building and functioning of it, the commonwealth now stood alone and, so these writers argued, rightly claimed the loyalty of all Englishmen. Here, in essence, was one of the important ideas set forth by many in support of the Commonwealth government.

How effective this concept actually was in rallying support for the government and influencing men to take the engagement is impossible to determine. Religious arguments based on Scripture and God's providence, or political arguments emphasizing the fact that the Commonwealth government was actually in possession and protecting the people, may well have been more persuasive. Nevertheless, the concept of England as a commonwealth or community to which men owed loyalty played a significant part in the arguments of many of the theorists and propagandists for the government. In addition to Enoch Grey, John Rocket, and others treated briefly in this chapter, this concept loomed large in the thinking of Ascham, Parker, Dury, and Elcock—four of the most important theorists or pamphleteers of the time. Moreover, there is clear evidence that some writers recognized the difference between commonwealth in the larger sense and the Commonwealth government. It seems reasonable to speculate that this difference must have helped some perplexed men resolve their dilemmas and take the engagement. To the royalist Filmer, this difference proved to be significant.

If this concept of a larger entity played an important part in the political thinking of a number of men from 1649 to 1653, its significance is even greater in the longer history of social and political ideas. To think about political society apart from the king, so long regarded as an integral and indispensable part of their polity, did not come easily for Englishmen. Their recognition in these years that the English community, whatever its form of government, was a viable entity possessing binding traditional ties, constitutes an important transition from older to more modern ways of viewing their polity. It was in the seventeenth century that there was, according to Professor Hanson,

> . . . the appearance of what may be called civic consciousness and loyalty. . . . the development, or better, perhaps, the recovery of consciousness of a uniquely public dimension in social life—public in the sense of general or common to the social order as a whole. The idea of civic consciousness refers to

the elementary perception that there is a public order, that the social order is in part a network of shared problems and purposes, and to the installation of that recognition at the center of political ideas and conduct.[106]

The concept of the age-old English commonwealth, set forth by a number of writers between 1649 and 1653, adds another chapter to the history of the development of "civic consciousness and loyalty" in the seventeenth century.

IV

IMPORTANCE OF GOVERNMENT AND ITS POSSESSION

With the execution of Charles and, more important, the abolition of monarchy, that institution so interwoven with Englishmen's political concepts and beliefs, some pamphleteers and preachers began to consider government itself apart from its traditional tie with monarchy. They saw in possession a government of doubtful validity to say the least, but clearly a government which performed in many respects as they had long believed a monarchical government should. Relative peace and order prevailed in England, as they had not since the outbreak of the civil war in 1642. The law courts now functioned, affording to many men of property the protection necessary to retain and enlarge their landed holdings. These essentials, so dear to the hearts of important Englishmen, were reasonably well provided by the new government. In less than three years the Commonwealth government subdued the enemies threatening its security in Ireland and Scotland and quickly won the respect of several foreign nations, Catholic Spain being the first to recognize the new government. The memories of England's disastrous Continental war in the 1620s and the continuing decline of English prestige abroad could be partly erased in men's minds as they contemplated the new government's successes in foreign affairs.

In the face of these achievements at home and abroad, a climate of opinion emerged in which a number of protagonists of the Commonwealth government ignored concepts which had traditionally conditioned much political thinking in England. These writers showed no regard for God or monarch, for the origins or legitimacy of the government. No longer did they ask how a monarch should perform or ideally should rule his subjects. Instead, in a frankly pragmatic fashion, the defenders of the Rump set forth the importance of government itself, whatever its form. They insisted that possession of the government, rather than its origin or legal claims, was the basic criterion by which it should be assessed. They asked probing questions about the nature of government per se, such as: What are the major functions and characteristics that can be found in any government? What is justice if a monarch is no longer the fount of justice? How does a man judge whether the government of a community is one to which he owes allegiance? What are the utilitarian benefits government provides? If it protects a man and serves his particular interests, does he not owe it obedience?

The writer who first concerned himself with some of these questions was Anthony Ascham, whose *Discourse* had appeared in 1648 before the execution of Charles. Beginning in the summer of 1649, as Skinner has shown, Ascham led the way in setting forth a secular theory supporting the new government and the engagement it required of more and more Englishmen.[1] Ascham undoubtedly influenced many pamphleteers, some of whom actually cited him. Ascham's own ideas, first enunciated in 1648, were sharpened by his contact with the views of Hobbes, whose *De Cive* he had read some time before November 1649. Earlier writings of Hobbes were published in England in 1650 and 1651. Skinner has shown that Hobbes himself deliberately entered the engagement controversy with the publication of the *Leviathan* in 1651,[2] and like Ascham influenced a number of preachers and pamphleteers. Exactly who read whom and appropriated whose ideas is not always easy to determine, for writers at this time often chose not to acknowledge their sources, particularly when it was the "atheist" Hobbes.[3] Nedham is an important writer in this period who formulated his views, Hobbesian in some respects, independently of Hobbes. Nedham was delighted, however, to find that the supposedly royalist Hobbes shared his opinions, and in the second edition of the *Case of the Commonwealth* Nedham added an appendix out of Salmasius and Hobbes.[4]

The purpose of this chapter and the next is not to trace, as Skinner has done so well, the important roles played by Ascham and Hobbes in the engagement controversy or to attempt specifically to discover and assess their influence upon other writers participating in this controversy. It is, rather, to examine the many different ways in which known and unknown writers viewed their government, now that England no longer had a monarch as its head, and in so doing to show that a new climate of opinion concerning government clearly emerged in these few years.[5]

In this changed climate of opinion the sheer need for government itself, whatever the form, is a favorite theme set forth by the Commons, by public officials, and in the pamphlets and sermons supporting the Rump. The Commons intended to preserve, they stated in their declaration of 17 March 1649,

> the laws and government of the nation; and that if those should be taken away, all industry must cease; all misery, blood, and confusion would follow; and greater calamities, if possible, than fell upon us by the late king's misgovernment, would certainly involve all persons, under which they must inevitably perish.[6]

Two charges given by Thomas Edgar, justice of the peace for the county of Suffolk, revealed the attitude of one public official on the necessity of maintaining government and suppressing crime.[7] Edgar insisted that those now "in public employment in a commonwealth, must not desert government, because the way or form doth not like them."[8] "Government itself," and not monarchy or any other form, "is of divine right."[9] Man needs government. It is true that in divine affairs who commands is important, but in human affairs, what is commanded counts.[10] If local officials objected "that the stamp or effigies of the seal is new," they needed to remember that "the effigies is not the virtue of the seale. But the honor and virtue of the great seal is because it passes all original proceedings of justice . . . and all public instruments of government and state."[11] Through the seal justice reached the people. "And therefore it is [now] called the great seal of England and not of any king or particular person."[12] To seek out crime, put down disorder, catch the thief, repair sewers, was as essential under this government as it was in the past under a king, if society was to be preserved. It was fortunate, Edgar pointed out, that the old laws still prevailed. "These laws, like truth, are very aged, yet very fresh and good, without wrinkles, of full beauty and strength, their age and duration show the strength of their constitution."[13] Both Edgar and the Commons in their March 1649 declaration linked the new government with the long-established laws, presumably to persuade people needing and loving those laws to accept this government which promised to preserve them.

Thus, the importance of government itself for man and human society became a note sounded increasingly by pamphleteers and preachers. J. Blackleach cautioned his readers not to be afraid of government because Charles had been a bad monarch.[14] He reminded his readers to consider "that God is the author of government" and "that from the excellency of government does arise the happiness and blessedness of the saints in the kingdom of heaven."[15] "How the change of government should be against the nature of government [Samuel Eaton] could not apprehend."[16] According to the anonymous author of the *Memorandums of the conferences*, "the being of a government was absolutely necessary for the preservation of human societies, and that of the being and existence thereof there could be no intermission with the safety of societies."[17] "Without government," the author of *The Engagement vindicated* wrote, "a second chaos must needs return upon the world."[18]

John Owen, as shown in chapter 2, said much on God's providence and man's response to it, yet in his famous sermon delivered upon Ireton after the latter's death, Owen made the following remarkable statement about government itself:

> Some things are universally unchangeable and indispensable among men, supposing them to live answerable to the general principles of their kind: as that a government must be; without which everyone is the enemy of everyone, and all tend to mutual destruction which are appointed of God for mutual preservation, that in government some do rule, and some be in subjection, that all rule be for the good of them that are ruled, and the like principles that flow necessarily from the very nature of political society.[19]

How Owen came to see government in such terms is impossible to determine. Was he influenced by Ascham, Hobbes, the climate of opinion, or the political realities in 1651? In any case, he demonstrated in this statement that he could think of government in essentially secular, not religious, terms.

Zacheus Mountagu and William Sclater were two preachers who still maintained that it was God who ordained government for man. It was government itself, however, and not monarchy or even the laws, which they eulogized in their assize sermons.[20] According to Mountagu, "If you take government out of the world, you take the sun out of the firmament and leave it no more a beautiful structure but a ruinous heap of confusion."[21] Sclater waxed eloquent on the benefits which government, ordained by God, provided for man. Government is, he explained,

> as an order to an army, without which it were but a crowd, it's as an hedge to a vineyard, which without it would be wasted by wild boars and other spoiling creatures, it's as an hem to a garment which without it would ravel out. . . . What is it that clothes you in scarlet with other delights and puts on ornaments of gold upon your apparel, is it not government? What is it that clothes your downs, your pastures, your valleys with flocks and store till they shout and sing for joy, is it not government?[22]

Since God ordains government, so essential for man,

> when men offer to reject that form of government which is by providence cast upon them, in the language and style of the Holy Ghost, they do not reject man, but God himself, that he should not rule over them [1 Sam. 8:7].[23]

Paralleling the emphasis upon the importance and need of government for man was the argument that actual possession of the government, rather than its origins or legality, was the essential fact Englishmen should remember. Writers stressing this point were fortunate that neither before nor after the execution of Charles was there any hiatus of power, but a government always in possession. Furthermore, even though no king now possessed the government, the idea of possession as an important factor in giving it validity had a goodly, even legal, heritage. Henry VII had picked up the crown on Bosworth Field, where Richard III lay dead, and had placed it on his own head. Once possessed of the kingship he had quickly acted to strengthen his dubious hereditary claim by marrying the right woman, calling Parliament, and legalizing his position by statute. Moreover, to believers in God's providence it was clear that God himself had sanctioned or chosen this government now in possession. For many reasons possession of the government was one of the strongest arguments used by a number of writers, both religious and secular, supporting the Rump.

In the summer of 1648, months before the execution of the king, Anthony Ascham wrote, "As for the point of right, it is a thing always doubtful, and would be ever disputable in all kingdoms. . . . Possession therefore is the greatest title."[24] The important question was "whether the invading party have us and the means of our subsistence in his possession or no?"[25] Ascham seemed to be preparing the way for men to accept as valid a government clearly in possession, though without a monarch. In *The bounds & bonds of public obedience*, purchased by Thomason 27 August 1649, Ascham quoted Grotius on the situation in one kingdom where the king had part of the power and "the people or senate the other [part]." If war took place between "such fundamental and supreme parties," Grotius explained (and Ascham agreed with him), "the king may lose all his share [of power] by the right of war."[26] No residual or mystical power remained to him as king. In England, Ascham pointed out, the war had been won by Parliament, "now sitting at Westminster," unquestionably the supreme power of the kingdom. Whether or not they "be a Parliament according to the old forms and composure of the Parliament," they should be obeyed.[27] Men should not question "how the change was made,"[28] but should accept the fact that a change actually had taken place.

It was probably in November 1649 that Ascham's 1648 *Discourse* was republished with certain additions.[29] Even more in these additions than in the earlier edition, Ascham emphasized possession, and discussed it specifically in relation to the oaths involving the king which many men were loath to break. "Possession," he insisted, "is the great condition for our obedience or allegiance."[30] "Mortal men" should conclude "that we of the people must be contented with these governors, into whose full possessions it is our destiny to fall."[31] In his last known writing, Ascham continued to assert that allegiance was dependent on possession, "original and legal assurance being a moral impossibility it is best and enough for our present obedience, to inform ourselves, whether the kingdom be plenarily possessed by those who at present exercise immediate command over it."[32] As for former "promissory oaths," Ascham explained, they "always have tacit conditions innate to them, in regard of their uncertain futurition. That the condition of political oaths is to obey whom God permits plenarily to possess kingdoms, which is the sense in which kings themselves understand them."[33]

Power and actual possession of the government were frequent themes of Nedham and Osborne. Nedham referred often to the fact that the authority of Henry VII was based upon the foundation of military power. "As for any just title, he could have none."[34] If the present government "had no other plea for possession than the power of the sword, it were just as good a title as any of our kings had since the conquest, as may be seen in all our chronicles."[35] Osborne also made possession and power a key factor in his arguments. He bluntly proclaimed "that no government extant this day could possibly be demolished by fouler hands than it was erected."[36] Osborne took pains to remind his readers that men in possession did not easily "part with their power" and those out of power would find it difficult to find friends.[37]

Other less well-known pamphleteers and ministers sounded the same note, that possession was the determing factor. As Richard Saunders declared in a sermon, man can only judge if power is of God if it "actually is." Saunders went even further, declaring in the title of his sermon that "plenary possession makes a lawful power."[38] The anonymous author of the *Northern subscriber's plea* said, "We can expect no operation of that which is not in being, let the title or right to power be never so highly pretended."[39] According to another pamphleteer, it was "the present juncture of affairs"[40] that demanded attention.

Edward Gee's *An exercitation concerning usurped powers*,[41] one of the most effective pamphlets denouncing the government, was rebutted by an anonymous writer in *The exercitation answered*.[42] Here the author insisted that men should weigh the present situation when considering obedience to government. He contended that "obedience is due to powers in possession though unlawfully entered."[43] This government, he argued, was securing peace and providing order, of which God approved. Since it was God who put the government in possession, how could man resist it?[44] Moreover, "neither can the obligation of an oath whatsoever invalidate a duty, or enforce a sin in this particular,"[45] as Gee and others had insisted. If God supported the government in possession, so did the statute of Henry VII and earlier court decisions.[46]

This interesting tract, *The exercitation answered,* ended with a long quotation from William Perkins's, *Treatise of callings* (p. 742). The author of *The exercitation answered* reminded his readers that Perkins was a "holy, impartial, and reverend author," writing before the present situation existed, and implored them to hear what Perkins had written "concerning the validity of the commands of an usurped power and the duty of obeying them."[47] According to Perkins, the author of *The exercitation answered* explained, "if there be no fault in the work the defective calling of the worker, doth not make a nullity of the action done. . . . For though he be called amiss, yet he stands in the room of one lawfully called."[48] Denying this truth would "over turn the regiments of kingdoms, churches, states, and societies, whatsoever."[49] Relying upon God's sanction, English law, and the teachings of a leading Puritan preacher of an earlier period, the unknown author of *The exercitation answered* insisted that the government in possession, whatever the means by which it had acquired power, had to be obeyed.

Many of the ideas related to possession which have been discussed up to now could be set forth in poetry, as the following ditty by R. F. illustrates:

> Crowns were but gallant robberies at first
> And conquerors heroic thieves that durst
> Attempt the worlds enslaving, why should we
> Repine them to behold a monarchy
> Rak'd up in dust?
> . . . .
> I must subscribe to and congratulate
> The sanctions of heaven, the hand of fate
> . . . .
> Present things
> and forms of state must be our laws and kings.
> . . . .
> And be reformed in this

To yield obedience to the state that is
. . . .
For Gods determination must be,
His yea, makes nay impossibility
. . . .
There's nothing wanting which we had before
Only our grievances are not so sore.[50]

Another ditty runs as follows:

What say he then if God new powers prepares
To present rule his word commands, ye bow.
Shall God's commands be crossed by your vow?
His word forbidding, oathes unlawful makes.
You'll say to such as have a legal call
But God himself doth bid submit to all
You'll say to good and just, not bad ye dare
But God bids yield unto the powers that are;
And in so doing, promises to bless
Men with a quiet life in Godliness
For they that titles do so far extend
Will kindle fires that burn unto the end
Who swears to future powers, doth strife increase
Who swears to present, is a friend of peace.
Thus heavenly wisdom doth direct to be.
Submiss 'neath present from past powers free,
Marking the streams in which his actings run,
Praying, thy will, O Lord, on earth be done.[51]

The message conveyed in these ditties is clear. Englishmen must cease to think of past powers or to yearn for their return. Instead they should obey God's command and accept the present power actually in possession of the government. By such action they would bring peace to a troubled land, enabling men to live "a quiet life in godliness."

Although this basic idea of possession of the government as determining its validity was a concept which had long played a part in men's thinking about kings in England, it took on added meaning in these critical years. Now it was applied, not to a king seizing the throne, but to a party forcibly taking over the government and maintaining itself in power. Now it acted to obliterate the sanctity of oaths which had long bound men in the most solemn fashion to their earthly monarch, the king. Undoubtedly when they wrote of possession, the pamphleteers and ministers knew that they were appealing to men of different beliefs who so longed for peace in their native land that the possession of government, rather than its legality, might be a persuasive argument in favor of their supporting the existing government. This emphasis on possession was one concerned with present reality, not with past traditions and rights. Consequently both the importance of the present and of sheer power loomed large in men's political thinking and played an important part in the changing criteria by which government was assessed.

V

PROTECTION AND OBEDIENCE, JUSTICE AND HUMAN INTERESTS

A significant number of the writers and preachers defending the government and justifying the engagement injected into their arguments certain basic problems and concepts concerning the nature and functions of government itself, whatever its original form. The more philosophically minded of these writers became concerned with political obligation, with the basic functions of any government, and with the nature of justice. Others, more practical in their approach, discussed the criteria men should use in assessing the value to them of the government under which they lived.

Again it was Anthony Ascham who led the way in exploring some of these more fundamental aspects of government itself. Undergirding much of Ascham's thought was his hatred of war and confusion and his profound desire for a stable, peaceful society.[1] When in 1649 the Levellers and those refusing to take the engagement seriously threatened the peace, Ascham came to the government's support, using his pen to answer its critics and to set forth a secular justification of it, as Skinner has shown.[2] In *Bounds & bonds* Ascham stated that "the administration of public justice and protection" were the "soul of a state," and that these were provided by the "present powers."[3] When men receive protection, he later wrote, they may "enjoy the fruits of their own labors, communicate with another's virtues, sleep composed (without any alarms in their beds) . . . they therefore who enjoy such a protection are indebted for a return of allegiance."[4] To Ascham the protection given by the government required in turn the obedience of men living under and benefitting from that protection.

Many writers at this time were undoubtedly influenced by Ascham, Hobbes, Nedham, or by all three. Fervent longing for peace and all its advantages must have been in their minds when they emphasized the importance of protection.[5] The anonymous author of *Essays upon several subjects* claimed that protection was the "end and essence of all government,"[6] while Drew remarked "it sufficeth us if the reason or foundation of allegiance be protection."[7] Drew insisted that in taking the engagement, men were bound only "to our actual protectors successively."[8] Price asked the clergyman preaching against the government, "have you not protection by this government? . . . Should a man seek to destroy that which preserveth him? . . . Cannot you live under them a peaceable and quiet life in all godliness and honesty?"[9] According to these writers and others the existing government, which gave protection to Englishmen, deserved their allegiance rather than a king who had failed in a monarch's responsibility to protect his subjects and give them peace, and instead had actually waged war on them and torn the country apart. "That power [i.e., the king]," wrote the author of *Essays upon several subjects*, "seems to be ceased, and consequently all engagements to it that hath no ability to protect those it claims allegiance from, nor they any means left to defend it, they are the powers in being we are commanded to obey. . . . Tis the exercise of government, not the title of the governors, that most concern us that are subjects. . . . Unless we desire to live alone in the world, or in continual war, we must acknowledge some power, from which upon our allegiance, we may expect protection, wherein the end and essence of all government seems to consist."[10]

According to the lawyer Cocke, "It is certain protection requires obedience."[11] John Dury, as usual employing almost any prevailing argument in support of the government, put it this way: "So that he who gives protection hath a right to challenge allegiance, and he that will not yield in just and lawful things, his allegiance hath no right to challenge protection."[12] Nedham made protection a favorite theme and Osborne insisted that the present government "having the only power of protection, cannot in justice be denied the duty of obedience."[13]

One of the most effective pamphlets, according to the scanty evidence available,[14] in persuading people to take the engagement was *A discourse concerning the Engagement: or the Northern subscriber's plea opposed to their dissenting Northern Neighbors importune animosities against Engaging to be true and faithful.*[15] The first argument presented by the anonymous author, and the one he himself stated was the most important, rested upon Providence. The second was based upon "the mutual relation of protection and allegiance." This mutual relation, "every benefit requiring some duty, presseth us to a cheerful owning the Parliament . . . as our actual protectors in subscribing to be true and faithful."[16] The author dismissed the sanctity of the oath of allegiance to the king, since "the ground of that oath we conceive to be our actual protection, and not merely the king's obligation to protect us. . . . If the king is not actually our liege lord, we cannot be termed his liege subjects, for relations stand and fall to-gether."[17] It was not necessary, according to this author, to "labor in specifying or aggravating the benefits of protection, they being so obvious a sense to all, who prize religion, life, liberty and prosperity."[18] The clarity with which this anonymous author distinguished between the traditional obligation of a king to protect his subjects and the protection the existing government actually provided, as well as his insistence that protection and allegiance were mutual, marked him as one who understood much about the nature of government itself.

The author of *The Engagement vindicated* paid at least theoretical respect to the older ideas of monarchy and oaths, and at the same time urged support for the new government. Admitting that "monarchy doth most resemble God's manner of government," the author insisted that "this doth not prove it the most accommodate to human affairs, unless we could attain to a succession of kings perpetually, that would exactly imitate God in his dispensation."[19] This author admitted "that oaths [i.e., those taken earlier to the king] that a man can be under" were of a "moral complexion," whereas engagements were of "an order inferior to oaths, not attesting God, not immediately eyeing religion or conscience, but obligatory by the law of mutual faith and honesty, the pillar of human converse."[20] The oaths concerned "conscience and religion," or God, while the engagement concerned man's "moral honesty and faith."[21] Could a clearer distinction be made between the traditional reliance upon a sanction based on an oath to God, and that resting on the "mutual faith" of man to man? This writer seems to have recognized that a transition from religious to secular ties binding society together was taking place in his own time.

No longer could this writer, and the other pamphleteers who argued that men should take the engagement to the existing government, consider the traditional and "mystical" ties between the English monarch and his subjects. Instead they came to understand and to set forth the mutuality between the services (particularly protection) provided by the government and the allegiance owed it by those living under it. They had come to grips with one of the most, if not the most fundamental question in political theory— that of political obligation.

The most philosophically minded of these writers, Anthony Ascham, dealt not only with political obligation but also with forms of government, insisting that there was no essential difference between them. Whether in monarchy, democracy, or mixed government, "the supreme acts of government were the same": in the first place "to make and take away a law, secondly to make war and peace, thirdly to judge of life and death, fourthly to fix all appeal in itself. . . . For what change is a change of government. It changes neither our human nature nor our spiritual relations, but only a ministerial circumstance of our mean civil station.[22] In a state, "every man must either command or obey, or else live by himself, by his own laws and his own militia."[23] In this new situation where no monarchy existed, Ascham analyzed the nature of government itself, whatever its form.

It was Ascham also who discussed political justice which, with protection, he regarded as the "soul of the state." His views on this vital subject reveal how completely he had abandoned traditional concepts concerning it. He was searching, so he announced, "after that sort of justice only, which is due to the people from any magistrate [whatever the form of government] and likewise to any magistrate from the people."[24] He called this political justice, which "consists in the reciprocalness of mutual human rights, paternal and filial duties, as we are congregated into commonwealths and public societies."[25] Political justice, in such a society, is that equity whereby a private man is rightly ordered under the public magistrate of his particular country, and collaterally toward his fellow citizens of that particular country by public care and inspection. Secondly, it is that equity whereby the magistrate likewise of that particular country employs his chiefest care according to his chiefest law for the safety of those fellow citizens in that country.[26]

The magistrate's function is to protect, the private man's to obey and to act officially within the framework the government has decreed. When protection is well given and allegiance reciprocally rendered in a "public society," there is political justice.[27] Although Ascham admitted that universal, private, and legal justice were important,

> yet none has such sad effects in this world as the violation of political justice. When this runs into a war, it disorders all the other relations of justice, the religion of God in universal justice is suspended, temples are fired, opportunities are given to revenge and to desolate a private neighbour. . . . Innocent families are desolated, and private vice or injustice has no limits. . . . many times ambitious or angry men form subtleties and pretences, and afterwards the poor people (who understand them not) are taken out of their houses . . . to fight and maintain them at the perils of one another's lives, and such wars not being of their interest, they are sure to reap nothing but desolation by them.[28]

Ascham's reversal of the concepts of justice is obvious when his ideas are compared with those set forth by St. Thomas Aquinas, who saw eternal justice flowing down to man through natural and divine justice. To Ascham, political justice on earth was primary—any basic failure of it overturned all other justice, even natural, divine, and eternal. God and his justice were no longer of real concern to this writer who so longed for peace, particularly for the common man, in his own time and land, so long torn by civil dissension, that he abandoned traditional ideas and concentrated on down-to-earth human realities. Ascham is the writer who best illustrates in a number of ways, which have been indicated in this essay, the new secular realistic thinking on political matters which had emerged in these few years when monarchy had been officially abolished.

The secular ideas set forth in support of the Rump government were many and varied. Those discussed up to now in this chapter delved deeply into the nature and functions of government itself. Others were primarily concerned with the practical question of how men should assess this new government. Some of its protagonists advised perplexed Englishmen that they should examine pragmatically the merits of this particular government, not in absolute but rather in relative terms, weighing its merits in comparison with those of King Charles's government.

The best known of such writers was Henry Robinson, who had argued persuasively during the forties in favor of religious toleration and parliamentary sovereignty. In *A short discourse between monarchical and aristocratical government,* Robinson did not defend the legality of the existing regime, but pointed out that in evaluating recent changes some had paid more attention to "how things are done than what is done."[29] Robinson believed that this present government should be judged pragmatically by its "justness and honest fruits." It is these which "will endear mens hearts to it."[30] Certainly the present government, which Robinson frankly labeled an aristocracy, was superior to that of King Charles who had brought misery upon his people.

To Robinson, "our liberty and his [i.e., Charles's] life were grown incompatible and inconsistent"[31] with each other. Monarchy as a form of government no longer fitted "the facts of political life in the community."[32] The present government, however, Robinson pointed out, had been careful not to change the laws or the "fundamentals of the former government, but only the persons and mal-administration of it."[33] It had done well, bringing more justice to the people than had prevailed under Charles. Be sensible, Robinson urged his readers, and accept this government as better than the king's. Even if it was not all they desired it was better to act with it "than to give encouragement to our common enemy [i.e., Prince Charles]."[34] Men should not expect perfection or that all wrongs would soon be righted, as Robinson implied the Levellers did. With that group in mind, Robinson pointed out to his readers the realistic difficulties of achieving the great changes the radicals desired.

74

It's easy to frame an idea of a new government, and as easy to live under it in peace, had we all but one mind; but not so easy . . . to alter an old one, where so many parties are engaged and disaffected and so much rubbish to be removed. Were we to begin the world again, and to choose for ourselves, having hearts, we should not need swords, and then an agreement of the people, though not according to the Levellers anarchical model, might be a foundation of peace.[35]

Many moderate men in and out of the government must have evaluated the existing government in the relative way Robinson did, but it is fortunate that this writer expressed his cool pragmatic beliefs in a pamphlet which has survived.

The unknown author of *Essays upon several subjects* clearly recognized the dilemma men faced in deciding whether or not to take the engagement. Earlier in the civil war, he explained, "many good men were at a stand what to do [because] the principles of government [were] divided among themselves."[36] This author came to believe the present government should be accepted because, for one reason, it was the one "the times [are] most capable of. . . . We seem to be fallen so far into the dregs of vice, that we are not capable of the best constitution; we must not expect to be governed by angels in this world, though we were better men than we are."[37] Men should accept the present government despite its imperfections. "We are not in the place of God to dispose of the events of affairs, and since things are fallen out so contrary to our expectation . . . we ought to consider rather what may concern us in this present juncture of affairs, than what may seem to be required of us as to former relations. . . . Tis the exercise of the government, not the title of the governors, that most concerns us that are subjects."[38] The unknown author of *Certain Particulars* admitted that he did not like all aspects of the present government. Nevertheless, "our case would be far worse if there were none [i.e., government] at all, and perhaps for such a time as this, the fittest expedient which could be found."[39]

John Price also looked at the existing government in cold, realistic terms. In a morning lecture he lashed out against "the Cloudy Clergie," those "London preachers, who . . . do corrupt the judgments of their seduced auditors, against the governors and government of the Commonwealth of England."[40] Price frankly admitted that the older government was "altered by force of arms," yet it is "impossible to find a lawful authority in the world."[41] Why should men hesitate to obey the present government? "Cannot you live under them a peaceable, and quiet life in all godliness and honesty? . . . Have you not protection by this government"[42] and all the benefits of protection such as recourse to the law when needed? According to Rous, it was "better to have some justice than none at all, some coercive power and government than that all be left to disorder, violence and confusion."[43]

The unknown author of *Vox Pacifica* freely admitted that conditions under the Commonwealth government were not perfect. Nevertheless, "the ship of this commonwealth is now near her harbor, fraught with peace, and the blessed means of plenty and freedom. . . . Trading is now in a fair way to flourish."[44] New elections would be held in which the peoples' desires and interests would count.[45] Remembering "how successless the last wars" were, let us not bring on a new war.[46] It is much easier to find fault than "a remedy."[47] Since we are "near our harbor" under this government, we should "compose our spirits" and resolve our doubts.[48]

The author of *The Engagement vindicated*, known only as T.B., freely admitted the criticisms and shortcomings of the government, but nevertheless stoutly defended it. If men criticized the government for the energy and money spent on the problem of Ireland, they should remember that its Irish policy had secured England's safety.[49] Of course they groaned over the taxes, "but let us consider the necessity of them. Can an army be maintained without these?"[50] Rather than complain that the government had not lived up to its promises to the people, they should remember that everything couldn't be done all at once but only "by degrees."[51] Instead of criticizing, "rather let us bless ourselves in that order and hope we sit under, by the protection and prudence of those faithful steerers, that have stood up for our safety, that have ventured and hazarded their all for us, and who are daily consulting a further settlement and assurance of our hopes."[52]

Thus a number of pamphleteers urged that men be sensible and judge the existing government pragmatically by its fruits. They should weigh its practical accomplishments and abandon their traditional belief in monarchy as well as their utopian hopes for the future. Illegal as this government's origins might be, limited as its achievements still were, Englishmen should realize that it was better for them than the government of King Charles, and in the future might even bring about more of their aspirations. This down-to-earth advice played a part in the changed climate of thinking about political society which emerged between 1649 and 1653.

As some pamphleteers urged that men should assess the present government in relative, not absolute or traditional, terms, others pointed out that in judging it men should consider its utility for themselves. They should ask whether this particular government was advantageous for their property, profession, and position in society—in short, their particular interests.

As early as 1642 a country rector, Charles Herle, had made such interests a central point in his arguments on behalf of Parliament and its sovereignty. He wrote:

> Experience shows that most men's actions are swayed most by their ends and interests . . . it was the wisdom of this government . . . to trust it rather to many independent men's interests [i.e., Parliament], than a few dependent men's oaths, every day's experience tells us that interests are better state security than oaths . . . our interests are entrusted [to Parliament] and so, subjected to their decisions.[53]

With the execution of the king and the abolition of monarchy, it was understandable that men should consciously weigh their own interests in deciding whether or not to accept this government cut off from ties with the past. As Robinson wrote in his *Short discourse,* on the "new foundation" provided by Providence, men now "have time to consider our own good," not the king's.[54] "Let our own interest prevail upon us" to accept the new government. If God's verdict "be too light, let earth be added to it to weigh down our judgements"[55] was the advice given by the author of *England's apology.* Dury freely admitted that the king's government had been legal, but this fact did not mean that "it is still most expedient for the public state."[56] Marchamont Nedham and Francis Osborne surveyed the situation in a realistic way. To them, as has been shown, the government's actual possession of power was a strong reason for its acceptance. To them also, the futility of resistance to the government and the realistic advantages of accepting it were telling arguments in its favor. The utility and benefit of a submission by all is the theme of Part II of Nedham's *Case of the Commonwealth of England Stated*. Since neither the royalists, Scots, Presbyterians, nor Levellers could succeed in overthrowing the government, as Nedham explained in considerable detail, it would be foolhardy for Englishmen to support the causes of any of these enemies of the regime.[57] Nedham's remarks about the gentry of royalist persuasion are particularly revealing. "It is not like that the gentry, men of estates, will stir in any considerable number to hazard their possessions, being yet scarce warm in them, after a purchase is made upon dear rates of composition."[58] In a similar vein, Osborne appealed to the gentry and nobility to accept the government. Not only would it be difficult for them to change it by another war, but they should be mindful of the fact that "a quiet and timely submission would estate them or their children in an undoubted capacity to share in what is or shall be established, enabling them to alter what they may find amiss."[59]

Many writers pointed out the special benefits which the Commonwealth government had or would provide, arguing as Robinson did, "that the justness and honest fruits of this government would endear men's hearts to it."[60] In the debate in the Commons in September 1651 concerning new elections, Colonel John Jones pointed out that more time was necessary before new elections could be held.

> Let there be patience used until burdens may be taken off, and the people enjoy some rest and opulency under the new change, let the old weeds that be dead on the ground have time to rot, let the Commonwealth have some time to take root in the interests of men, before it be transplanted or grafted on another stock. . . .[61]

John Price, a clergyman, and Albertus Warren, a lawyer, appealed to different groups in society to support the government on the basis of their interests, rather than their traditional loyalties. Speaking to the "cloudie clergie" (mainly Presbyterians) who were stirring up the people, Price reminded them of their own clerical interests. He cautioned them to remember that if their words should "charm up among the common people a spirit of scorn and contempt upon our governors" which might lead to rebellion against them, "do you suppose that you can charm them into a reverential and awful respect of your cloth?"[62] The clergy should look to their own interests and stop stirring up the people to revolt and upset the peace.

The lawyer, Albertus Warren, appealed to the interests of the clergy and also of gentlemen and lawyers, explaining that their acceptance of the present authority was "rational and necessary."[63] In his advice to gentlemen, he deplored the fact that too much had been made "of the indispensable necessity of monarchy." Gentlemen paid too much attention to "other men's doctrines," whereas "examples teach better than cold logic persons now-a-days are most to be studied."[64] Again, the emphasis was upon the present situation and not upon older ideas and traditions. Gentlemen also, Warren explained, had to change their way of thinking and realize that their place in society did not in reality depend upon the royal court. In fact their troubles in the past had come from the court itself and from the church.[65] In the future, however, under a democracy without a court, "a noble mind may climb up 'honors temples' by virtue's stairs."[66] Rather than hoping for a return of monarchy, gentlemen should realize that they could fare well under a democracy. Moreover, they should look at the situation realistically, and cease to hope for the return of monarchy. They should do nothing to prejudice themselves "from places of trust in the Commonwealth." Otherwise there would be danger that "inferior men of truth and breeding [would] ingross all places of honourable civil command and most gentlemen for ever afterwards [would] walk up, and down, like useless pageants."[67]

In the same utilitarian way, Warren reminded the Episcopal clergy that only by accepting the government's authority would they have any opportunity to preach God's word.[68] To the lawyers, "men of mine profession,"[69] Warren pointed out that the present government allowed them to carry on their profession. "The common lawyer above all men [has no] cause to repine at present fixing of our state, for that his craft or mystery is preserved entire, his road toward subsistence the same."[70] Men whose interests were, or could be, served by this government should support it.

To view a government through the eyes of self-interest was a point of view expressed by John Thurloe, certainly no theorist. In 1653 Thurloe urged Cromwell "to fix the nation's interest and your own upon some valid fundamentals in reference to the state oath of religion and polity . . . so that men may be self interested to adhere to you."[71] Joseph Lee, a minister, pushed the concept of self-interest into the heavenly realm. Even saints, Lee asserted in 1656, were motivated by self-interest, working both for "God's glory and their own advantage, viz. the salvation of their souls."[72]

Men's interests, whether in this world or the next, had clearly come to play a significant part in the political thinking of many pamphleteers who appealed to those interests in their efforts to persuade men to accept the government. Hobbes's *Leviathan*, published in 1651, was constructed on the basis of men's interest in self-preservation. As this chapter has shown, however, Hobbes was not alone in this period in placing a high priority on the earthly interests of men in considerations of government.

In these few years, then, pamphleteers set forth new and different ways of looking at government. Some, like Warren, advised that Englishmen should look to their own particular material interests, while others, like Robinson, that a relative rather than a traditional criterion be used in evaluating the government. Writers who were more philosophically minded, such as Ascham, the anonymous author of the *Northern subscriber's plea*, and others cited in the first part of this chapter, delved more deeply into the question of government itself. No longer concerned with the mysteries of monarchy, abandoning God and traditional loyalties, origins and legal rights, they concentrated on the nature of government, whatever its form. They analyzed its basic functions and the reciprocal relation to it of men who benefitted by such functions. These writers therefore did more than provide ideological support for a particular government at a particular time. Because they asked probing questions concerning government itself and gave fundamental answers to their own questions, they added a significant chapter to the history of political ideas in England in the seventeenth century.

CONCLUSION

In the few years between 1649 and 1653 Englishmen experienced an ideological shock much greater than that which they had faced in the civil war when Parliament had challenged the extent of the king's authority. The new government not only had executed the king but had abolished monarchy, for centuries the keystone of their society and government.

How could this new illegal government possibly be one to which Englishmen owed their allegiance? This was the fundamental question faced by those writers who used their pens and pulpits to provide ideological support for the Rump. The many pamphleteers and preachers who came to the support of the new government can not be listed among the giants in the history of religious or political thought. Neither Anthony Ascham, Marchamont Nedham, nor Henry Parker, probably the best-known of these men, approaches the stature of Hobbes or Harrington. The numerous repetitive pamphlets of the ubiquitous John Dury provide dull reading for the modern student, compared to the lively challenging tracts of John Lilburne, Gerrard Winstanley, and other radicals who attacked this government. John Owen has a deserved reputation today for his belief in religious toleration, but who has heard of

Richard Saunders or John Rocket, who used their pulpits to try to persuade their congregations to accept the new government, or of Ephraim Elcock, penetrating thinker though he was? Or of Thomas Edgar or Robert Bennet, who used the quarter sessions as their forum for the same purpose? The ideas of the anonymous authors of *England's apology*, the *Northern subscriber's plea*, and *The exercitation answered* also played a significant part in that broad spectrum of thought considered in this essay. Incomplete and scattered, often inconsistent and borrowed, as their arguments were, those pamphleteers and preachers supporting the government deserve to be recognized for meeting the new situation with a wealth of ideas—some traditional, and others breaking new ground in the way Englishmen viewed their society and government.

The more traditionally minded turned to Scripture, finding in the Old Testament proof that God had denounced monarchical government, and in the New Testament that God had proclaimed that men should "obey the powers that be." It was God's providence, as numerous writers defending the Commonwealth government reminded their readers, which had brought about the new government and continued to endorse it. In battle after battle, from Naseby to Worcester, it was God and not man who triumphed, clearly demonstrating His support of this government. A number of writers who turned to God's providence reminded their readers that Englishmen too had a vital part to play. They needed to respond actively to the opportunity afforded by God and cooperate with him, thereby doing "their own generation's work" here and now.

Writers less traditionally minded advanced primarily secular arguments in their ideological support of the government. The upsurge of secular thought in this period is one of its outstanding characteristics. A number of writers saw, some clearly and others dimly, that despite the civil wars and the abolition of monarchy, the age-old commonwealth of England still lived. Consequently it was to this organic whole, built up over the centuries, that Englishmen now owed their allegiance. Some writers explained that the community of England no longer needed a monarch as its head, for English customs and laws, language and liberties, long extolled as vital components of the English nation, remained as binding cohesive ties in their society. This concept that the English commonwealth now existed on its own, without a monarch as its head and builder, is a significant one. In the history of ideas it crosses the frontier between the traditional medieval way in which Englishmen had long viewed their polity, and the more modern way of conceiving of a community or society of men.

In analyzing the new government of this age-old commonwealth, writers coolly and pragmatically turned to the facts of its existence. Their concern became not the government's origins or legality, but present realities such as the fact that the Rump was in possession, the power it wielded, and the utilitarian benefits it provided for men who valued their own interests. They pointed out that protection for man became the first responsibility of any government, and allegiance to a government affording protection the corollary duty of man. Thus the relation between government and man was explained in purely secular terms as a mutual one, and not one dependent on special, almost mystical ties between a king and his subjects. A man's loyalty to a government should be determined by the ends or purposes for which it strives, and the functions it actually performs, rather than by sacred oaths he had traditionally sworn to a monarch.

When these secular approaches to human government and society are viewed cumulatively, it becomes evident that within a very short span of time a significant change took place in the way a number of Englishmen wrote about their polity. Instead of justifying the cause they espoused by looking back to Anglo-Saxon laws and customs, to Magna Carta, to the Petition of Right—an approach which had been so characteristic a pattern of English thought over the centuries—these writers turned from tradition to political reality. Constitutional thought concerning the English polity, which had loomed large in the medieval, Tudor, and early Stuart periods, no longer provided the basis for the arguments and ideas needed to meet the new situation. In turning to political thought to justify a particular government, these writers set forth basic concepts concerning the nature of government itself with which political thinkers in succeeding ages became increasingly concerned.

NOTES

Notes to Introduction

1. Milton was secretary of state to the council for foreign languages.

2. Perez Zagorin, *A History of Political Thought in the English Revolution* (London, 1954).

3. John Wallace, "The Engagement Controversy 1649-1652: An Annotated List of Pamphlets," *Bulletin of the New York Public Library*, LXVIII (1964): 384-405; John Wallace, *Destiny His Choice: The Loyalism of Andrew Marvell* (Cambridge, 1968).

4. Quentin Skinner, "Conquest and Consent," in *The Interregnum: The Quest for Settlement, 1646-1660*, ed. Gerald E. Aylmer (London, 1972); idem, "History and Ideology in the English Revolution," *The Historical Journal* VIII (1965): 151-78; idem, "The Ideological Content of Hobbes's Political Thought," *The Historical Journal* IX (1966): 286-317.

5. My own study is based in considerable measure upon the interpretation I made more than twenty years ago when I first read many of the Thomason Tracts written between 1649 and 1653.

6. Ivan Roots, *The Great Rebellion, 1642-1660* (London, 1966); David Underdown, *Pride's Purge: Politics in the Puritan Revolution* (Oxford, 1971), and *Somerset in the Civil War and Interregnum* (Hamden, Conn., 1973); Blair Worden, *The Rump Parliament, 1648-1653* (Cambridge, 1974); Gerald E. Aylmer, *The State's Servants: The Civil Service of the English Republic, 1649-1660* (London and Boston, 1973).

7. Douglas Brunton and Donald H. Pennington, *Members of the Long Parliament* (London, 1954), pp. 38-53; William L. Sachse, "English Pamphlet Support for Charles I, November 1648-January 1649," in *Conflict in Stuart England: Essays in Honour of Wallace Notestein*, ed. William A. Aiken and Basil D. Henning (New York, 1960); Cicely Veronica Wedgwood, *A Coffin for King Charles: The Trial and Execution of Charles I* (New York, 1964), pp. 107ff.

8. Worden, *Rump Parliament*, p. 379. See also pp. 10, 26.

9. Ibid., p. 123.

10. HMC, 13th Rep., app. IV, p. 400, as quoted by George S. Yule, *The Independents in the English Civil War* (Cambridge, 1958), p. 64.

11. *The Parliamentary or Constitutional History of England*, 24 vols. (London, 1763), XIX:189 (hereafter cited as *O.P.H.*).

12. Worden, *Rump Parliament*, p. 18.

13. Ibid., p. 209.

14. *O.P.H.*, XIX:7.

15. Ibid., p. 79.

16. *The exercitation answered* (London, 1650), p. 7. The anonymous author explained that many members of the Commons "possess their seats within these walls by virtue of an election unquestionably legal and by the sanction of a law to perpetuate them till themselves shall consent to their own dissolution, as unquestionable."

17. See, for example, *O.P.H.*, XIX:81, 82.

18. John P. Kenyon, ed., *The Stuart Constitution, 1603-1688: Documents and Commentary* (Cambridge, 1966), p. 324.

19. Charles H. Firth and Robert S. Rait, eds., *Acts and Ordinances of the Interregnum, 1642-1660*, 3 vols. (London, 1911), II:122 (hereafter cited as *F. and R.*).

20. Ibid., pp. 120-21. The question may be asked whether the Commons or the council of state was supreme. I agree with most modern historians (W. C. Abbott is an exception) who hold that the Commons was supreme. Some historians have claimed that in reality the army was supreme. For purposes of this essay, there will be no attempt to explore that question. Despite the great influence of the army, it should be remembered that for many months in 1649 and 1650 the army was in Ireland or Scotland. Not until after Worcester (September 1651) did the leaders of the government and army come to disagree increasingly on basic issues. See Worden, *Rump Parliament*, pt. IV.

21. Worden, *Rump Parliment*, p. 248. See also pp. 223ff.

22. Joseph Frank, *The Beginnings of the English Newspaper* (Cambridge, Mass., 1961), pp. 174-75. Some radical tracts did appear.

23. Marchamont Nedham, *The Case of the Commonwealth of England Stated*, ed. Philip A. Knatchel (Charlottesville, Va., 1969). For Nedham's career and writings see Knatchel's excellent introduction.

24. *F. and R.*, II:325.

25. See *Journal of the House of Commons* (hereafter cited as *Commons Journal*) for 11 and 12 October 1649, and 2 January 1650. Also see *F. and R.*, II:325. The word *subscribe* is the one most frequently used.

26. The extent to which the engagement was actually effective in securing support for the government is another story. See particularly Underdown, *Pride's Purge,* chap. 10, "The Revolution and the Communities." Underdown shows how difficult it often was for the government to secure the compliance of local officials.

27. Among the earlier historians who did recognize many of the achievements of the Rump are Charles H. Firth, *Oliver Cromwell and the Rule of the Puritans in England* (New York, 1900), and Frederick A. Inderwick, *The Interregnum, A.D. 1648-1660. Studies of the Commonwealth, legislative, social and legal* (London, 1891).

28. Bulstrode Whitelocke, *Memorials of the English Affairs,* new ed., 4 vols. (Oxford, 1853), III:168, 171, as quoted by Inderwick, *Interregnum,* p. 322. See also idem, *Interregnum,* p. 323, n.6.

29. Worden, *Rump Parliament,* p. 378.

30. *O.P.H.,* XIX:72, 75.

31. C. M. Williams, "The Political Career of Henry Martin" (D.Phil. thesis, Oxford University, 1954).

32. In these writings I believe Vane was more concerned with principles of right government than with forms of government. He did not necessarily oppose a monarchical form as such. See Margaret A. Judson, *The Political Thought of Sir Henry Vane, the Younger* (Philadelphia, 1969), pp. 58-68.

33. A leading literary scholar speaks of the inconsistencies of the *Defense* (Don M. Wolfe, *Complete Prose Works of John Milton,* 8 vols. [New Haven, Conn., 1953-66], IV, pt. 1, "Introduction," p. 115). In recent years historians have not regarded Milton as an important political theorist. See Zagorin, *Political Thought,* pp. 106-21; Austin Woolrych, "Milton and Cromwell: 'A Short But Scandalous Night of Interruption'?" in Michael Lieb and John T. Shawcross, *Achievements of the Left Hand: Essays on the Prose of John Milton* (Amherst, Mass., 1974), pp. 185-219; and Hugh R. Trevor-Roper, "The Elitist Politics of Milton," *The Times Literary Supplement,* 1 June 1973.

34. Wallace, *Destiny His Choice,* p. 69.

35. See John T. Shawcross, "The Higher Wisdom of *The Tenure of Kings and Magistrates,*" in Lieb and Shawcross, *Achievements of the Left Hand,* pp. 142-60, for a perceptive and illuminating essay on the "philosophic and enduring significance" (Ibid., p. 143) of the *Tenure.* Shawcross shows that in the *Tenure* Milton made "a contribution which underlies all of his poetic and prose attempts at engendering lasting liberty in the minds and hearts of all the people (Ibid., p. 152).

36. See chapters 4 and 5. Nedham's book, *The Excellency of a Free State,* was not published until 1656.

37. *Mercurius Politicus,* nos. 70, 85.

38. See Worden, *Rump Parliament,* p. 252.

39. See Margaret A. Judson, "Henry Parker and the Theory of Parliamentary Sovereignty," in *Essays in History and Political Theory in Honor of Charles Howard McIlwain* (Cambridge, Mass., 1936), and Wilbur K.

Jordan, *Men of Substance: A Study of the Thought of two English Revolutionaries, Henry Parker and Henry Robinson* (Chicago, 1942). Jordan's chapter 2 deals with Parker's life, chapter 4 with his religious thought, and chapter 5 with his political thought. In chapter 3 of this present study I discuss Parker's ideological support of the engagement required by the Commonwealth government. When Parker returned from Hamburg in 1649, he was given the registrarship of the prerogative office and later was made secretary to the army in Ireland.

40. Anthony Ascham, *A Discourse wherein is examined what is particularly lawful during the confusions and revolutions of government* (London, [28 July] 1648). It is not clear whether the government was rewarding Ascham for his writings when he was sent to Spain as envoy for the Rump. In Spain he was assassinated.

41. John Dury, *A case of conscience resolved: concerning ministers medling with state-matters in their sermons* (London, 1649).

42. Whitelocke, *Memorials*, III:74.

43. *D. N. B.*, s.v. Owen, John.

44. *Calendar of State Papers, Domestic Series, 1651*, p. 281 (hereafter cited as *Cal. St. P. Dom.*).

45. Ibid., p. 282. See also p. 440.

46. The ideas of Thorpe, Sclater, Saunders, and Price will be discussed in subsequent chapters.

47. Joseph M. Batten, *John Dury: Advocate of Christian Reunion* (Chicago, 1944). Batten lists all Dury's writings. For the activities of Dury and his importance before 1649, see also Hugh R. Trevor-Roper, "The Fast Sermons of the Long Parliament," in *Religion, the Reformation and Social Change*, ed. Hugh R. Trevor-Roper (London, 1967), pp. 251-52.

48. The writings of Thomas Brooks, John Goodwin, and Francis Rous will be discussed in subsequent chapters.

49. See George L. Mosse, *The Holy Pretence: A Study in Christianity and Reason of State from William Perkins to John Winthrop* (Oxford, 1957), chaps. 4 and 5. Both Perkins and Ames were exponents of the covenant theology.

50. Skinner, "Conquest and Consent," p. 97.

Notes to Chapter I

1. Edward Nicholas, *Proceedings and Debates in the House of Commons in 1620 and 1621*, 2 vols. (Oxford, 1766), II:238.

2. Henry Robinson, *Certain considerations in order to a more speedy . . . distribution of justice throughout the nation* (London, 1651), epistle dedicatory.

3. *F. and R.*, I:1262.

4. Ibid., p. 1263.

5. Ibid., II:1.
6. Ibid., p. 5.
7. Ibid., p. 6.
8. Ibid., p. 18.
9. Ibid., p. 122.
10. Whitelocke, *Memorials,* III:373.
11. "Monarchy Asserted to be the Best, Most Ancient and Legal Form of Government," in *Somers Tracts,* ed. Sir Walter Scott, 13 vols. (London, 1809-15), VI:355.
12. Ibid., p. 356.
13. Ibid., p. 358. There is some controversy over which man was the speaker.
14. Ibid., p. 371. For a full discussion of the belief in monarchy of both royalists and parliamentarians in the first decades of the seventeenth century, see Margaret A. Judson, *The Crisis of the Constitution: An Essay in Constitutional and Political Thought in England, 1603-1645* (New Brunswick, N. J., 1949), chap. 1.
15. Jerrilyn Green Marston, "Gentry Honor and Royalism in Early Stuart England," *Journal of British Studies* XIII (1973-74): 22. See this article for a valuable discussion of the relation between honor and royalism.
16. Gordon J. Schochet, "Patriarchalism, Politics, and Mass Attitudes in Stuart England," *The Historical Journal* XII (1969): 413-41.
17. Williams, "Political Career of Henry Martin," p. 139.
18. Cicely Veronica Wedgwood, "European reaction to the death of Charles I," in *From the Renaissance to the Counter Reformation: Essays in Honor of Garrett Mattingly,* ed. Charles H. Carter (New York, 1965), p. 41.
19. Wolfe, *Complete Prose Works of John Milton,* IV, pt. 1:13.
20. Wilbur C. Abbott, *The Writings and Speeches of Oliver Cromwell,* 4 vols. (Cambridge, Mass., 1937-47), I:3.
21. Samuel Rawson Gardiner, *The Constitutional Documents of the Puritan Revolution, 1625-1660,* 3d ed., rev. (Oxford, 1906), p. 269.
22. William Prynne, *Brief Memento,* as cited by Sachse, "English Pamphlet Support for Charles I," p. 162.
23. Nathaniel Ward, *Discolliminium or A most obedient reply to a late book called Bounds and Bonds* (London, 1650). In this tract Ward was replying to Ascham, almost certainly the author of *Bounds & bonds.* In June 1647 Ward, who had returned to England and had preached before Parliament, revealed in his sermon that at that time he believed in monarchy. See Hugh R. Trevor-Roper, "The Fast Sermons of the Long Parliament," p. 326.
24. Ward, *Discolliminium,* p. 50.
25. Ibid., p. 13.
26. Ibid., p. 50.
27. Ibid., pp. 39, 14.
28. Ibid., p. 42.
29. Ibid., p. 8. I am deliberately not citing the writings of extreme royalists here.

30. Ibid., p. 22. Ideas similar to those in Ward's *Discoliminium* were set forth in *A religious demurrer, concerning submission to the present power* [London, 1649]. According to Wallace, this earlier (26 May 1649) pamphlet may also have been written by Nathaniel Ward. I believe that Ward was almost certainly the author of *A religious demurrer*.

31. Albertus Warren, *The royalist reform'd or considerations of advice to gentlemen, divines, lawyers* . . . (London, 1650), p. 2.

32. T. B., *The Engagement* [*of Allegiance to the Commonwealth*] *vindicated; from all the objections, cavils, scruples, that wilfull opposers, or doubtful, unresolved judgements, may cast upon it* (London, 1650), p. 7.

33. Valerie Pearl, "London's Counter-Revolution," in *The Interregnum: The Quest for Settlement, 1646-1660,* ed. Gerald E. Aylmer (London, 1972), p. 37. John S. Morrill, in *The Revolt of the Provinces: Conservatives and Radicals in the English Civil War, 1630-1650* (London and New York, 1976), gives numerous examples of the desire for peace.

34. See Roger Howell, Jr., *Newcastle upon Tyne and the Puritan Revolution: A Study of the Civil War in North England* (Oxford, 1967). The great desire for peace is brought out by Philip A. Knatchel in his introduction to Nedham, *The Case of the Commonwealth,* and by John M. Wallace in the introduction of *Destiny His Choice.* Gardiner himself wrote, "we shall hardly be wrong in supposing that for every hundred convinced Royalists or Republicans, there were at least a thousand who were ready to accept whatever government was actually in existence, rather than risk disturbance of the peace by a fresh civil war." Samuel Rawson Gardiner, *History of the Commonwealth and Protectorate, 1649-1656,* 4 vols. (London, 1903), I:251.

35. *O.P.H.,* XIX:80.

36. Ibid., pp. 177, 197-98.

37. *Cal. St. P. Dom., 1650,* p. 78.

38. Ibid., 1651, p. 68.

39. *The Weekly Intelligencer of the Commonwealth* 21-28 October 1651, p. 51.

40. Thomas Carte, ed., *A Collection of Original Letters and Papers Concerning the Affairs of England, from the year 1641 to 1660 found among the Duke of Ormonde's Papers* . . . , 2 vols. (London, 1739), I:430.

41. HMC, 14th Rpt., app. II, *Duke of Portland,* p. 172. (III, 1894).

42. *The Life of Adam Martindale,* ed. Richard Parkinson (Chetham Society, 1845), p. 94. Martindale recounted his decision to take the engagement and then his doubts over his decision.

43. Robert Bennet, *Kings Charles' Trial Justified* . . . *being the sum of a charge given at the last sessions held at Truro* . . . *April 4* (London, 1649), p. 3. Bennet was a magistrate appointed by the Rump for Cornwall.

44. Frank, *Beginnings of the English Newspaper,* p. 185.

45. John Owen, *The Works of John Owen,* ed. William Goold, 16 vols. (London, 1850-55), IX:216.

46. *Vox Pacifica or a Pervasive to Peace* (London, 1649), p. 1.

47. Richard Saunders, *Plenary possession makes a lawful power* . . .

preached before the judges in Exeter, March 23, 1651 (London, 1651), p. 26. Saunders was "Preacher of the Gospel at Kentisbeer in Devon."

48. Ibid.

49. Enoch Grey, *Vox coeli, containing maxims of pious policy: wherein several cases of conscience are briefly discussed* (London, 1649), p. 25.

50. Ibid., p. 50.

51. See Batten, *John Dury*.

52. [John Dury], *A disengaged survey of the Engagement. In relation to public obligations* (London, 1650).

53. Ibid., p. 8.

54. John Rocket, *The Christian subject . . . Wherein are answered those ordinary objections, of heresy, tyranny, usurpation, breach of covenant. Which some make as a sufficient plea to take them off from a chearful obedience to this present government* (London, 1651), p. 19.

55. Ibid., p. 102.

56. Ibid., pp. 133, 151.

57. Ascham, *A Discourse*, p. 7. On Ascham's profound desire for peace, see Irene Coltman, *Private Man and Public Causes* (London, 1962), pp. 197-242.

58. [Anthony Ascham] *A combat between two seconds* (London, 1649), p. 15.

59. [Anthony Ascham] *The bounds & bonds of public obedience. Or, a vindication of our lawful submission to the present government, or to a government supposed unlawful, but commanding lawful things. . . . In all which a reply is made to the three answers of the two demurrers, and to the author of the grand case of conscience, who profess themselves impassionate Presbyterians* (London, 1649), p. 18. I agree with Wallace and Skinner that Ascham, and not Rous, is the author of this pamphlet.

60. Anthony Ascham, *Of the confusions and revolutions of governments.* (London, 1649), p. 18.

61. Ibid., p. 146.

62. Francis Osborne, "A Persuasive to a mutual compliance under the present government" (Oxford, 1652), in *Somers Tracts*, VI:157.

63. Nedham, *The Case of the Commonwealth*, pp. 102, 110-11.

Notes to Chapter II

1. John Blackleach, *Endeavours aiming at the Glory of God* (London, 1650), p. 87. This tract was a reply to a recent speech by Prynne in the House of Commons. No other tract by Blackleach is listed in Wing. Blackleach stated that he was no actor in the king's death (p. 15).

2. Ibid., title page.

3. Ibid., pp. 124, 99.

4. Ibid., p. 138.

5. John Cook, *Monarchy no Creature of God's making. Wherein is proved by Scripture and Reason, that Monarchical government is against the mind of God* (Waterford, 1652). John Cook was chief justice of the province of Munster in Ireland.

6. Ibid., p. 115.

7. Ibid., p. 102.

8. *The Moderate Mercury*, 21-28 June 1649.

9. Francis Rous, *The lawfulness of obeying the present government. Proposed by one that loves all Presbyterian lovers of truth and peace, and is of their communion* (London, 1649). A second and longer edition appeared in the summer of 1649, in which Rous refers to "Master Ascham's *Discourse* that hath in it both judgement and learning concerning possession" (p. 15). Rous was in the parliaments of 1625-26, 1628-29, 1640, and the Long Parliament, 1654 and 1656.

10. Ibid., pp. 2-6.

11. Ibid., p. 7.

12. Ibid., p. 8.

13. Skinner, "Conquest and Consent," pp. 87ff.

14. *A discourse concerning the Engagement: or the Northern subscriber's plea opposed to their dissenting Northern Neighbors importune animosities against Engaging to be true and faithful* (London, 1650), p. 7. This important tract was generally known as the *Northern subscriber's plea*.

15. Osborne, "A Persuasive," p. 159.

16. John Dury, *Objections against the taking of the Engagement answered. Or some scruples of conscience, which a godly minister in Lancashire did entertain against the taking of the Engagement* (London, 1650), p. 2.

17. Saunders, *Plenary possession*.

18. Ibid., p. 7.

19. Ibid., p. 8.

20. See William Haller, *Foxe's Book of Martyrs and the Elect Nation* (New York, 1963) and Christopher Hill, *God's Englishman: Oliver Cromwell and the English Revolution* (London, 1970), chap. 9.

21. See Judson, *The Crisis of the Constitution*, chap. 9, and Trevor-Roper, "The Fast Sermons of the Long Parliament."

22. *O.P.H.*, XVIII:504, 505.

23. *England's apology, for its late change: or, a sober perswasive, of all disaffected or dissenting persons, to a seasonable engagement, for the settlement of this commonwealth; Drawn from the workings of providence, The state of affairs, The danger of division* (London, 1651), p. 29. Professor Gerald E. Aylmer, in n. 6 of his article "England's Spirit Unfoulded, or an Incouragement to take the Engagement: A newly discovered pamphlet by Gerrard Winstanley," *Past and Present*, XL (1968): 4, cites *England's apology* as follows: "anon. [John Goodwin], Englands Apologie, . . ." Aylmer has since told me that he was mistaken in attributing this pamphlet to Goodwin.

24. Ibid., p. 30.

25. Ibid., p. 1.

26. *O.P.H.*, XIX:178.

27. Ibid., p. 68.

28. *England's apology*, p. 6.

29. *Anglia Liberata, or the rights of the people of England maintained against the pretences of the Scottish King* (London, 1651), p. 66.

30. Ibid., p. 67.

31. William Cooper, *Jerusalem fatal to her assailants* (London, 1649), p. 29.

32. *England's apology*, p. 10.

33. Thomas Brooks, *The hypocrite detected, anatomized* . . . (London, 1650), p. 13. Brooks was one of the more radical ministers.

34. George Wither, *Carmen Eucharisticon: a private thank-oblation exhibited to the glory of the Lord of Hosts, for the timely and wonderfull deliverance, vouchsafed to this nation, in the routing of a numerous army of Irish rebels before Dublin, by the sword of his valiant servant, Michael Jones, Lieutenant-Generall for the Parliament of England* (London, 1649).

35. This ditty was found in E669, fol. 15 (73), Thomason Tracts, British Library.

36. Henry Robinson, *A short discourse between monarchial and aristo-cratical government, or a sober persuasive of all true hearted Englishmen to a willing conjunction with the Parliament of England in setting up the Government of the Commonwealth* (London, 1649), p. 18. See chapter 5 of this study for a discussion of Robinson's ideas.

37. See chapter 5.

38. *A discourse concerning the Engagement*, pp. 11, 7.

39. John Drew, *The Northern subscribers plea, vindicated* (London, 1651), pp. 17, 21.

40. *England's apology*, pp. 4, 28.

41. Ibid., pp. 28, 3.

42. Ibid., p. 18.

43. John Warren, *The Potent Potter* (London, 1649), p. 13. One of his texts was Ps. 127:1, "Except the lord build the house they labor in vain that build it."

44. Ibid., p. 18.

45. Cooper, *Jerusalem fatal to her assailants*, p. 2.

46. [Dury], *A disengaged survey*, p. 9.

47. Ibid., pp. 22, 10.

48. *Certain Particulars, further tending to satisfy the tender consciences of such as are required to take the engagement, written by a godly and learned divine* (London, 1651), p. 6.

49. Ibid., pp. 6-7.

50. *A word of councel to the disaffected* (n.p., n.d.), as quoted in Wallace, "The Engagement Controversy," p. 402.

51. Michael Walzer, *The Revolution of the Saints: A Study in the Origins of Radical Politics* (New York, 1968), p. 167.

52. Ibid. For an outstanding discussion of covenant theology see Perry Miller, *The New England Mind: The Seventeenth Century* (New York, 1939), chap. 13.

being greater than a part." In citing this doctrine, Grey clearly seemed to approve of it.

37. Rocket, *The Christian subject*, p. 131.

38. Shaw of Christ's College, Cambridge, and "now preacher of God's Word at Kingston upon Hull," *Surtees Society*, LXV (1877): 405. For further information about Shaw see n. 64 of chap. 2.

39. Ascham, *A Discourse*, pp. 70-71. Ascham followed Grotius in many of the ideas he set forth in this book. I am citing pages from *Of the confusions* (1649), but these statements are in *A Discourse* (1648). After the execution of the king Ascham continued to believe in the society or community of Englishmen, but shifted his emphasis to the government of that community. See chapters 4 and 5 of this essay.

40. *Anglia Liberata*.

41. The following statement by Sir William Macdonnell is given in *Cal. St. P. Dom.*, Jan. 1651, p. 31. "Reasons and motives against [the States of Holland] acknowledging the present power in England a republic by Sir Wm. Macdonnell." Macdonnell also stated that the king is "the undoubted proprietor of the crown, though not in possession."

42. *Anglia Liberata*, p. 21 the Dutchman speaking.

43. Ibid., p. 50. The Englishman was familiar with both Grotius and Bodin. Like Dury and others, he used many different arguments to prove his case.

44. Henry Parker, *Scotlands holy war . . . as also an answer to a paper, entitled Some considerations in relation to the Act of 2 Jan: 1649, for subscribing the Engagement* (London, 1651), p. 47. Beginning on p. 66 (of the Harvard second edition of the tract) there is a heading in capitals *Of the Engagement*.

45. Parker, *Of the Engagement*, p. 68.

46. Ibid.

47. Ibid., pp. 70-71.

48. Ibid., pp. 72-73.

49. John Dury, *Considerations concerning the present Engagement, whether it may lawfully be entered into; yes or no?* (London, 1649). This pamphlet went through four editions. In "The Engagement Controversy" (p. 394), Wallace states that the *Considerations* was "the most read" of Dury's engagement pamphlets.

50. Dury, *Considerations*, p. 2.

51. John Dury, *Conscience eased: or, the main scruple which hath hitherto stuck most with conscionable men against the taking of the Engagement removed, etc.* (London, 1651), p. 12.

52. Dury, *Considerations*, p. 17.

53. Ibid., p. 5.

54. Ibid.

55. Dury, *Objections*, p. 22.

56. Ibid.

57. John Dury, *Two Treatises concerning the matter of the Engagement* (London, 1650), p. 58.

58. See the part which Dury played in the publication of Elcock's treatise and the *Memorandums*, pp. 50, 53.

59. Ephraim Elcock, *Animadversions on a book, called, A plea for non-scribers* (London, 1651), Introductory letter.

60. Ibid.

61. Ibid., p. 9.

62. Ibid., pp. 37-38.

63. Ibid., p. 14.

64. Ibid., p. 45.

65. Ibid., pp. 37-38.

66. Although in his pamphlet Elcock often uses the term people, he does not discuss them apart from their representatives in Parliament. On page 19, for example, he quotes Sir Thomas Smith's statement that in Parliament "every Englishman is presumed to be either by himself, or by his proxy." Again on page 23 he refers to the Commons as the "representatives of the whole people." He did not question the fact that in reality "the whole people" were not represented in the Commons.

67. In *A Plea for non-scribers. Or the grounds and reasons of many ministers in Cheshire, Lancashire and the parts adjoining for their refusal of the late Engagement* (London, 1650), Edward Gee used this argument, claiming that the Commons announed their belief in coordinate government in their declaration of 17 April 1646.

68. Elcock, *Animadversions*, p. 14

69. Ibid., p. 19.

70. Ibid., pp. 49-50.

71. Ibid., p. 45. Elcock regarded the Lords as not really coordinate but as creatures of the king, who sat in a "personal" not a "corporate" capacity. On page 23 he wrote, "So many single persons cannot equal the representatives of the whole people."

72. See Margaret A. Judson, "Development of the Theory of Parliamentary Sovereignty (Ph.D. diss., Radcliffe College, 1933).

73. Elcock, *Animadversions*, p. 48.

74. According to Wing, *Animadversions* was Elcock's only pamphlet, and it only appeared in one edition. Elcock denied that king, Lords, and Commons were actually coordinate, but insisted that even if they were, the Commons possessed final power in an emergency. "For the end of coordination of powers is, that if one [i.e., king, Lords, or Commons] should prove pernicious to the commonwealth, there not be wanting a power to restrain it, and if necessary require the taking of it away, there might be a face of public authority remaining" (Elcock, *Animadversions*, p. 24).

Charles Herle, as early as 1642, had written in terms of the "end or purpose" of coordination. See my *Crisis of the Constitution*, pp. 409ff. Elcock did not quote Herle, but may well have been influenced by him. Elcock made no reference to Ascham, but did quote Aristotle, Prynne, Rutherford, Junius, Brutus, and Ames.

75. The tract is entitled *A Religious Scrutiny concerning unequal Marriage*, but attached to this discourse in the second (1650) edition which I used at Harvard is one with a separate frontispiece entitled *A Faithful and*

Conscientious Account for Subscribing to the engagment (London, 1650). Whether or not Paget was the author I do not know. Wing lists a separate tract (no author given) entitled *A Faithful and Conscientious Account*, to be found at Oxford and Union Theological.

76. *A Faithful and Conscientious Account*, p. 9.
77. Ibid., p. 11.
78. Ibid., pp. 12-13.
79. Ibid., p. 13.
80. Ibid., pp. 13-14.
81. *Certain Particulars*, p. 2.
82. Ibid.
83. Ibid. In contrast to Elcock, the author of *Certain Particulars* admitted that the present government should be more representative yet was perhaps "the fittest expedient which could be found" at that time when some government was necessary (p. 13). Like Elcock, however, he failed to discuss what he meant by *people*.
84. *Memorandums of the conferences held between the brethren scrupled at the Engagement; and others who were satisfied with it On Feb. 15 and March 1, 1650* (London, 1650). For further information concerning "the conferences held between the brethren," see Worden, *Rump Parliament*, pp. 230-31.
85. Ibid., p. 16.
86. *Conscience puzzled, about subscribing the new Engagement* (London, 1650).
87. Ibid., p. 4.
88. The author of *A Plea for non subscribers* . . . (London, 1650) warned his readers against the argument that in taking the engagement subscribers would only be pledging loyalty to the larger entity. Citing page 4 of the tract *Conscience puzzled* in the margin, he wrote on page 34: "Some to molify and facilitate the engagement tell us that by the commonwealth may be meant the whole company of men within the bounds of these dominions, or the commonwealth, or the commonality, or the public good, or common safety."
89. I am referring to the ideas Filmer expressed in an unpublished tract dealing with the problem of taking the engagement. The manuscript is in the Bodleian, Tanner MS, 233. One scholar told me that Filmer later changed his mind concerning taking the engagement. I have not, however, been able to document his changed position. See Filmer's "Directions for Obedience to Government in Dangerous or Doubtful Times," in Thomas Peter R. Laslett, ed., *Patriarcha and Other Political Works of Sir Robert Filmer* (Oxford, 1949), pp. 231-37.
90. Robert Filmer, Tanner MS, 233, p. 3, Bodleian Library, Oxford, England.
91. Ibid., p. 4. Filmer admitted on that page that in a popular state commonwealth could be "by the unanimous and universal consent of all the members of it, incorporating and submitting themselves by their personal consent or free suffrage to certain laws and a select form of

government for the preservation of human society." This, however, had not been done in the present situation.

92. Ibid., p. 5.

93. Ibid., p. 4.

94. Ibid., p. 7.

95. Ibid., p. 6.

96. Ibid., p. 9.

97. Ibid., p. 12.

98. Ibid., p. 13.

99. *The Engagement vindicated & explained, or the reasons upon which Lieut. Col. John Lilburne, took the Engagement* (London, 1650), p. 2.

100. Ibid., p. 5.

101. Ibid., p. 6.

102. Ibid., pp. 3-4. Lilburne cites Magna Carta in support of some of his assertions.

103. See Aylmer, "England's Spirit Unfoulded." The pamphlet was found in the Clark MSS in Worcester College, Oxford.

104. Ibid., pp. 9-10.

105. Ibid., pp. 10-11.

106. Donald Hanson, *From Kingdom to Commonwealth: The Development of Civic Consciousness in English Political Thought* (Cambridge, Mass., 1970), p. 1.

Notes to Chapter IV

1. Skinner, "Conquest and Consent," pp. 87ff.

2. Ibid., p. 97.

3. Skinner, "Ideological Content of Hobbes's Political Thought," p. 304.

4. Nedham, *The Case of the Commonwealth*, pp. 129-39.

5. Inevitably in chapters 4 and 5 I cite a number of the pamphlets which Skinner did, and also discuss some of the ideas concerning government which he brought out. My essay, however, which, as one of its objectives, is concerned to show the range and variety of ideas set forth in defense of the government between 1649 and 1653, would be incomplete without these two chapters. Not only is my approach different from Skinner's, but these chapters also include some ideas and some writings concerning government which were not relevant to his work.

6. *O.P.H.*, XIX:79-80. Two thousand copies of this declaration were distributed.

7. Thomas Edgar, *Two charges, as they were delivered by T. E. Esquire, justice of the peace for the county of Suffolk* (London, 1650). The first charge was delivered at a quarter session in Ipswich 6 April 1649, the second on 5 September 1649 also in Suffolk, at the "first public sitting upon the commission of sewers," pp. 13ff.

8. Ibid., p. 3.

9. Ibid., p. 17.

10. Ibid., p. 1.

11. Ibid., p. 16.

12. Ibid.

13. Ibid., p. 4.

14. Blackleach, *Endeavours aiming at the Glory of God*, p. 75.

15. Ibid., pp. 76, 103.

16. Samuel Eaton, *The oath of allegiance and the national convenant proved to be non-obliging: or, three several papers on that subject* (London, 1650), p. 10. Eaton was "teacher of the church of Christ in Duckenfield in Cheshire," according to the title page of this pamphlet.

17. *Memorandums of the conferences*, p. 7.

18. B., *The Engagement vindicated*, p. 15.

19. Owen "The Laboring Saint's dismission to rest," p. 350. Owen did know some of Grotius's writings.

20. Zacheus Mountagu, *The Jus Divinium of Government or Magistracy Proved to be God's Ordinance and Justice the Magistrate's Duty. In a plain sermon preached before the Judges of Assize at East Grimstead in the County of Sussex* (London, 1652); William Sclater, *Civil Magistracy by Divine Authority asserted and laid forth in a Sermon, Preached at the Assize holden at Winchester for the County of South Hampton on Thursday, the 4th day of March 1652* (London, 1653). Sclater was "Preacher of the Word of God" in Broad Street, London.

21. Mountagu, *Jus Divinium*, p. 17.

22. Sclater, *Civil Magistracy*, pp. 7, 16.

23. Ibid., p. 26.

24. Ascham, *A Discourse*, pp. 32, 10. The pages cited are taken from the 1649 *Of the Confusions*, but in the cases cited, the statements are the same in both pamphlets.

25. Ibid., p. 12. In this statement Ascham was referring specifically to a king invading the territory of another state, but in taking this idea from Grotius, upon whom he relied heavily, Ascham applied it to a situation where a party seized power in the same kingdom.

26. [Ascham] *Bounds & bonds*, p. 6.

27. Ibid., p. 12.

28. Ibid., p. 11.

29. Ascham, *Of the confusions*. In large part this is a reissue of the 1648 *A Discourse*, but there are some additions. See Skinner, "Conquest and Consent," for the development of Ascham's thought.

30. Ascham, *Of the confusions*, p. 95 This is not in the 1648 edition.

31. Ibid., p. 115. This is not in the 1648 edition.

32. Anthony Ascham, *A reply to a paper of Dr. Sandersons, containing a censure of Mr. A. A. his book Of the confusions and revolutions of government* (London, 1650), p. 5.

33. Ibid., p. 7.

34. Nedham, *The Case of the Commonwealth*, p. 27.

35. *Mercurius Politicus,* 14-21 November 1650, p. 389. This paper was written by Nedham.

36. Osborne, "A Persuasive," p. 157.

37. Ibid., p. 159.

38. Saunders, *Plenary possession,* p. 14. Saunders, "preacher of the gospel at Kentisbeer in Devon," took as his text Titus 3:1: "Put them in mind to be subject to principalities and powers."

39. *Northern subscriber's plea,* p. 5.

40. *Essays upon several subjects . . .* (London, 1651), p. 16.

41. Edward Gee, *An exercitation concerning usurped powers wherein the difference betwixt civil authority and usurpation is stated* (London, 1650).

42. *The exercitation answered* (London, 1650). This pamphlet might have been written by Charles Herle. The author quotes Herle's *Fuller Answer* (London, 1642) frequently. Moreover, some of his ideas are similar to Herle's. For a discussion of Herle's ideas in the forties see my *Crisis of the Constitution,* pp. 409-33.

43. *The exercitation answered,* p. 42.

44. Ibid., pp. 16-18.

45. Ibid., p. 18.

46. Ibid., p. 32.

47. Ibid., p. 54. For a discussion of Perkins's theology and influence, see Mosse, *The Holy Pretence,* chap. 4.

48. Ibid., pp. 54-55.

49. Ibid., p. 55.

50. R. F., *Mercurius Heliconius or, the result of a safe conscience: whether it be necessary to subscribe to the government now in being* (London, 1651), pp. 3, 4, 6. R. F. may be Richard Farnsworth.

51. British Library Thomason Collection E669f.15 (73), 24 Jan. 1651, p. 9.

Notes to Chapter V

1. See chapter 1.

2. Skinner, "Conquest and Consent," pp. 87ff.

3. Ascham, *Bounds & bonds,* p. 27.

4. Ascham, *Of the confusions,* p. 146.

5. See Skinner, "Conquest and Consent," pp. 90ff., for the pamphleteers in 1650 and 1651 who must have been influenced by Ascham's secular defense of the engagement. Also see Skinner, "Ideological Content of Hobbes's Political Thought," p. 305, for the influence of Hobbes in 1650 and 1651 upon some of the same pamphleteers.

I have no intention of attempting to assess again the specific influence of Ascham or Hobbes or Nedham upon a particular writer. Skinner brings out convincingly that some of the pamphleteers I am citing on the subject of protection and allegiance must have been indebted in some measure to these writers. Because Nedham's ideas can be seen in Knatchel's edition of *The Case of the Commonwealth*, I have deliberately chosen not to refer to them in any detail in this study.

6. *Essays upon several subjects*, p. 21.

7. Drew, *Northern subscribers plea, vindicated*, p. 58. In this pamphlet Drew frequently refers to W. Ames's *De Conscienca*.

8. Ibid., p. 52.

9. [John Price or Prise] (in ink on British Library pamphlet), *The Cloudie Clergy or a morning lecture . . . intended for a weekly antidote against the Daily Infection of those London Preachers who . . . do corrupt the judgments of their seduced auditors, against the Governors and Government of the Commonwealth of England* (London, 1650), pp. 17, 14. These preachers were undoubtedly Presbyterian. Worden states that Price was "a city politician and assiduous Commonwealth supporter," and "an ally" of Heselrige *(Rump Parliament*, p. 256).

10. *Essays upon several subjects*, pp. 20, 21.

11. Charles Cocke, *English Law or a Summary Survey of the Household of God on Earth* (London, 1651), p. 73. Cocke, a civil lawyer, studied at the Inner Temple and in 1652 became a member of the commission to reform the laws. In 1655, he made it clear that he wished only moderate and gradual changes in the law. See Stuart E. Prall, *The Agitation for Law Reform during the Puritan Revolution, 1640-1660* (The Hague, 1966), pp. 121-23.

12. Dury, *Objections*, p. 16.

13. Osborne, "A Persuasive," p. 161.

14. See *The Life of Adam Martindale*, p. 98. Martindale stated that the *Northern subscriber's plea* "gave many satisfaction and something furthered mine."

15. By N. W., a friend to the Commonwealth.

16. *Northern subscriber's plea*, p. 11.

17. Ibid., pp. 20, 22.

18. Ibid., p. 11.

19. B., *The Engagement vindicated*, p. 7.

20. Ibid., pp. 4, 8.

21. Ibid., p. 8.

22. Ascham, *Of the confusions*, pp. 131, 134. (This is not in the 1648 edition.) Bodin may have influenced Ascham's statement here. Richard Saunders, who emphasized the secular aspects of government, also wrote, "Powers then [are] when they give laws to the people and the people receive laws from them. This is a most visible and undoubted sympton of the life and being of a governing power. When we see this, we may say a government . . . is, or a power is, as safe as we may say, there is life where we see breathing" (Saunders, *Plenary possession*, p. 11). There are no helpful marginal references to authorities in Saunders's printed sermons.

23. Ascham, *Of the confusions*, p. 138. (This is not in the 1648 edition.)

24. Ibid., p. 141. The statements of Ascham cited on justice are not in his 1648 work.

25. Ibid., pp. 141-42. In the trial of Love, Prideaux, the attorney general,

said, "I think justice is a political interest, the preservation of the general" (Howell, *Cobbett's Complete Collection of State Trials*, V:20).

26. Ascham, *Of the confusions*, p. 143.
27. Ibid.
28. Ibid., pp. 143-44.
29. Robinson, *A short discourse*, p. 4. See Jordan, *Men of Substance*, for a discussion of Robinson's political and economic ideas.
30. Ibid., p. 11.
31. Jordan, *Men of Substance*, p. 182.
32. Ibid., p. 185.
33. Robinson, *A short discourse*, p. 18.
34. Ibid., p. 20.
35. Ibid., p. 19. Robinson did believe in moderate reforms.
36. *Essays upon several subjects*, p. 16.
37. Ibid., pp. 18, 20. This statement sounds as if he had read Machiavelli.
38. Ibid., pp. 16, 21.
39. *Certain Particulars*, p. 3.
40. [Price], *The Cloudie Clergy*, title page.
41. Ibid., pp. 6, 11.
42. Ibid., pp. 14, 17.
43. Rous, *The lawfulness*, p. 19. According to Wallace on page 390 of "The Engagement Controversy," this second edition appeared some time before 27 August 1649.
44. *Vox Pacifica*, pp. 1, 15.
45. Ibid., p. 22.
46. Ibid., pp. 23, 36.
47. Ibid., p. 41.
48. Ibid., p. 15.
49. B., *The Engagement vindicated*, p. 11.
50. Ibid., p. 12.
51. Ibid.
52. Ibid., p. 13.
53. [Charles Herle] *A Fuller answer* . . . (London, 1642), pp. 17-18. See Judson, *Crisis of the Constitution*, chap. 10, for a fuller discussion of Herle's ideas. For the best general discussion of the public interest in this period see John A. W. Gunn, *Politics and the Public Interest in the Seventeenth Century* (London, 1969).
54. Robinson, *A short discourse*, p. 7.
55. *England's apology*, p. 28.
56. Dury, *Objections*, p. 2.
57. Nedham, *The Case of the Commonwealth*, pp. 51ff.
58. Ibid., p. 60.
59. Osborne, "A Persuasive," p. 157.
60. Robinson, *A Short discourse*, p. 11. I have not included here, for reasons given in the introduction, some of the stock republican arguments set forth in these years. An example of these arguments is that trade would improve in a republic, and England, like the Netherlands and Venice, would flourish on the seas.

61. J. Mayer, "Inedited letters of Cromwell—and other regicides," *Transactions of the Historical Society of Lancashire*, n.s. I (1860-62): 190-91, as quoted in Worden, *Rump Parliament*, p. 288.

62. [Price], *The Cloudie Clergie, p.* 18.

63. Warren, *The royalist reform'd*, title.

64. Ibid., pp. 2-3.

65. Ibid., pp. 4-5.

66. Ibid., p. 5. Warren was obviously stating a typical Renaissance idea.

67. Ibid., p. 19.

68. Ibid., p. 26.

69. Ibid., p. 35.

70. Ibid., p. 42.

71. John Thurloe, *A collection of state papers of John Thurloe, Esq. Secretary to the Council of State and the two Protectors Oliver and Richard Cromwell: to which is prefixed the life of Mr. Thurloe,* ed. Thomas Birch, 7 vols. (London, 1742), vol. I.

72. Joseph Lee, "Vindication of a Regulated Enclosure" 1656, Goldsmith's Library, as quoted by Margaret James, *Social Problems and Policy during the Puritan Revolution* (New York, 1966), p. 33.

Bibliography

I. Manuscript Sources.

Oxford. Bodleian Library. Tanner MS, 233. Robert Filmer.

II. Pamphlets, Sermons, Newsbooks, Speeches, and Diaries.

Anglia Liberata, or the rights of the people of England maintained against the pretences of the Scottish King. London, 1651.

[Ascham, Anthony.] *The bounds & bonds of public obedience. Or, a vindication of our lawful submission to the present government, or to a government supposed unlawful, but commanding lawful things.... In all which a reply is made to the three answers of the two demurrers, and to the author of the grand case of conscience, who profess themselves impassionate Presbyterians.* London, 1649.

[————.] *A combat between two seconds.* London, 1649.

————. *A Discourse wherein is examined what is particularly lawful during the confusions and revolutions of government.* London, 1648.

107

———. *Of the confusions and revolutions of governments.* London, 1649. (This pamphlet is a second edition of the earlier 1648 *Discourse,* but with significant additions.)

———. *A reply to a paper of Dr. Sandersons, containing a censure of Mr. A. A. his book Of the confusions and revolutions of government.* London, 1650.

B., T. *The Engagement* [*of Allegiance to the Commonwealth*] *vindicated; from all the objections, cavils, scruples, that wilfull opposers, or doubtful, unresolved judgements, may cast upon it.* London, 1650.

Bennet, Robert. *King Charles' Trial Justified . . . being the sum of a charge given at the last sessions held at Truro . . . April 4.* London, 1649.

Blackleach, John. *Endeavours aiming at the Glory of God.* London, 1650.

Brooks, Thomas. *The hypocrite detected, anatomized . . .* London, 1650.

Cardell, John. *God's Wisdom justified and Man's Folly condemned.* London, 1649.

Certain Particulars, further tending to satisfy the tender consciences of such as are required to take the engagement, written by a godly and learned divine. London, 1651.

Cocke, Charles. *English Law or a Summary Survey of the Household of God on Earth.* London, 1651.

Conscience puzzled, about subscribing the new Engagement. London, 1650.

Cook, John. *Monarchy no Creature of God's making. Wherein is proved by Scripture and Reason, that Monarchical government is against the mind of God.* Waterford, 1652.

Cooper, William. *Jerusalem fatal to her assailants.* London, 1649.

Drew, John. *The Northern subscribers plea, vindicated.* London, 1651.

Dury, John. *A case of conscience resolved: concerning ministers medling with state-matters in their sermons.* London, 1649.

———. *Conscience eased: or, the main scruple which hath hitherto stuck most with conscionable men against the taking of the Engagement removed, etc.* London, 1651.

———. *Considerations concerning the present Engagement, whether it may lawfully be entered into; yes or no?* London, 1649.

[_____.] *A disengaged survey of the Engagement. In relation to public obligations.* London, 1650.

_____. *Just re-proposals to humble proposals.* London, 1650.

_____. *Objections against the taking of the Engagement answered. Or some scruples of conscience, which a godly minister in Lancashire did entertain against the taking of the Engagement.* London, 1650.

_____. *Two Treatises concerning the matter of the Engagement.* London, 1650.

_____. *The unchanged, constant and single-hearted peace-maker drawn forth into the world.* London, 1650.

Eaton, Samuel. *The oath of allegiance and the national covenant proved to be non-obliging: or, three several papers on that subject.* London, 1650.

Edgar, Thomas. *Two charges, as they were delivered by T. E. Esquire, justice of the peace for the county of Suffolk.* London, 1650.

Elcock, Ephraim. *Animadversions on a book, called, A plea for non-scribers.* London, 1651.

The Engagement vindicated & explained, or the reasons upon which Lieut. Col. John Lilburne, took the Engagement. London, 1650.

England's apology, for its late change: or, a sober perswasive, of all disaffected or dissenting persons, to a seasonable engagement, for the settlement of this commonwealth; Drawn from the workings of providence, The state of affairs, The danger of division. London, 1651.

Essays upon several subjects . . . London, 1651.

The exercitation answered. London, 1650.

F., R. *Mercurius Heliconius Or, the result of a safe conscience: whether it be necessary to subscribe to the government now in being.* London, 1651.

A Faithful and Conscientious Account for Subscribing to the engagement. London, 1650. It is attached to the second edition at Harvard of Thomas Paget's *A Religious Scrutiny concerning unequal Marriage* (London, 1649).

Fisher, Payne, *Veni, Vidi, Vici . . .* London, 1652.

Gee, Edward. *An exercitation concerning usurped powers wherin the difference betwixt civil authority and usurpation is stated.* London, 1650.

————. *A Plea for non-scribers. Or the ground and reasons of many ministers in Cheshire, Lancashire and the parts adjoining for their refusal of the late Engagement.* London, 1650.

Goodwin, John. *Right and Might well met . . .* London, 1648.

The grand case of conscience concerning the Engagement stated and resolved. Or, a strict survey of the Solemn League & Covenant . . . in reference to the present Engagement. London, 1650.

Grey, Enoch. *Vox coeli, containing maxims of pious policy: wherein several cases of conscience are briefly discussed.* London, 1649.

[Herle, Charles.] *A Fuller answer . . .* London, 1642.

The Life of Adam Martindale. Edited by Richard Parkinson. Chetham Society, 1845.

Memorandums of the conferences held between the brethren scrupled at the Engagement; and others who were satisfied with it On Feb. 15, and March 1, 1650. London, 1650.

Mercurius Politicus, 14-21 November 1650.

Mercurius Politicus, no. 70 [1651] and no. 85 (1652).

The Moderate Mercury, 21-28 June 1649.

"Monarchy Asserted to be the Best, Most Ancient and Legal Form of Government." In *Somers Tracts,* edited by Sir Walter Scott. London, 1809-15. Vol. VI.

Mountagu, Zacheus. *The Jus Divinium of Government or Magistracy Proved to be God's Ordinance and Justice the Magistrate's Duty. In a plain sermon preached before the Judges of Assize at East Grimstead in the County of Sussex.* London, 1652.

Nedham, Marchamont. *The Case of the Commonwealth of England Stated.* Edited by Philip A. Knatchel. Charlottesville, Va., 1969.

Osborne, Francis. "A Persuasive to a mutual compliance under the present government." Oxford, 1652. In *Somers Tracts,* edited by Sir Walter Scott. London, 1809-15. Vol. VI.

Owen, John. "The advantages of the kingdom of Christ in the shaping of the kingdoms of the world or providential alterations in their subserviency to Christ's exaltation," preached to Parliament 24 October 1651. In *The Works of John Owen,* edited by William Goold. London, 1850-55. III:310-44. Epistle dedicatory to this sermon only in *The Works of John Owen,* edited by Thomas Russell. London, 1826. XV:416.

————. "Human Power Defeated, preached before Parliament

June 7, 1649." In *The Works of John Owen*, edited by William Goold. London, 1850-55. IX:197-217.

_____. "The Laboring Saint's dismission to rest . . . preached at the funeral of Ireton . . . at Westminster, Feb. 6, 1651." In *The Works of John Owen*, edited by William Goold. London, 1850-55. VIII:342-63.

_____. "The Steadfastness of the Promises and the Sinfulness of Staggering, a sermon preached before Parliament Feb. 28, 1650." In *The Works of John Owen*, edited by William Goold. London, 1850-55. VIII:207-41.

A pack of old puritans. Maintaining the unlawfulness & inexpediency of subscribing the new engagment. London, 1650.

Parker, Henry. *Jus Populi* . . . London, 1644.

_____. *Observations upon some of his Majesties late Answers and Expresses*. London, 1642.

_____. *Scotlands holy war . . . as also an answer to a paper, entitled Some considerations in relation to the Act of 2 Jan: 1649, for subscribing the Engagement*. London, 1651.

A Plea for non subscribers . . . London, 1650.

[Price or Prise, John.] *The Cloudie Clergy or a morning lecture . . . intended for a weekly antidote against the Daily Infection of those London Preachers who . . . do corrupt the judgments of their seduced auditors, against the Governors and Government of the Commonwealth of England*. London, 1650.

Rectifying Principles About the Power and Sovereignty of Kingdoms. London, 1649.

A religious demurrer, concerning submission to the present power. London, 1649.

Robinson, Henry. *Certain considerations in order to a more speedy . . . distribution of justice throughout the nation*. London, 1651.

_____. *A short discourse between monarchical and aristocratical government, or a sober persuasive of all true hearted Englishmen to a willing conjunction with the Parliament of England in setting up the Government of the Commonwealth*. London, 1649.

Rocket, John. *The Christian subject . . . Wherein are answered those ordinary objections, of heresy, tyranny, usurpation, breach of covenant. Which some make as a sufficient plea to take them off from a chearful obedience to this present government*. London, 1651.

Rous, Francis. *The lawfulness of obeying the present government. Proposed by one that loves all Presbyterian lovers of truth and peace, and is of their communion.* London, 1649. A second and longer edition appeared in the summer of 1649.

Saunders, Richard. *Plenary possession makes a lawful power . . . preached before the judges in Exeter, March 23, 1651.* London, 1651.

Sclater, William. *Civil Magistracy by Divine Authority asserted and laid forth in a Sermon, Preached at the Assize holden at Winchester for the County of South Hampton on Thursday the 4th day of March 1652.* London, 1653.

Shaw, John. "Britannia Rediviva," a sermon. In *Surtees Society, Yorkshire diaries and autobiographies* XV (1877).

Vox Pacifica or a Pervasive to Peace. London, 1649.

W., N. *A discourse concerning the Engagement: or the Northern subscriber's plea opposed to their dissenting Northern Neighbors importune animosities against Engaging to be true and faithful.* London, 1650.

Ward, Nathaniel. *Discolliminium or A most obedient reply to a late book called Bounds and Bonds.* London, 1650.

Warren, Albertus. *The royalist reform'd or considerations of advice to gentlemen, divines, lawyers. Digested into three chapters. Wherein their former mistakes are examined, and their duties of obedience, unto the present authority, succinctly held forth as rational, and necessary.* London, 1650.

Warren, John. *The Potent Potter.* London, 1649.

The Weekly Intelligencer of the Commonwealth, 21-28 October 1651.

Winstanley, Gerrard. "England's Spirit Unfolded, or an Incouragement to take the Engagement." London, 1650. In Aylmer, Gerald E. "England's Spirit Unfoulded, or an Incouragement to take the Engagement: A newly discovered pamphlet by Gerrard Winstanley." *Past and Present* XL (1968).

Wither, George. *Carmen Eucharisticon: a private thank-oblation exhibited to the glory of the Lord of Hosts, for the timely and wonderfull deliverance, vouchsafed to this nation, in the routing of a numerous army of Irish rebels before Dublin, by the sword of his valiant servant, Michael Jones, Lieutenant-Generall for the Parliament of England.* London, 1649.

A word of councel to the disaffected. In Wallace, John. "The

Engagement Controversy 1649-52, An Annotated List of Pamphlets." *Bulletin of the New York Public Library.* June, 1964.

III. BOOKS.

A. Primary.

Abbott, Wilbur C. *The Writings and Speeches of Oliver Cromwell.* 4 vols. Cambridge, Mass., 1937-47.

Calendar of State Papers, Domestic Series, Commonwealth, 1649-1653.

Carte, Thomas, ed. *A Collection of Original Letters and Papers Concerning the Affairs of England, from the year 1641 to 1660 found among the Duke of Ormonde's Papers* . . . 2 vols. London, 1739.

Firth, Charles H., and Rait, Robert S., eds. *Acts and Ordinances of the Interregnum, 1642-1660.* 3 vols. London, 1911.

Gardiner, Samuel Rawson. *The Constitutional Documents of the Puritan Revolution, 1625-1660.* 3d ed., rev. Oxford, 1906.

Historical Manuscripts Commission. 14th Report, Appendix II. *Duke of Portland,* III, London, 1894.

Howell, Thomas B., ed. *Cobbett's Complete Collection of State Trials and Proceedings for High Treason and Other Crimes and Misdemeanours From the Earliest Period to the Present Time.* Vols. IV and V. London, 1809-14.

Husband, Edward. *An Exact Collection of the Remonstrances, Declarations* . . ., *Dec. 1641-March 1643.* London, 1643.

Hyde, Edward, earl of Clarendon. *The History of the Rebellion and Civil Wars in England* . . . Edited by W. D. Macray. 6 vols. Oxford, 1888.

Journals of the House of Commons.

Kenyon, John P., ed. *The Stuart Constitution, 1603-1688: Documents and Commentary.* Cambridge, 1966.

Laslett, Thomas Peter R., ed. *Patriarcha and Other Political Works of Sir Robert Filmer.* Oxford, 1949.

Malham, J., ed. *The Harleian Miscellany: A collection of scarce, curious, and entertaining pamphlets and tracts* . . . *found in the late Earl of Oxford's library.* 12 vols. London, 1808-11.

113

Muddiman, Joseph G., ed. *Trial of King Charles the First.* London, 1928.

Nalson, John. *An Impartial Collection of the Great Affairs of State, from the beginning of the Scotch Rebellion in 1639, to the murder of King Charles I. . . . wherein . . . the whole series of the late troubles in England, Scotland, & Ireland are faithfully represented.* 2 vols. London, 1682-83.

————. *A true copy of the Journal of the High Court of Justice for the trial of K. Charles I.* London, 1684.

Nichols, John. *Letters and Papers of State addressed to Oliver Cromwell.* London, 1743.

The Parliamentary or Constitutional History of England. 24 vols. London, 1763. Generally known as the *Old Parliamentary History.*

Rushworth, John. *Historical Collections.* 8 vols. London, 1721.

Thurloe, John. *A collection of state papers of John Thurloe, Esq. Secretary to the Council of State and the two Protectors Oliver and Richard Cromwell: to which is prefixed the life of Mr. Thurloe.* Edited by Thomas Birch. 7 vols. London, 1742.

Whitelocke, Bulstrode. *Memorials of the English Affairs.* 4 vols. New ed. Oxford, 1853.

Wolfe, Don M. *Complete Prose Works of John Milton.* 8 vols. New Haven, Conn., 1953-66.

B. *Secondary.*

Aylmer, Gerald E., ed. *The Interregnum: The Quest for Settlement, 1646-1660.* London, 1972.

————. *The State's Servants: the Civil Service of the English Republic, 1649-1660.* London and Boston, 1973.

Batten, Joseph M. *John Dury: Advocate of Christian Reunion.* Chicago, 1944.

Brunton, Douglas, and Pennington, Donald H. *Members of the Long Parliament.* London, 1954.

Chrimes, Stanley B. *English Constitutional Ideas in the Fifteenth Century.* Cambridge, 1936.

Coltman, Irene. *Private Man and Public Causes.* London, 1962.

Everitt, Alan M. *The Local Community and the Great Rebellion.* London, 1969.

Firth, Charles H. *Oliver Cromwell and the Rule of the Puritans in England.* New York, 1900.

Frank, Joseph. *The Beginnings of the English Newspaper.* Cambridge, Mass., 1961.

Gardiner, Samuel Rawson. *History of the Commonwealth and Protectorate, 1649-1656.* 4 vols. London, 1903.

Gunn, John A. W. *Politics and the Public Interest in the Seventeenth Century.* London, 1969.

Haller, William. *Foxe's Book of Martyrs and the Elect Nation.* New York, 1963.

Hanson, Donald. *From Kingdom to Commonwealth: The Development of Civic Consciousness in English Political Thought.* Cambridge, Mass., 1970.

Hill, Christopher. *God's Englishman: Oliver Cromwell and the English Revolution.* London, 1970.

Howell, Roger, Jr. *Newcastle upon Tyne and the Puritan Revolution: A Study of the Civil War in North England.* Oxford, 1967.

Inderwick, Frederick A. *The Interregnum, A. D. 1648-1660. Studies of the Commonwealth, legislative, social and legal.* London, 1891.

James, Margaret. *Social Problems and Policy during the Puritan Revolution.* New York, 1966.

Jordan, Wilbur K. *Men of Substance: A Study of the Thought of two English Revolutionaries, Henry Parker and Henry Robinson.* Chicago, 1942.

Judson, Margaret A. *The Crisis of the Constitution: An Essay in Constitutional and Political Thought in England, 1603-1645.* 1949. Reprint. New York, 1976.

_____. "Henry Parker and the Theory of Parliamentary Sovereignty." In *Essays in History and Political Theory in Honor of Charles Howard McIlwain.* Cambridge, Mass., 1936.

_____. *The Political Thought of Sir Henry Vane, the Younger.* Philadelphia, 1969.

Maitland, Frederic W. "Crown as Corporation." In *The Collected Papers of Frederic William Maitland.* Edited by H. A. L. Fisher. 3 vols. Cambridge, 1911. Vol. III.

Miller, Perry. *The New England Mind: The Seventeenth Century.* New York, 1939.

Morrill, John S. *The Revolt of the Provinces: Conservatives and Radicals in the English Civil War, 1630-1650.* London and New York, 1976.

115

Mosse, George L. *The Holy Pretence: A Study in Christianity and Reason of State from William Perkins to John Winthrop*. Oxford, 1957.

Pearl, Valerie. "London's Counter-Revolution." In *The Interregnum: The Quest for Settlement, 1646-1660*, edited by Gerald E. Aylmer. London, 1972.

Prall, Stuart E. *The Agitation for Law Reform during the Puritan Revolution, 1640-1660*. The Hague, 1966.

Roots, Ivan. *The Great Rebellion, 1642-1660*. London, 1966.

Sachse, William L. "English Pamphlet Support for Charles I, November 1648-January 1649." In *Conflict in Stuart England: Essays in Honour of Wallace Notestein*, edited by William A. Aiken and Basil D. Henning. New York, 1960.

Schochet, Gordon J. *Patriarchalism in Political Thought*. New York, 1975.

Shawcross, John T. "The Higher Wisdom of *The Tenure of Kings and Magistrates*." In Lieb, Michael, and Shawcross, John T. *Achievements of the Left Hand: Essays on the Prose of John Milton*, Amherst, Mass., 1974.

Skinner, Quentin. "Conquest and Consent." In *The Interregnum: The Quest for Settlement, 1646-1660*, edited by Gerald E. Aylmer. London, 1972.

Trevor-Roper, Hugh R. "The Fast Sermons of the Long Parliament." In *Religion, the Reformation and Social Change*, edited by Hugh R. Trevor-Roper. London, 1967.

Underdown, David. *Pride's Purge: Politics in the Puritan Revolution*. Oxford, 1971.

———. *Somerset in the Civil War and Interregnum*. Hamden, Conn., 1973.

Wallace, John M. *Destiny His Choice: The Loyalism of Andrew Marvell*. Cambridge, 1968.

Walzer, Michael. *The Revolution of the Saints: A Study in the Origins of Radical Politics*. New York, 1968.

Wedgwood, Cicely Veronica. *A Coffin for King Charles: The Trial and Execution of Charles I*. New York, 1964.

———. "European reaction to the death of Charles I." In *From the Renaissance to the Counter Reformation: Essays in Honor of Garrett Mattingly*, edited by Charles H. Carter. New York, 1965.

Woolrych, Austin. "Milton and Cromwell: 'A Short But Scandalous Night of Interruption'?" In Lieb, Michael, and Shawcross, John T. *Achievements of the Left Hand: Essays on the Prose of John Milton*. Amherst, Mass., 1974.

Worden, Blair. *The Rump Parliament, 1648-1653*. Cambridge, 1974.

Yule, George S. S. *The Independents in the English Civil War*. Cambridge, 1958.

Zagorin, Perez. *The Court and the Country: The Beginning of the English Revolution*. New York, 1970.

————. *A History of Political Thought in the English Revolution*. London, 1954.

IV. ARTICLES AND UNPUBLISHED MANUSCRIPTS.

Judson, Margaret A. "Development of the Theory of Parliamentary Sovereignty." Ph.D. dissertation, Radcliffe College, 1933.

Marston, Jerrilyn Green. "Gentry Honor and Royalism in Early Stuart England." *Journal of British Studies* XIII (1973-74):21-43.

Russell, Conrad. "The Theory of Treason in the Trial of Strafford." *English Historical Review* LXXX (1965):30-50.

Schochet, Gordon J. "Patriarchalism, Politics, and Mass Attitudes in Stuart England." *The Historical Journal* XII (1969):413-41.

Skinner, Quentin. "History and Ideology in the English Revolution." *The Historical Journal* VIII (1965):151-78.

————. "The Ideological Content of Hobbes's Political Thought." *The Historical Journal* IX (1966):286-317.

Trevor-Roper, Hugh R. "The Elitist Politics of Milton." *The Times Literary Supplement*. 1 June 1973.

Wallace, John M. "The Engagement Controversy 1649-1652: An Annotated List of Pamphlets." *Bulletin of the New York Public Library* LXVIII (1964):384-405.

Williams, C. M. "The Political Career of Henry Martin." D.Phil. thesis, Oxford University, 1954.

117

INDEX

118